PARADOXES OF NEOLIBERALISM

From the rise of far-right regimes to the tumult of the COVID-19 pandemic, recent years have brought global upheaval as well as the sedimentation of longstanding social inequalities. Analyzing the complexities of the current political moment in different geographic regions, this book addresses the paradoxical persistence of neoliberal policies and practices, in order to ground the pursuit of a more just world.

Engaging theories of decoloniality, racial capitalism, queer materialism, and social reproduction, this book demonstrates the centrality of sexual politics to neoliberalism, including both social relations and statecraft. Drawing on ethnographic case studies, the authors show that gender and sexuality may be the site for policies like those pertaining to sex trafficking, which bundle together economics and changes to the structure of the state. In other instances, sexual politics are crucial components of policies on issues ranging from the growth of financial services to migration. Tracing the role of sexual politics across different localities and through different political domains, this book delineates the paradoxical assemblage that makes up contemporary neoliberal hegemony. In addition to exploring contemporary social relations of neoliberal governance, exploitation, domination, and exclusion, the authors also consider gender and sexuality as forces that have shaped myriad forms of community-based activism and resistance, including local efforts to pursue new forms of social change. By tracing neoliberal paradoxes across global sites, the book delineates the multiple dimensions of economic and cultural restructuring that have characterized neoliberal regimes and emergent activist responses to them.

This innovative analysis of the relationship between gender justice and political economy will appeal to: interdisciplinary scholars in social and cultural studies; legal and political theorists; and the wide range of readers who are concerned with contemporary questions of social justice.

The authors are all part of the Gender, Justice, and Neoliberal Transformations Project at the Barnard Center for Research on Women, Barnard College, Columbia University, USA.

Part of the SOCIAL JUSTICE series

Series editors

Sarah Keenan, *Birkbeck College, University of London, UK*
Davina Cooper, *University of Kent, UK*
Sarah Lamble, *Birkbeck College, University of London, UK*

for information about the series and details of previous and forthcoming titles, see https://www.routledge.com/Social-Justice/book-series/RCSOCJ

A GlassHouse book

PARADOXES OF NEOLIBERALISM

Sex, Gender, and Possibilities for Justice

Edited by Janet Jakobsen and Elizabeth Bernstein

LONDON AND NEW YORK

First published 2022
by Routledge
4 Park Square, Milton Park, Abingdon, Oxon OX14 4RN

and by Routledge
605 Third Avenue, New York, NY 10158

Routledge is an imprint of the Taylor & Francis Group, an informa business

© 2022 selection and editorial matter, Elizabeth Bernstein and Janet R Jakobsen; individual chapters, the contributors

The right of Elizabeth Bernstein and Janet R Jakobsen to be identified as the authors of the editorial material, and of the authors for their individual chapters, has been asserted in accordance with sections 77 and 78 of the Copyright, Designs and Patents Act 1988.

All rights reserved. No part of this book may be reprinted or reproduced or utilised in any form or by any electronic, mechanical, or other means, now known or hereafter invented, including photocopying and recording, or in any information storage or retrieval system, without permission in writing from the publishers.

Trademark notice: Product or corporate names may be trademarks or registered trademarks, and are used only for identification and explanation without intent to infringe.

British Library Cataloguing-in-Publication Data
A catalogue record for this book is available from the British Library

ISBN: 978-1-032-18072-4 (hbk)
ISBN: 978-0-367-51159-3 (pbk)
ISBN: 978-1-003-25270-2 (ebk)

DOI: 10.4324/9781003252702

Typeset in Bembo
by Deanta Global Publishing Services, Chennai, India

For Christina,
Thanks for everything.

CONTENTS

Notes on contributors	*viii*
Acknowledgments	*xii*

1 Introduction: Gender, justice, and the paradoxical
persistence of neoliberal times   1
Elizabeth Bernstein and Janet Jakobsen

2 Gender justice and economic justice: Production,
reproduction, and survival   34
Janet Jakobsen, Mark Padilla, and Maja Horn

3 Neoliberal vulnerability and the vulnerability of neoliberalism   71
*Kerwin Kaye, Ana Amuchástegui, Abosede George, and
Tami Navarro*

4 The productive incoherence of "sex trafficking"   109
*Elizabeth Bernstein, Sealing Cheng, Sine Plambech, and
Mario Pecheny*

5 Borders and boundaries: Thinking migration, sexuality
and precarity in a neoliberal age   134
Sine Plambech, Mark Padilla, Sealing Cheng, and Svati Shah

6 Political power and practices of resistance   159
Mario Pecheny, Janet Jakobsen, Ana Amuchástegui, and Maja Horn

Index   *189*

CONTRIBUTORS

Elizabeth Bernstein is Professor of Women's, Gender, and Sexuality Studies and of Sociology at Barnard College, Columbia University. Her research and teaching focus on the political economy of the body, gender, and sexuality. She is the author of the award-winning books *Brokered Subjects: Sex, Trafficking, and the Politics of Freedom* (University of Chicago Press 2018) and *Temporarily Yours: Intimacy, Authenticity, and the Commerce of Sex* (University of Chicago Press 2007), and co-editor of the volume *Regulating Sex: The Politics of Intimacy and Identity* (Routledge 2004). She is currently beginning research for a new book project entitled *Imagining Immunity: Precarious Bodies and the Governance of Gendered Disease*, a feminist analysis of the immunological metaphors that guide common conceptions of bodily risk and suffering, as well as biopolitical interventions designed to address conditions ranging from allergies to autoimmune disorders to infectious disease.

Janet Jakobsen is Claire Tow Professor of Women's Gender and Sexuality Studies at Barnard College, Columbia University. She served for 15 years as Director of the Barnard Center for Research on Women (BCRW). As Director of BCRW, Professor Jakobsen founded the webjournal *Scholar & Feminist Online*, along with the New Feminist Solutions series of activist research projects with community-based organizations, such as the National Domestic Workers Alliance, Queers for Economic Justice, the New York Women's Foundation, and A Better Balance: Work and Family Legal Center. She is the author of *The Sex Obsession: Perversity and Possibility in American Politics* and *Working Alliances and the Politics of Difference: Diversity and Feminist Ethics*. With Ann Pellegrini, she co-wrote *Love the Sin: Sexual Regulation and the Limits of Religious Tolerance* and co-edited *Secularisms*. With Elizabeth Castelli, she co-edited *Interventions: Academics and Activists Respond to Violence*.

Contributors **ix**

Ana Amuchástegui is Professor of Education and Communication Department at Universidad Autónoma Metropolitana–Xochimilco, Mexico City. She was a Postdoctoral fellow at the Program for the Study of Sexuality, Gender, Health, and Human Rights (Columbia University, USA) and Member of the National System of Researchers Level II. She has done extensive qualitative research on subjectivity, sexuality, and rights in Mexico. She has published in the *Routledge Handbook of Sexuality, Health, and Rights* (edited by Peter Aggleton and Richard Parker), and in journals such as *Culture, Health and Sexuality*, *Citizenship Studies*, *Sexualities*, and *Reproductive Health Matters*. She is part of the International Research Group *Gender Justice and Neoliberal Transformations* (Barnard College, USA). She has worked with civil society organizations like Catholics for Free Choice, and government agencies like the National Center for AIDS Prevention and Control. Currently, she leads *Yantzin: Women Peer Advisors in HIV*, an action/research project in collaboration with public clinics in Oaxaca, Cuernavaca, and Mexico City.

Sealing Cheng is Associate Professor in the Department of Anthropology, The Chinese University of Hong Kong. Before joining The Chinese University, she was Associate Professor in the Department of Women's and Gender Studies of Wellesley College in Massachusetts. She began research on migrant entertainers in US military camp towns in South Korea in 1997, and analyzed the politics of human trafficking policies, women's human rights, and transnational activism in the Asia-Pacific region. After relocating to Hong Kong, she started research on asylum seekers and refugees, specifically on their intimate relationships with local women. Her works have appeared in journals including *Current Anthropology*, *Anthropological Quarterly*, *Social Politics*, *Feminist Theory*, *Feminist Studies*, and *Journal of Ethnic and Migration Studies*. Her first book, *On the Move for Love: Migrant Entertainers and the U.S. Military in South Korea* (University of Pennsylvania Press 2010) received the Distinguished Book Award of the Sexualities Section of the American Sociological Association in 2012.

Abosede George is Associate Professor of History at Barnard College and Columbia University in New York. She teaches courses on migration, historical mapping, urban history, childhood and youth, and the study of women, gender, and sexuality in African History. Her book, *Making Modern Girls: A History of Girlhood, Labor, and Social Development* was published by Ohio University Press and received the Aidoo-Snyder Book Prize in 2015 from the Women's Caucus of the African Studies Association, as well as an honorable mention from the New York African Studies Association. Her writings have appeared in the *American Historical Review*, the *Journal of Social History*, *Comparative Studies in South Asia, Africa, and the Middle East*, *Meridians*, *Women's Studies Quarterly*, and *The Washington Post* among other outlets.

Maja Horn is an Associate Professor in the Department of Spanish and Latin American Cultures and an affiliate of the Department of Africana Studies at Barnard

x Contributors

College, USA. She researches contemporary Caribbean cultures with a focus on contemporary literature, visual and performance art, and gender and sexuality studies. She published *Masculinity after Trujillo: The Politics of Gender in Dominican Literature* (University Press of Florida 2014), which won an honorable book prize mention from the Haitian-Dominican Section of the Latin American Studies Association (LASA). She has published in scholarly journals such as *Small Axe: A Caribbean Journal of Criticism*, *GLQ: A Journal of Lesbian and Gay Studies*, and *Latino Studies Journal*, as well as in various art magazines in the US and in the Dominican Republic. She is currently completing a second monograph on queer Dominican literature, visual, and performance arts.

Kerwin Kaye is an Associate Professor of Sociology, American Studies, and Feminist, Gender, and Sexuality Studies at Wesleyan University in Connecticut. He is the author of *Enforcing Freedom: Drug Courts, Therapeutic Communities, and the Intimacies of the State* (Columbia University Press 2020). He teaches courses on social theory, the sociology of sexualities, sex work, the sociology of mental health and psychiatry, the sociology of drug use, and the criminal justice system.

Tami Navarro is the Associate Director of the Barnard Center for Research on Women (BCRW) and Editor of the journal *Scholar and Feminist Online*. She is a cultural anthropologist whose work has been published in *Cultural Anthropology*, *American Anthropologist*, *Transforming Anthropology*, *Small Axe Salon*, *The Caribbean Writer*, *Social Text*, and *Feminist Anthropology*. She serves on the Board of the St. Croix Foundation and is a member of the Editorial Board for the journal *Small Axe: A Caribbean Journal of Criticism*. She is the co-host of the podcast, "Writing Home: American Voices from the Caribbean," and her book, *Virgin Capital: Race, Gender, and Financialization in the US Virgin Islands*, will be published by SUNY Press in 2021.

Mark Padilla is a Professor of Anthropology in the Department of Global and Sociocultural Studies at Florida International University in Miami. He is a medical anthropologist with research and teaching interests in issues of gender, sexuality, race, migration, political economy, commercial or transactional sex, theories of tourism, and critical HIV/AIDS and drug research. His ethnographic research has been conducted primarily in the Hispanic Caribbean, including *Caribbean Pleasure Industry: Tourism, Sexuality, and AIDS in the Dominican Republic* (University of Chicago Press 2007), and *Love and Globalization: Transformations of Intimacy in the Contemporary World* (Vanderbilt University Press 2007). More recently, he has been conducting research on transgender women as well as critical disaster research in Puerto Rico. His work seeks to shift research, dialogue, and policy by amplifying the voices and experiences of the communities he studies to raise awareness of social inequalities and provide directions for policy change, community engagement, and social transformation.

Contributors **xi**

Mario Pecheny holds a Ph.D. in Political Science from the University of Paris III. He is Professor of Political Science and Sociology of Health at the University of Buenos Aires, Argentina, and is Principal Researcher at CONICET. He has conducted research on health, gender, sexuality, rights, and politics in Latin America. Some of his publications include: *Legalización del aborto en la Argentina: científicas y científicos aportan al debate* (with M. Herrera 2019), *Prevención, promoción y cuidado. Enfoques de vulnerabilidad y derechos humanos* (with J.R. Ayres et al. 2018), *Políticas del amor: derechos sexuales y escrituras disidentes en el Cono Sur* (with F. Blanco and J. M. Pierce 2018), *Travestis, mujeres transexuales y tribunales: Hacer justicia en la Ciudad de Buenos Aires* (with B. Radi 2018), *Esperar y hacer esperar* (with M. Palumbo 2017), *Abortus Interruptus* (with S. Correa 2016), *The Politics of Sexuality in Latin America* (with J. Corrales 2010), and *Todo sexo es político* (with C. Figari & D. Jones 2008).

Sine Plambech is Senior Researcher at DIIS – the Danish Institute for International Studies. She has held visiting professorships at Barnard College and in Yale University's program in Race, Ethnicity, and Migration Studies. Dr. Plambech is an anthropologist and scholar of international migration, engaged in questions of critical migration studies, women's migration, trafficking, transnational feminism, and sex work migration. Over the past fifteen years, she has carried out fieldwork in migrant communities, border areas, red light districts, and along migrant routes from and within Nigeria, Thailand, Sicily, and northern Europe. Plambech is also an award-winning filmmaker, merging her academic work with documentary film-making. Her films have been broadcast by the BBC and her articles have been published in *Social Politics, Feminist Economics, Journal of Ethnic and Migration Studies, Security Dialogue*, and *The Anti-Trafficking Review.*

Svati P. Shah is an Associate Professor of Women's, Gender and Sexuality Studies at the University of Massachusetts, Amherst, with adjunct appointments in Anthropology, Afro-American Studies, and the Social Thought and Political Economy Center. Dr. Shah also holds research affiliations at the African Centre for Migration and Society and the Wits Institute for Social and Economic Research, both at the University of Witwatersrand, South Africa. Dr. Shah's research addresses questions of sexuality, gender, political economy, migration, state-sanctioned violence, and social recognition in South Asia. Their first book, *Street Corner Secrets: Sex, Work and Migration in the City of Mumbai* (Duke University Press 2014), was drawn from a long-term ethnographic study of sex work and other forms of sexual commerce in Mumbai's informal economies. Their forthcoming book is on LGBTQI movements, the Indian new left, and anti-democratic governance.

ACKNOWLEDGMENTS

Paradoxes of Neoliberalism is dedicated to gender justice. The book is based on a collaborative intellectual practice that has been undertaken as part of the Transnational Feminisms Initiative (https://bcrw.barnard.edu/projects/transna tionalfeminisms) at the Barnard Center for Research on Women (BCRW) (https://bcrw.barnard.edu/). We began with a one-day symposium on gender, justice, and neoliberalism that led to a special issue of BCRW's webjournal *Scholar and Feminist Online* (http://sfonline.barnard.edu/gender-justice-and-neoliberal-transformations/), in which participants published short articles on their individual research projects. The capaciousness of their thinking and the expansiveness of their expertise were exhilarating – so much so that it made Elizabeth Bernstein and Janet Jakobsen, as editors of the special issue, excited about continuing the conversation. In particular, could further discussions move the analysis from case-by-case analysis to a more synthetic approach that would bring together thinking across our various research sites and particular case studies?

A common method of social analysis is to think of each case study as an instance of a more general phenomenon, to think of national austerity programs, for instance, as particular facets of a global neoliberal political economy. And yet as our analysis throughout the book shows, there is no singular and general phenomenon that can encompass all specific instances of neoliberal economics or politics. Instead, in pursuing our collaborative discussions, we found that we were working not with a general phenomenon and a set of particular instances in which that phenomenon was realized, but rather with a set of dynamic, complex, overlapping, contradictory, and yes, paradoxical, inter-relations. Together, these relations might materialize neoliberal*ism*, but they did so through overlapping practices and policies, through the travels of specific tropes and mechanisms of governance to different areas of the world, and through the type of "resemblance" that might, as Wittgenstein points out, allow us to recognize a social undertaking as a game even if there is no single characteristic common to all games.

To analyze these dynamically crisscrossed relations took more than the collected set of essays offered in *Scholar & Feminist Online*. It took reading together – both each other's work and that of many other scholars. It took a series of meetings in different locations over five years, meetings that included not just our scholarly discussions but also conversations with local activists who had been negotiating the paradoxes of neoliberalism on behalf of sexual and gender justice. It took another full-day conference to discuss what we had learned with a broader audience of scholars and public advocates. And it took the process of writing and editing our book chapters as a collective endeavor. Pursuing this rigorously collaborative method was strenuous; life and loss intervened more than once in our efforts to bring this book to completion. But through our interactions, we also learned to think differently about gender and justice, about neoliberalism, about research itself, and about social change.

One of the greatest challenges of the entire process was producing a book that could provide even a semblance of the synthetic richness of our discussions. Although no book could fully represent all the themes that we considered, our hope is that the book does provide our readers with some new understandings and some inspiration about the possibilities for collaborative intellectual work. Thus, our greatest thanks are to one another, and to each of the participants who made the discussions over the years so abundant: Ana Amuchástegui, Elizabeth Bernstein, Sealing Cheng, Abosede George, Maja Horn, Janet Jakobsen, Kerwin Kaye, Tami Navarro, Mark Padilla, Mario Pecheny, Sine Plambech, and Svati Shah.

The chapters demonstrate our commitment to collaborative thinking and action, even as the institutional environments that we inhabit as scholars tend to value individual contributions over collaboration. It is also often the case that successful collaborative projects require a coordinator to bring together different intellectual and institutional trajectories. Elizabeth Bernstein, who was the scholarly leader for the initial BCRW symposium, has fulfilled this coordinating role for the project as a whole. Janet Jakobsen, who was Director of BCRW when this project was initiated, worked to bridge the connections between our intellectual work and the material realities of trying to coordinate twelve interdisciplinary scholars working at different institutions in various regions of the world. BCRW also provided invaluable administrative labor for all of the meetings. We are particularly grateful to Pamela Phillips, Tami Navarro, Catherine Sameh, Tina Campt, and Elizabeth Castelli for their support of the project at each of its different stages.

Another exuberant set of thank yous is due to the participants who organized our meetings. We began with a meeting in 2013 organized by Mario Pecheny through the University of Buenos Aires, in conjunction with the International Association for the Study of Sexuality, Culture, and Society. Mario also arranged

xiv Acknowledgments

for members of our research group to meet with a group of activists in Buenos Aires who were working at the intersection of advocacy for gender justice (at that time with a specific focus on transgender rights) and resistance to neoliberalism. This conversation provided crucial insight into how political and economic power works in neoliberal settings, and strategies for resistance. It also set up the format for our future meetings in which we conjoined the discussions of the research group and discussions with local activists. Ana Amuchástegui was similarly generous in organizing a meeting for us in Mexico City in conjunction with the Universidad Autónoma Metropolitana-Xochimilco. The conference, "*Sexo, Poder y Dinero: Perspectivas Críticas sobre la 'Trata de Mujeres'*" ("Sex, Power, and Money: Critical Perspectives on 'Trafficking in Women'") (https:// www.youtube.com/watch?v=5OJF19LYjtY and (https://www.youtube.com/ watch?v=kzJAQfNjCIA), was organized by Ana and by Marta Lamas of the National Autonomous University of Mexico (UNAM). Our meeting that year was enriched by both the conference and meetings with members of the Brigada Callejera (whose innovative activist projects we discuss in Chapter 1). Sine Plambech organized the concluding conference, "Sex, Migration and New World Disorder," (https://www.diis.dk/en/event/sex-migration-and-new-world-disorder) through the Danish Institute for International Studies in Copenhagen. As a public conference to share some of our emerging analysis with a broader public, this conference proved particularly helpful. In addition to Sine, we are grateful to the invited scholars who participated and shared their research in this setting: Bridget Anderson, Lisa Duggan, Eric Fassin, Inderpal Grewal, and Kamala Kempadoo. At this meeting, we also were fortunate enough to be able to meet with the research team from the Centre for Women's and Gender Research at the University of Bergen, Norway, to discuss their related research project, WAIT, "Waiting for an Uncertain Future: The Temporalities of Irregular Migration" (https://www.uib.no/en/project/wait). During the period of our work together, the BCRW sponsored two additional meetings in New York, one in conjunction with the "For the Public Good" conference (http://bcrw.barnard.edu/event/ for-the-public-good-conference/), which also included a panel discussion with New York gender justice advocates Kate D'Adamo, Amber Hollibaugh, Tiloma Jayasinghe, Sydnie Mosley, Penelope Saunders, and Tourmaline (http://bcrw .barnard.edu/videos/gender-justice-and-activisms-in-new-york-city/).

While this brief description of our meetings may provide some indication of the ampleness of our discussions, it also indicates how difficult it was to move from wide-ranging intellectual engagement to lucid prose. In addition to the editorial work provided by each member of our research team, we benefited from the generosity and wisdom of everyone who read the manuscript. Sine Plambech helped to edit early versions of the initial chapters, and the first draft of the manuscript was read by Randi Gressgård from the University of Bergen and Cecelia Varela from the University of Buenos Aires. Their insights led us to strengthen our understanding of paradoxes (as discussed in Chapter 1) and to think through what Cecelia Varela termed the "deep intersectionality" formed by the interlocking histories of neoliberal social relations. The reviewers for Routledge Press similarly spurred us to deepen our analysis of the genealogies and current relations among and within racial capitalism, decoloniality, and feminist and queer materialism (as discussed in Chapter 2). The editors of the Social Justice series at Routledge, particularly Davina Cooper, guided us through the process of revising the book so as to bring these insights to the fore in the midst of a far-reaching analysis produced by an interdisciplinary group of scholars. Our exceptionally capable research assistants, Erin Ward and Aneliza Ruiz, helped us with a wide array of tasks in order to prepare the final manuscript for publication, and the work of Svetlana Kitto was crucial in the final stages of proofreading and copy-edits.

We undertook this collaborative book project because our initial discussions showed that no single framework of analysis could comprehend neoliberalism. We offer not a comprehensive and global account of neoliberalism, but one that is necessarily partial and paradoxical, one that reflects the differences among neoliberal policies and practices in our specific field sites, and one that synthesizes diverse modes of scholarship. Here, at the conclusion of the project, we have come to understand that collaborative action, along with collaborative knowledge production, is necessary to gender justice. We are thankful for the support of all the people and organizations named in these acknowledgments for the generosity, patience, intelligence, and insight that has allowed a project of this scope and complexity to come to fruition. None of us knew the challenges we were taking on in agreeing to be part of this project, but we are so glad to have been participants in collaborative knowledge production. We hope that our efforts will be part of expanding movements of collaborative and synthetic intellectual labor.

Finally, we have dedicated the book to Christina Crosby, who died unexpectedly from pancreatic cancer just as we were completing the manuscript and who contributed significantly to the editing process. Christina's words were often moving, and they have moved us to live on in the struggle for justice. We are infinitely grateful that some of those words are included in this book.

Janet Jakobsen and Elizabeth Bernstein

1

INTRODUCTION

Gender, justice, and the paradoxical persistence of neoliberal times

Elizabeth Bernstein and Janet Jakobsen

In the early months of 2020, as the COVID-19 pandemic extended its reach, it initially seemed as if the frenzied pace of global capitalist exchange had come to an eerie standstill. By April of 2020, nearly one-third of the world's population was living under conditions of lockdown, national borders had been sealed shut, and the social organization of both productive and reproductive forms of labor had been radically upended. For many, the abrupt changes brought about by the pandemic made the longstanding inadequacies of public health care systems, social safety nets, and more general relations of care impossible to ignore.

These changes also ushered in a series of bewildering paradoxes: the common designation of some forms of labor as "essential," whereas the workers in question (disproportionately Black and brown, migrants, and female) were treated as disposable.[1] While vast numbers of people became unemployed and faced conditions of food insecurity, the wealthiest tiers of the population, both across and within nation-states, amassed unprecedented wealth.[2] With much of the population confined to the home, the importance of caring labor became visible as never before, yet there were few public provisions for domestic work or childcare.[3] At the same time, stay-at-home directives, issued in the name of protection, had little to offer those trapped in homes with abusers, or the growing numbers of people who were insecurely or inadequately housed.[4]

This book is dedicated to unraveling paradoxes such as these, and to using this understanding to guide the pursuit of social justice. Our particular contribution is to think through how sex and gender relations contribute to multiple systems of injustice, and, concomitantly, how attending to gender and sexuality – particularly in times as perilous as ours – might also contribute to the creation of a more just world.

The project began as a set of conversations among scholars working in different regions of the world, both in the Global South and the Global North,

DOI: 10.4324/9781003252702-1

2 Elizabeth Bernstein and Janet Jakobsen

conversations focused on how to understand gender justice given current systems of economic injustice. These systems are often termed "neoliberalism," and so we hoped to bring together possibilities for justice across gender and sexual identities with an in-depth analysis of neoliberalism in its various facets. In order to produce such a wide-ranging and complex analysis, the Gender Justice and Neoliberal Transformations research team met together for five years in different contexts and wrote the chapters in small groups to develop a jointly authored book manuscript. As our discussions proceeded, the group moved to add synthetic insights to a comparative method, thus allowing for broad yet focused discussions of the intersections of gender, sex, and political economy in contemporary global relations.

The purpose of the project in contributing to movements for justice had initially seemed clear enough. It turned out, however, that this project of seeking justice in the face of injustice was quite paradoxical. For instance, our conversations were given context as part of a "transnational feminisms" project sponsored by the Barnard Center for Research on Women, but both feminism and transnational activism have paradoxical aspects. As many of the participants have demonstrated in their research and as this book documents, feminist projects can often produce gender regulation along with or even instead of gender justice. For example, as Ana Amuchástegui shows in her study of peer support groups for women living with HIV/AIDS in Mexico (discussed in Chapters 3 and 6), the peer groups produce both a sense of empowerment for the participants and a need to enact the imperatives of a regulatory state and disciplinary capitalism as the conditions of sustaining the participants' lives. Svati Shah's research (discussed in Chapter 5) argues that the discourse of sexuality in India produces both an expansion of sexual possibility and a discourse of narrowing nationalism (Shah 2015). Furthermore, project co-director Elizabeth Bernstein has shown how the discourse of sex trafficking can expand state violence precisely through its invocation and development of an anti-violence rhetoric about sexuality (Bernstein 2018). As we will discuss further below, rather than taking up a simple version of feminism with a singular subject (the "global woman," for example), we approach these paradoxes as the necessarily complicated substance of any feminist project.[5]

We find similar paradoxes in our engagement across locations, an engagement that is at once grounded in specific local contexts and attendant to international relations and transnational discourses that become embodied in complex ways in these localities. It is not simply, for example, that transnational discourses have different effects in different locations, but rather that there is no single relation between the local and the inter- or transnational. The transnational does not directly determine what happens locally, even as it can have profound effects. Those effects are various, and they may be formed by the immediate pressures of local policies and/or the long-standing histories of global relations. Moreover, the transnational is not necessarily made from the top down, simply from the edicts of transnational institutions, but also from thickly woven mats of local policies and practices that hold hegemonic relations in place across localities, even as these patterns may differ from mat to mat and place to place.

Notably, what began as a project under one set of conditions with a set of case studies developed over years of conversation (and, in some cases, decades of critical and ethnographic work by collective members) is being completed under what can seem like a totally different set of material and cultural conditions – thanks in no small part to the profound disruptions that have been wrought by the effects of COVID-19.[6] When doing work about contemporary social relations, scholarship is always published as the history of the recent past, but the question of the relation between the recent past and the current moment is thrown into high relief by converging crises that include (but are not limited to) the global pandemic caused by the novel coronavirus, accelerated climate change, and the deadly and racist effects of militarization and policing.[7]

As these crises have flared, we have found that some of the case studies in this book seem more pertinent than ever, while others can serve as crucial background and context. Taken together, the cases we consider illuminate the means by which we got here – i.e., how neoliberal policies and practices have created the conditions of these crises. They also reveal both the abrupt changes and the deep continuities between the past and the present that have produced these crises. Some of our case studies show how neoliberal governance was developed transnationally, even as this apparatus is now being used to promote or solidify a phase of "nationalist neoliberalism."[8] We also demonstrate that some phenomena that now seem new were already happening in embryonic form, even as so many familiar patterns of social and economic life have been upended. For example, in Chapter 2, through case studies in the Dominican Republic and the United States (US) we document the role of gender (in)justice in the formation of mainstream productive economies, in social reproduction, and in survival economies inhabited by and sustaining many marginalized people. Throughout this book, we focus particular attention on those whose lives have been made most precarious by neoliberal policies and practices, often those disempowered by relations of social difference in the context of neoliberal political economy. By bringing the study of survival economies to the fore as a necessary part of any economic analysis, we also shift understandings of reproductive and productive economies, while focusing on those whose lives have been most affected by the injustice of neoliberal policies and practices. Notably, in relation to the COVID-19 pandemic, much of the service sector and informal economies on which marginalized people depend have come to a virtual standstill, even as public discussions of the important and, indeed, essential aspects of service work have moved to the fore.

In tracking these shifts in our case studies, we ask: how is it that the forms of neoliberal governance of the past several decades have produced this set of global responses to current crises? The path has been paradoxical, and we will argue it is particularly worthwhile to attend to those paradoxes. And in our view, it remains necessary to think about possibilities for justice, even in the midst of devastating

4 Elizabeth Bernstein and Janet Jakobsen

crises. Disaster capitalism, so clearly named by Naomi Klein (2007), is not the only possible outcome. Tracing paradoxical effects can also point to interstices, interventions, and inter-relations that might provide the ground for something other than the devastating problems of the current moment (whatever they may be when and where you are reading this).

Neoliberalism

As this book will show, there are many paradoxes of neoliberalism, perhaps not least of which is the paradox of its continuation in many areas of the world. The demise of neoliberalism has been repeatedly proclaimed (and we have at different points in this project thought about shifting our point of reference). But the import and, indeed, urgency of analyzing neoliberal governmentality has also persistently reasserted itself. After the financial crisis of 2008, it seemed that perhaps governments would have to respond to the poisoned fruits of neoliberalism by shifting away from such policies and practices. As Janet Jakobsen and Ann Pellegrini noted in 2009: "At the World Economic Forum in Davos, for example, one of the panel discussions asked directly, 'Is Neoliberalism Dead?' The assembled captains of industry and finance, however, decided (much to their apparent relief) that neoliberalism was very much alive."[9] Although there were indeed some shifts after 2008, major components of neoliberal formations, including the dominance of financial markets over industrial production, a focus on shareholder wealth, growing inequality, and the imposition of austerity measures, continued and often intensified.

As discontent with neoliberal policies and practices also continued apace, it seemed that the middle of the next decade might see a major shift in governmentality. Did the installation of new "strongmen" in some countries along with growing nationalist populism point to a profound change in approach? Insofar as neoliberalism is a transnational phenomenon, were different areas of the world shifting in their fundamental political-economic framework? And if so, were they all shifting in the same direction? Did the 2016 election of Donald Trump as president of the US represent a rejection of the neoliberal policies that had dominated US economics and politics for over three decades? Or alternatively, was Trump's election an intensification of those very same policies as enacted through tax cuts favoring the rich (the major legislative victory of his administration)? Had the world renewed its embrace of neoliberal austerity wrapped in promises of freedom, or had it instead moved into the authoritarian thrall of "thug love"? (Amar 2013, 2016).

The comparative and synthetic work of this project suggests that the answer to such questions is "all of the above." In some regions, there has been an intensification of existing neoliberal conservatism (e.g., India, South Korea), while other places (e.g., Argentina) have managed the paradoxes of neoliberalism through repeated political change *via* the early adoption of neoliberalism, a subsequent move to what contributing author Mario Pecheny (2012/2013) has termed "post-neoliberalism," a recent return to neoliberal practices, and an uncertain political future. Latin American economist James M. Cypher summarizes this complex history as follows: "[S]ince 1973, (excepting the complex case of Venezuela), Latin America has shifted into and out of and then sometimes back into mutating neoliberal economic structures. While in power, left governments have been conditioned by prior neoliberal reforms that they have been unable to shake. Neoliberalism has thrived, died, and been resurrected in a dizzying sequence that defies linear interpretation ... . In late 2018, the two largest nations in Latin America – Brazil and Mexico – moved in opposite directions, with Mexico's new president declaring the end of neoliberalism while Brazil's burning Amazon became another textbook expression of [Milton] Friedman's possessive individualism – 'free' unregulated land grabbers were left unhindered to clear land to implement ecology-destroying agribusiness operations" (Cypher 2019, 22).

Since the onset of the global pandemic created by the novel coronavirus, however, Brazil and Mexico, despite their political differences, have hewn closer to the same line with a resistance to mitigation efforts driven by economics as well as politics. Up to 60% of people living in Mexico make their incomes through unregistered businesses, street sales, and other survival economies (Linthicum 2020). A nationwide lockdown in Mexico would have thrown large numbers of people, who were already in highly precarious economic positions, into a totally unsustainable situation, and yet this resistance to mitigation has allowed the virus to spread almost as widely as it has through Brazil's full political embrace of the same authoritarian denial that has followed the ecological effects of agribusiness in the Amazon.

Amongst these different – and, as Cypher (2019) suggests, "dizzyingly" nonsynchronous – formations we find no single set of policies or universal set of stages through which all political formations move, but rather a set of complex interrelations, such as those between de-industrializing areas of the Global North and the areas of the Global South where capitalism and markets are newly ascendant. Divergent enactments of neoliberal policies and practices are embedded in complex histories and continuations of colonial relations between North and South. Many analyses of neoliberalism still develop their frameworks from the perspective of the Global North. For example, David Harvey (2007) famously centers his "brief history of neoliberalism" on developments in Great Britain and the US, downplaying precedents in Chile and throughout Latin America.

Centering the Global South within the frame produces much more than a bi-focal analysis, however. Major differences remain within and among sites in the Global South. In some areas, such as Chile, neoliberalism has depended on a strong, even an authoritarian state, whereas, in other areas, such as Nigeria, neoliberal practices in relation to a weak central government are more focused on non-governmental organizations (NGOs). In some areas of the Global South, neoliberalism has involved direct structural adjustment policies imposed by global institutions like the International Monetary Fund (IMF) and the World

6 Elizabeth Bernstein and Janet Jakobsen

Bank, whereas, in other areas, structural adjustment has not been institutionally imposed but nonetheless many of the same effects have been produced through the operations of the market.

To understand contemporary political economy and social relations adequately, then, requires a wide lens that does not simply divide the world between "neoliberal" and "populist," or between North and South.[10] What is needed, instead, is a view of the multiple relations and flows across different local formations, as well as differences within particular localities.

Analyzing the current political moment in different areas of the world, we describe both political and affective ambivalences, but even in areas moving toward authoritarian leadership, neoliberal economics and policies often remain active. What is most prevalent are recombinant formations, which place neoliberal economics in relation to new political formations or which intensify some neoliberal policies while attenuating others. Following neoliberal paradoxes as they travel across sites also allows us to understand how various issues, including especially the relation between sexual politics and political economy, are managed by various political actors – politicians, media commentators, and activists – in response to these fraught political formations.

Not only does "neoliberalism" name a paradoxical bundle of policies and practices, but contemporary governmentality is also produced by practices that have been layered over time. One of the major arguments of our project is that neoliberal transformations both maintain the old contradictions of capitalism and democracy, and, at the same time introduce new taxing levels of incoherence. Part of what we demonstrate throughout this book is the persistence of classically liberal formations, including gender and race relations, which do not simply disappear, even as new policies and practices reshape and reconfigure these older approaches so as to produce a particularly lethal form of capitalism.

In this sense, we analyze neoliberalism along epistemological lines suggested by Annemarie Mol's (2002) conceptualization of a "body multiple." Adapting Mol's concept to that of a "social body multiple" allows for an analysis that recognizes the concatenation of policies and practices that make up a social phenomenon, like neoliberalism, without making any single attribute the leading or definitive indicator of the overall phenomenon.[11] Instead, we understand the various policies and practices of neoliberalism as imbricated, often overlapping without any singular characteristic holding all social relations together.

Rather than try to define a singular version of neoliberalism, we are interested in its capacity to designate so many distinct processes and entities. For neo-Marxists, it is an agenda of upward economic redistribution, one that is characterized by structural adjustment policies and the relocation of industrial production from North America and Europe to Global South markets. For Foucaultians, neoliberalism has been imagined as a cultural project, premised upon marketized governmentalities which produce self-regulating and calculative "good subjects." And for political sociologists, neoliberalism has often been conjured as a new mode of statecraft, with privatization, the shift from the welfare state to the carceral state, and the attendant rise of new governing institutions (including NGOs, religious organizations, and corporate entities) among its most significant features. For queer, feminist, and critical race theorists, neoliberalism allows for the (re)deployment of social hierarchies and violence through legal recognition and institutional incorporation.[12]

Neoliberalism is so uneven in part because it is enacted through such a wide range of accumulative mechanisms. We canvas just a few here so as to show the complexity of neoliberal formations along with the dangers of focusing on a single phenomenon as indicative of the social formation itself.[13] From the 1970s through the 1990s, for example, neoliberalism was often associated with *structural adjustment policies* enforced by transnational institutions like the IMF and the World Bank, but many countries that were not subjected to these specific policies nevertheless felt the effects of neoliberal austerity plans, sometimes from their own national governments, and sometimes with more international or transnational enforcement.

In order to explain the effects of neoliberalism in locations that were not the direct object of neoliberal enforcement, analysts have pointed to a number of shifts in economic organization (both within nation-states and globally) that have changed economic and political relations. *Financialization* is sometimes taken to be the leading edge of neoliberalism, an edge that can create financial crises like the "Asian" crisis of 1997–98 and the US and European crisis of 2008.[14] Although consumerism continues to be important to capitalist accumulation, much consumer spending is now powered by debt instead of the Taylorist compromise of the twentieth century, in which factory jobs provided not just production but the wages enabling consumption. Even with production diminished and wages stagnant, economic value may still be created not through production and consumption but through the development of financial instruments that allow for the sale of and profit from the trading of many types of debt. These financial instruments also allow for the financialization and trading of risk well beyond the traditional insurance industry or the twentieth-century commodity "futures" markets.

For actors whose profits depend on financial markets alone, it can seem as if people are no longer necessary to economic value, at least not in the ways they were in a market organized around production and consumption. And, importantly, it is possible to track neoliberal policies that make similar assumptions about no longer needing people (at least not people whose lives do not contribute to financial markets), not even in a "reserve army of labor." Gargi Bhattacharyya in *Rethinking Racial Capitalism: Reproduction and Survival* (2018, 19) makes the point that contemporary economic relations, particularly in postcolonial nations, do not necessarily create and maintain potential laborers for imperial or urban centers: "The inhabitants of the necropolis may no longer represent a reserve of labor, if they ever did, and we may need to think again about whether symbolic others, holding spaces and unmarked territories constitute the same kinds of reserve at all." And, indeed, as discussed in Chapter 5 of this volume, "Borders

8 Elizabeth Bernstein and Janet Jakobsen

and Boundaries," many of our collaborative conversations focused on the time that people spend waiting as a primary marker of neoliberal social relations. Even those who do manage to migrate to imperial centers may find themselves in a different geopolitical place, but still waiting.

This sense of no longer needing to sustain people's lives in even marginal ways is another marker of neoliberal policies and practices, often summarized as focusing on *individualism* and *personal responsibility* instead of society and public goods.[15] Public policy is understood only to support the operation of the market and perhaps those individuals who can support themselves. Any number of commentators have shown that those who think of themselves as autonomous individuals are, however, not self-sufficient but rather dependent upon service economies for everything from cooking and cleaning to washing their clothes and managing their schedules. But, nonetheless, those who are not imagined as individuals or who are not part of the service sector upon which these "individuals" depend have widely come to be considered disposable (Wright 2006; Tadiar 2012/2013).

In other words, it is not just factory workers who are now disposable because there is a reserve army of laborers available to replace them. Rather, as the economic base moves from industrial production to financial markets, entire populations are excluded from any possibility of access to factory work or even to service work and so become disposable *tout court*, as Neferti Tadiar suggests about some communities in the Philippines that can access neither subsistence factory work nor migration for service work (Tadiar 2012/2013). We also saw proclamations of precisely this form of disposability in the US and Britain early in the coronavirus pandemic, when, for example, various US politicians in a number of states, including the Texas Lieutenant Governor and a member of the US House of Representatives from Indiana, suggested it was best to let people die rather than to harm the economy (LeBlanc 2020; Yong 2020). And, specifically, whole populations, including people of color and elderly and disabled people, were imagined as more of a burden on the economy than as contributors to economic value or even potential consumers. This line of reasoning was made explicit by one local politician in northern California who stated directly that, "We would have significant loss of life, we would lose many elderly, that would reduce burdens on our defunct Social Security System, health care cost (once the wave subsided), make jobs available for others, and it would also free up housing in which we are in dire need of ... We would lose a large portion of the people with immune and other health complications. I know it would be loved ones as well. But that would once again reduce our impact on medical, jobs, and housing" (Prieve 2020). Thus, neoliberal economies are hardly the liberal political economy that depended on "citizens" and "workers," even as the liberal categories dividing people into different populations and some of the architecture of colonial formations that constituted liberalism also continue in the neoliberal era.

Global trade, with increasingly interconnected communications, supply chains, and financial relations, is another marker that is sometimes taken to be paradigmatic of neoliberalism. And, certainly, in the 1970s the move to globalization *via* the expansion of supply chains and the outsourcing of jobs beyond national borders led to many of the economic effects that produced the end of the era of Keynesian political economies, which had predominated in many countries since the global depression of the 1930s. For example, "stagflation" in the US in the 1970s resulted in part because the effectiveness of Keynesian policies in favor of government stimulus was reduced. If every dollar in government spending had once multiplied many times as it moved through a national economy, government action could hold up economic growth in the face of threatened downturns. And then, as growth heated up, the government could reduce the stimulus to control inflation. But, with a global economy, each dollar of spending by a national government might well move into other areas of the world, leaving the (national) Gross Domestic Product (GDP) stagnant, even as inflation, driven in part by, for example, the global effects of the oil and gas industry, might grow despite the lack of growth in GDP: stagflation.

Although globalization was central to the development of neoliberal policies in many areas of the world, going forward it may not remain so central. As we have noted, the response to the problematic recovery from the 2008 financial crisis may have already led to a turn toward "nationalist neoliberalism," and responses to COVID-19 have also taken a nationalist turn, whether toward nationalist travel bans enforced by many countries, or in the national stockpiling of ventilators, PPE, and vaccine technologies, or even in the more federalist response of the European Union (EU) to the economic consequences of the pandemic.[16] Nationalist neoliberalism can name the ways in which policies can turn away from global relations, like trade and migration, even as other aspects of neoliberalism, like financialization and marketization, are continued or intensified. We will consider nationalist neoliberalism in some depth in several of our chapters, in particular Chapters 2 and 6, but our discussion here signals the danger of taking a single characteristic as being indicative of neoliberalism as a whole.

The value of our approach to neoliberalism as a paradoxical social body multiple is that it enables an analysis of hegemonic relations without requiring unsustainable claims to epistemological coherence. Even while taking multiplicity seriously, we can show how neoliberal practices affect power relations, including the ambivalences and paradoxes of those relations. Such an approach also allows for the disarticulation of neoliberalism and any single characteristic, whether it is that of imposed austerity or that of globalized economies. Our analysis traces such paradoxes and outlines how the very incoherence created by multi-layered and crisscrossing policies can be productive for powerful elites.

Paradoxes

We adopt the analytic possibilities offered by the idea of "paradoxes of neoliberalism" in order to bring some of these generative ambivalences to the fore.

10 Elizabeth Bernstein and Janet Jakobsen

Sealing Cheng brought this term into our conversations for one of our first video presentations as a means to describe her research on neoliberal government responses to sex workers in South Korea (2012/2013, and Chapter 4 of this volume).[17] The South Korean government took up a de-regulatory attitude typical of much neoliberal governance, letting the market operate more "freely." At the same time, the market for sexual commerce was subjected to more intense regulation, including policies that limited the neighborhoods and spaces in which sexual commerce could operate. Cheng notes a similar paradox in her research on migration to Hong Kong, as she describes in Chapter 5. Migration is often understood as the site of a new global mobility concomitant to neoliberal globalization, and, in part, this is true. But Cheng's research in Hong Kong shows that, even before the coronavirus pandemic, migrants often experienced years of immobility while waiting without access to jobs. In this case, sexual relationships and specifically marriage provided one of the only means to change one's status, whether by simply allowing for work and money to survive or, in the case of marriage, a move into a government-legitimated migration status that would also open doors to new labor markets.

The particular paradox between mobility and stasis was echoed in conversations between Abosede George and Sine Plambech at the final conference for our project, regarding migration to Europe from Nigeria. The experience of migrants can be as much one of stasis and waiting as of motion. George discussed the extended "waiting" for a deferred adulthood, delayed indefinitely by the unavailability of jobs with wages that might sustain an adult living as part of the social forces prompting migration, even as the experience of migration itself may be one of more waiting – waiting to be able to leave, waiting to arrive in a new destination, and waiting for a conclusion to the migratory journey, such as that provided by a new status. Movement may itself be blocked by being returned "home" at various points along the way to start a new round of waiting. Mark Padilla documents a related mobility-for-stasis (discussed in Chapter 5) in which migrants from the Dominican Republic to the US might be deported back to the Dominican Republic, only to find life no longer sustainable there, initiating a return to the US in a process that may be repeated more than once. In this formulation, mobility is a paradoxical experience that may either directly result in a static experience of waiting or in a more complex, but nonetheless similarly static experience of never-ending mobility.

And, indeed, Cheng's sense of paradox is apparent in many of the commonly identified characteristics of neoliberal social formations. For example, what is usually called neoliberal "privatization" is generally understood as a move from government service provision to the private sector. The phenomenon is apparent in the move from public education to privately run charter schools, or when public hospitals are absorbed into networks of corporately run hospitals. In neoliberal terms, privatization is supposed to provide more efficient service provision based on market principles and increased competition, that is also supposed to lower costs. And the shift from the public sector to private enterprise is also supposed to create the leaner and more efficient government that conservatives promise their constituents. Paradoxically, though, while privatization may turn many institutions and services over to corporate control, this move does not necessarily entail operation by market principles and concomitant smaller government. Instead, privatization may also involve an expansion of government contracting. Charter schools, for instance, often depend on government-owned and -operated school buildings, various forms of state support, including tax breaks, and government help in controlling or removing unionization. And, when these government-provided privileges might be removed, corporations fight hard for them to be sustained, indicating corporate dependence on the government.

We see a similar paradox in the move toward service provision through non-governmental organizations. Many commentators have noted an exponential expansion of NGOs since the advent of neoliberalism, particularly beginning in the 1990s. Josephine Ho (2008) has pointed out the ways in which transnational hegemonic power comes to bear on everyday life in many parts of Asia through a proliferation of different not-quite-governmental agencies – NGOS, Business Organized NGOs (BONGOs), etc. And, as Sine Plambech argues in Chapter 4, one of the main manifestations of neoliberal governance in Nigeria and places with weaker central states is through the expanded activity and power of both local and transnational NGOs. One of the effects of this NGO-ization can be that activism that has historically been autonomous from the state is now undertaken in terms regulated by the government and with a focus shifted from changing the structure of the state to greater integration into those structures while doing the work of the state through service provision. Sonia Alvarez (2010) has tracked this in documenting the relation between formerly autonomous feminist movements, NGOs working with major transnational funders like the Ford Foundation, and government action, including by professionalized governmental feminists. Similarly, in the US, social movements like those for gender and sexual liberation, which often started with strong critiques of state power and of policing, in particular, can become arms of that very power, when, for example, domestic violence work shifts from a model of mutual aid to one focused on policing "perpetrators." Paradoxically, then, as Siobhan Brooks (2012/2013) points out, one way to define neoliberalism is not through privatization and smaller government, but "as the investment and integration of social movements into state-sponsored institutions, such as electoral power, market power, marriage, citizenship, and the military."

We were able to locate the discussion of paradoxes within our research group in a conceptual genealogy deriving from David Scott's (2004) foundational *Conscripts of Modernity: The Colonial Tragedy of Enlightenment* and flowing through J Kēhaulani Kauanui's (2018) dazzling *Paradoxes of Hawaiian Sovereignty: Land, Sex, and the Colonial Politics of State Nationalism*. Kauanui draws upon Scott's analysis of the ways in which both colonial practices and enlightenment thought accompanying colonialism create conditions of possibility that do not enable simple or clear distinctions. Nor do these paradoxes permit easy choices for activism. One cannot make a "simple choice for or against" enlightenment, or, in the case considered by Kauanui (2018, 20), for or against sovereignty. Kauanui (2018, 20) is interested in the ways in which sovereignty is both an inescapable part of what Scott calls the "permanent legacy" of colonialism and also a possibility drawn from a "precolonial past" and open to a decolonial future: "Indigenous resurgence is a liberatory framework grounded in distinct precolonial epistemes."[18] Similarly, as we will discuss in Chapter 2, domestic workers organizing in the US through the National Domestic Workers Alliance have argued both for a Domestic Workers Bill of Rights and for a total revaluing of capitalist social relations that includes a critique of capitalism and the structure of global political economy. Their strategy shows how the paradoxes of neoliberalism can be taken up in organizing strategies that are not trapped within, but which rather build in creative ways from the point of paradox.

The realization of such creativity often depends on being able to identify the ambivalences created by paradoxical relations so as to shift them to an ambi-valent opening to different possibilities. Scott (2004, 22) develops the analytic import of paradoxes through his reading of CLR James's *The Black Jacobins*: "We look back, today, through the remains of a postcolonial present that James looked forward to in *The Black Jacobins* as the far-off horizon of an imagined sovereignty. Of course, the future when it came, came touched by suffering and ambiguity; it was not exactly the future James might have envisioned." Taking up Scott's sense of paradox allows Kauanui to emphasize the ambiguity, not just the suffering.[19] And by placing our conversations about neoliberalism in a conceptual genealogy established by Scott and Kauanui, we are able to attend not only to the suffering resultant from the effects of hegemonic power but also to the ambiguities – and the ambi-valent possibilities.[20]

Part of our analysis considers the material effects of rhetorics in which gender and sex are treated as both crucial to contemporary political life and utterly irrelevant. The invocation of this particular paradox allows sexual politics to provide key elements of the kaleidoscopic common sense that constitutes neoliberalism.[21] As politicians proclaim that saving women remains a key justification for state violence – whether *via* the Trump Administration's initial travel ban with its invocation of "honor crimes," the regulation of public restrooms so as to exclude transgender people who are positioned as intrinsically dangerous, or the militarization of Mexico's border with Guatemala so as to stop "sex trafficking" – they also argue that gender justice is disposable in relation to "more important" issues, such as economics or war and peace.[22] The ability to move from one position to the other – from claims about the importance of gender and sex to the dismissal of sexual politics – allows political actors to highlight questions of gender and sexuality on behalf of a range of issues, while also containing the possible effects of this discourse once these issues are mobilized.

Our analysis suggests that sexual politics are centrally constitutive of neoliberal formations and that analyzing the complexity of that constitutive role is crucial to a broad conception of social justice. Engagement with gender and sexuality is, for example, central to theorizing the feminization of migration, the growth in affective labor as part of the market, neoliberal transformations of the welfare state, and the increasing precarity of workers. Comparative study highlights the varying and complex roles played by gendered and sexual politics as crucial joists in the scaffolding of neoliberal hegemony, including both economic relations and statecraft.

Gendered labor markets are one of the major apparatuses that connect different areas of the world in neoliberal relations. Gendered labor is, for example, central to the landscape of de-industrialization in the Global North with the loss of masculinized industrial jobs in relation to the expansion of a feminized service sector, while feminized industrial production has arisen in the developing markets of the Global South. Gender and sexuality are also deeply entwined with the affects that instantiate neoliberal policies and practices. Sometimes the promises linking neoliberalism, gender and sexuality are direct – i.e., the idea that neoliberal policies will open new opportunities for women in the workforce, one of the neoliberal promises that have deeply informed economic policies in parts of the Caribbean (the Dominican Republic and the US Virgin Islands in this volume). Sometimes the promises are more indirect – such as promises to "save" women from sex trafficking through policies that are compatible with neoliberal governmentality (Bernstein 2018).

The paradoxes and contradictions of these promises are apparent almost immediately. For example, as authors Kerwin Kaye, Ana Amuchástegui, Abosede George, and Tami Navarro argue in Chapter 3, at the same time that neoliberalism creates heightened conditions of vulnerability for many sectors of the population – and in profoundly gendered and sexualized ways – discourses of gender and sexuality are deployed to delineate the scope of what is understood to constitute this vulnerability, making only certain forms of gendered harm and precarity (often focused only on a singular or binary gender) recognizable or actionable. Conversely, sexual progress on abortion or transgender rights may be invoked to support different formations in different places (progressive neoliberalism in Mexico or post-neoliberalism in Argentina).

The very development of a transnational feminist movement, sometimes conceptualized as a single global women's movement, over the course of the neoliberal period has foregrounded the figure of the "global woman" as representative of this supposedly singular entity. Sometimes, gender and sexuality are the site for policies like those pertaining to "sex trafficking" (see Chapter 4) that bundle together economics and changes to the structure of the state. In other instances, sexual politics are an implicit dimension of broader policies on issues ranging from the relations among formal and informal sectors (Chapter 2) to the growth of financial services (Chapter 3) to instruments of governance (Chapter 4) to migration (Chapter 5) to practices of resistance (Chapter 6). Tracing the role of sexual politics across different localities and through different policies allows for a delineation of the paradoxical assemblage that makes up neoliberal hegemony.

14 Elizabeth Bernstein and Janet Jakobsen

In so doing, we build upon the work of scholars of gender and sexuality who have also sought to emphasize what Lisa Duggan (2003) has described as "the dense interrelations" among neoliberalism's economic, political, social, and cultural projects. We argue that it is impossible to disentangle economic and cultural projects, such that political economy is also sexual politics and *vice versa*. For example, writing about the World Bank in Ecuador in the 1990s, Kate Bedford (2009) observed that the promotion of complementary love within heterosexual sharing couples was a central part of the Bank's anti-poverty programs. In her ethnographic study of the Grameen Bank's heralded microcredit program in Bangladesh, Lamia Karim (2011) similarly demonstrated how micro-lending programs relied on, and ultimately came to reinforce, pre-existing gender inequities. Consistent with the analytic approach we are advocating, various feminist and queer scholars have examined the intertwined economic, gendered, and sexual interests that coalesce in corporate campaigns around seemingly progressive causes such as global campaigns for LGBT rights and the fight against breast cancer, or in the neoliberal state's appropriation of formerly liberationist discourses (of feminism and queerness) in fomenting sexual nationalisms, carceral politics, and securitized borders.[23]

Most importantly, sex is not simply a function of the relations with which it is imbricated. An analysis that cannot account for the relative autonomy of sexual politics cannot account for much that happens in social life and public debate, including the ways in which people's commitments regarding gender and sexuality (whether conservative or progressive) may be the driving force of their politics and the ways in which sexual politics may be the leading edge and model for – rather than distraction from – other forms of political action.[24] As Roger N. Lancaster (2017, 93) has argued, for example, "the techniques used for marking, shaming, and controlling sex offenders have come to serve as models for laws and practices in other domains." In an ethnography of "intimate economies" in Thailand, Ara Wilson (2004) has similarly shown some of the ways in which sex is productive of (not just productive for) capitalism in Thai society. From the familial and kinship ties that made possible the shift from personal shops to impersonal retail sales on a large scale, to sex work as a tourist industry, Wilson shows that it is just as much sexual relations that have made possible the development of capitalism as it is that capitalism has made certain sexual relations possible. And, in the US, racialized gender and sexuality contribute to the historical development of racial capitalism and also to neoliberal shifts in the structure of the welfare state, particularly through "welfare reform" in the 1990s (Bernstein and Jakobsen 2009) and the expansion of domestic work as a paid and precarious form of neoliberal labor (Bernstein and Jakobsen 2009; Crosby and Jakobsen 2020).

In addition to exploring contemporary social relations of neoliberal governance, domination, exclusion, and oppression, this volume considers gender and sexuality as forces that have shaped myriad forms of community-based activism and resistance, including local efforts to pursue new forms of social change in

Buenos Aires, Copenhagen, Mexico City, and New York. Through collaborative research and theorizing, the contributors to this volume analyze the multiple dimensions of economic and cultural restructuring that have characterized neoliberal and neoliberalizing regimes, as well as emergent activist responses to them, as they interactively circulate across the globe.

Serious consideration of the ways in which relations of gender and sexuality are themselves materially generative of political-economic possibilities allows for reimagining conventionally understood "feminist questions" (such as those pertaining to gendered violence, reproductive rights, transactional sex, or intimate labor) within a broader field of political context and historical transformation. It also allows for a reimagination of political possibility writ large. How, for example, could a shift to imagining the paradigmatic worker as a domestic worker (rather than an industrial worker) also shift possibilities for global labor organizing? How might sexual democracy (rather than the reification of traditional gender roles) contribute to anti-poverty projects? How can social justice feminism contribute to new possibilities for coalitions and alliances amongst, for example, anti-racist, anti-capitalist, and pro-environmental movements?

It is thus that we attend to *paradoxes*. The paradoxes of neoliberalism come in many different forms. They are layered and uneven, as many different systems of social relations are juxtaposed, often violently so.

Gender and justice

Gender and justice are similarly layered, heterogeneous, and compounded. In these pandemic times, when a global crisis is intensified by political and economic domination, and even as the crisis itself can be conceptualized as enabled by the injustice of climate change, we suggest that any possibility for justice demands a capacious imagination of how social relations might be changed. The relations of injustice are so globally expansive, so inextricably entwined, and so profoundly urgent that, when thinking about gender and justice, we must attend to gender in its myriad forms and in its many imbrications. And given these conditions, moving toward social justice, including gender justice, seems the only way to avert catastrophe.

Gender relations, variously constituting and constraining women, men, transgender and gender non-conforming people, are imbricated with all of the social relations we will consider throughout this book: those of colonialism, of race, of nation, and of class.[25] Maria Lugones argues, for example, that gender is "a key part of how gender fuses with race in the operations of colonial power. Colonialism did not impose precolonial, European gender arrangements on the colonized. It imposed a new gender system that created very different arrangements for colonized males and females than for white bourgeois colonizers. Thus, it introduced many genders and gender itself as a colonial concept and mode of organization of relations of production, property relations, of cosmologies, and ways of knowing" (Lugones 2007, 186). We analyze the multifarious ways in

16 Elizabeth Bernstein and Janet Jakobsen

which gender hierarchies organize, materialize, and affectively sustain colonialism, racism, and capitalism. But, as Lugones (2008) also points out, many of the analytic frameworks used to consider these relations draw upon modern, colonialist ideas of gender, even when these frameworks are otherwise dedicated to social justice. Lugones considers the ways in which the decolonial framework of sociologist Aníbal Quijano focuses gender analysis on "biological dimorphism and heterosexual patriarchy" in ways that are common to white European gender relations but, if taken to represent gender relations *tout court*, can also obscure "the ways in which "non-white" colonized women were subjected and disempowered" (Lugones 2008, 2). Such an analysis can, for example, narrow the meaning of gender to disputes over (hetero)sexuality, effectively eliding the work that gender does in organizing human labor relations or relations between humans and the natural world.

If we are to develop an analysis of gender justice, it becomes important to consider the ways in which gender relations take forms well beyond those related to "disputes/struggles over control of 'sexual access, its resources, and products'" (Quijano quoted by Lugones 2008, 2). In the next chapter, for example, our analysis considers the "ungendering" that Hortense Spillers has explicated in "Mama's Baby, Papa's Maybe" as part of the colonial relations of slavery in which enslaved people were often treated as outside either biological dimorphism or heterosexual patriarchy. Not only is an expansive and dynamic gender analysis necessary to do justice to the breadth and complexity of social relations, but it is also key to developing a vision of gender justice that does not simply reiterate the very dominations – colonialist, racist, and gendered – that justice would challenge. Our engagement with Spillers' analysis as central to understanding colonial power and enslavement leads us to join social reproduction theorists in challenging those versions of gender justice that depend upon a dimorphic split between production and reproduction in labor relations. The material effects of this problematic analysis can be seen in labor movements (both liberal and Marxian) that do not take the reorganizing of reproductive labor as necessary, along with the reorganization of productive labor. We show, for example, that domestic labor is central to contemporary, capitalist production on a global scale, even as labor movements in both national and global contexts have rarely taken the organizing of domestic workers as being central to economic justice. The complexity of social relations entangled in conditions of injustice thus necessitates complex analysis and action for any project seeking justice.

The relational contexts of neoliberal paradoxes

We address this challenge through our method of extended conversations across locations in the Global South and North, a method that also crosses epistemological frameworks. Decoloniality, analyses of racial capitalism, social reproduction theory, and feminist and queer materialism are all directly relevant to this project.[26] It is clear, for example, that racialized systems of colonialism and imperialism are enacted and extended in important ways through neoliberal policies and practices, such that Kamala Kempadoo (2017) has argued that neoliberalism should not be considered a new formation, but rather yet another episode of colonialism. As such, any study of neoliberalism must take into account the imbrication of capitalism and these racialized systems, including both the expropriation of indigenous lands and natural resources and the development of economic systems on the basis of slavery.

It is also clear that social reproduction theory remains relevant, including to an analysis of racial capitalism. In both classical economics and Marxian theory, it often seems as though human beings arrive in the world fully grown and ready to work. Social reproduction theory seeks to make visible the labor necessary to reproduce those workers. But, as José Esteban Muñoz (2009) has pointed out in *Cruising Utopia: The Then and There of Queer Futurity*, not all futures are reproductive futures, and not all gendered and sexualized labor is for reproductive purposes. A feminist and queer analytic allows for a focus on nonnormative economic relations – not just those, like housework, that don't fit into waged labor, but also those that do not fit into the usual understanding of reproduction. In other words, connecting queer, as well as feminist and anti-racist, approaches to materialism attends to labor that doesn't reproduce human beings and that is often treated as a threat to, rather than a necessary (if often unpaid) part of, society.

The analytic division between productive and reproductive labor can follow traditional divisions even as it can exclude economic activity that does not fall into either category. We not only add survival economies, but also trace the ways in which gender, race, and sex actively constitute productive, reproductive, and survival economies. In *Black Sexual Economies: Race and Sex in a Culture of Capital*, for instance, Adrienne D. Davis and the Black Sexual Economies Collective (2019) bring to the fore the range of sexualized labor enforced under slavery, including social reproduction through enforced pregnancy and the feminized labor of domestic work, and the way in which women were also involved in the a- or even un-gendered agricultural labor of the fields.[27] The analytic of slavery as a "Black sexual economy" can also show how entire industries are sexualized, even as this sexualization is based in both the racist dominations of colonialism and the expropriation and exploitation of capitalism. For example, in Chapter 2, we consider the ways in which tourism to the Dominican Republic represents precisely such a sexualized economy, in which tourism itself has been sexualized and through various colonial tropes, as have the Dominican Republic and the Caribbean more generally.

In *Rethinking Racial Capitalism: Social Reproduction and Survival*, Bhattacharyya cites the work of Kalyan Sanyal in order to bring into view economic activity outside of the traditional productive/reproductive pairing.[28] As Bhattacharyya (2018, 15) notes, "Although Sanyal arrives at his analysis through an encounter with development economies, his account of the postcolonial wasteland echoes many aspects of the experiences of racially subordinated groups in other settings." Battacharayya (2018, 44) not only connects analyses of colonialism, racial capitalism, social reproduction, feminist, and queer materialism, but also recognizes the ways in which social reproduction, along with work in survival economies, may not go to the end of simply reproducing bodies for the labor market, but may be undertaken for "reasons of love, care, community, survival."

Our analysis attends to these inter-relations and overlaps. We do so by following a line of analysis offered by Cathy Cohen (2005, 31) in her essay "Punks, Bulldaggers, and Welfare Queens," which has been foundational for "Left intersectional analysis." Cohen (2005, 37) suggests that "to realize its 'radical potential,' queer analysis must look beyond a division between gays and straights to 'the ways in which nonnormative heterosexuality has been controlled and regulated through the state and systems of marginalization.'" One way to respond to this important exhortation is to attend to nonnormative labor in relation to systems of marginalization, labor that takes place in survival economies rather than in recognized industries, labor that is not done in factories or offices but in homes, and labor that is intimate, even as it is part of market commerce.

Nonnormative labor is often done by those who are politically and economically marginalized by social relations of race, gender, and nation. Thus, analyzing this labor intersects with the violence of racial capitalism and the removal of social reproduction from paid labor. Because such intersections are complex, our approach also suggests that they do not resolve into a coherent whole. This is true working within any of these paradigms, as well as working across them. A decolonial approach, for instance, recognizes enactments of neocolonialism, postcolonial elite domination, neoliberalism, *and* post-neoliberalism as potentially simultaneous.[29] Take, for example, Mario Pecheny's (2012/2013) analysis of the dynamic shifts amongst different formations of liberal neocolonialism, neoliberalism, and post-neoliberalism. Pecheny's understanding of the effects of such dynamics forms the framework of Chapter 6. In particular, Pecheny argues that these multiple formations produce a "fractured" experience of the social, as different forms of governmentality are enacted, not just one after another, but often simultaneously, despite their disjunctions. And that disjunctive simultaneity elicits complex responses from activists, as well as from those simply trying to move from one day to the next.

Our analysis follows economies of nonnormative labor across the Global North and Global South, as well as the travels of governmental efforts to regulate these economies, such as the effects of "anti-trafficking" policies, as described in Chapter 4. We also follow the governmental deployment of borders and boundaries in ways that ease the flow of capital while blocking the movement of people, so as to make a major marker of migrant experience neither production nor reproduction, but waiting (see Chapter 5). And we trace shifts in neoliberal and post-neoliberal economies, like that of Argentina, in which issues, framed in terms of gender and sexuality, are sometimes invoked as supports of and sometimes as threats to neoliberal governance.

Global comparisons and global synthesis

To answer these questions has required a different approach to the study of neo-liberalism, one that can take into account the policies and practices that make up neoliberal governmentality in a specific locality, and one that can trace relations across uneven geopolitical terrain. Much work on neoliberalism can be divided into two approaches: either site-specific engagements or systems-level synthetic analyses.[30] Our project recognizes the contributions and limitations of both of these approaches, as the former provides specificity and depth at the expense of breadth, while the latter privileges structural forces while obscuring the par-ticularities of place and positioning. For instance, despite the valuable insights on the global continuities of power provided by analyses of global systems, this work does not sufficiently attend to the important ways people are variously positioned within their local contexts. Alternatively, scholarship on the lived effects of structural adjustment in specific locations may poignantly demonstrate the myriad failings of these economic policies, but rarely provides a way to relate these shortcomings to the broader array of changes occurring in other regions of the world.[31]

Our model brings together empirical and theoretical investigations that are situated in particular contexts, while at the same time presenting a synthetic framework for theorizing the global transformations that have been wrought by neoliberalism. This analysis emphasizes the geopolitical unevenness and dif-ferential distribution of the myriad changes that neoliberalism has ushered in. In turn, these different experiences of neoliberalism are both powerfully informed by and themselves also imply new formations of gender and sexuality.

Our project stresses the significance of insights gained by deep engagement with particular field sites, and simultaneously provides a more capacious con-ceptual framework in which differently located accounts can be read in relation to each other. The comparative element of our project allows us to maintain the necessary focus on place and relations of power, whereas the synthetic ele-ment provides a much-needed framework through which we might apprehend the structural inequalities propelling neoliberalism across the globe. Forging an analysis of social relations that can traverse issues, field sites, and existing inter-pretive frameworks has been a key ambition of this project.

Aiming to build a robust picture of context that includes key points of global comparison, we have chosen to focus upon sites and issues that highlight crucial aspects of the disparate phenomena that have been called "neoliberalism," while also drawing upon the substantive expertise of the scholars in our collabora-tion. In contrast to conventional academic anthologies, comprised of individual chapters that focus upon single case studies, *Paradoxes of Neoliberalism* presents an overarching argument comprised of six chapters which have been collabo-ratively written and which have been workshopped by the entire team, with each chapter considering a constellation of geopolitical regions and substantive issues.

20 Elizabeth Bernstein and Janet Jakobsen

This method has allowed us to build a unique analysis of neoliberalism as neither simply "local" nor overarchingly "global." Instead, through our comparative and synthetic work together, we have come to understand neoliberalism as a concatenation of policies and practices that both circulate widely and come to form sometimes dense networks of relation. So, for example, in Chapter 4, we show how the language of "sex trafficking" has circulated globally to instantiate neoliberal remedies such as heightened border control and policing, promising to reform transactional versions of sexuality and gender *via* alternative models of gendered empowerment and freedom. In Chapter 5, "Borders and Boundaries," we show that sexuality unfolds within kaleidoscopic configurations of border regimes that are structured by the global system of nation-states but are also varied in form and logic, producing gender and sexuality differently depending on the specific social characteristics that emerge as salient at a particular time and place. Our collective work draws on our ongoing ethnographic discussions across disparate sites so that the variations we describe in each of our ethnographic settings are the scaffolding on which we build our thinking. As with the specific analysis in any given chapter, the progression among the chapters is arranged so that each chapter builds upon that which precedes it to advance the principal argument of the book about the pertinence of gender and sexuality to understanding contemporary neoliberal transformations in both their general contours and paradoxical manifestations.

Justice from the ground up

This method of analysis, combined with attention to sexual politics and gender justice, helps us to bring to the fore new approaches to resistance and revolt in neoliberal times. The paradoxes of neoliberalism set up a series of double binds that are structurally enforced, while individuals are left to resolve them. Even for those who are dedicated to resistance, activism, or movements for social change, daily life is likely to be organized through instruments of governmentality that make any course of action ambivalent and paradoxical. What relation to the state should one claim or advocate when the state acts as both a source of oppression, and as one of the few avenues toward a solution to individual and global problems? These paradoxes, ambivalences, and incoherencies imply that traditional forms of resistance – e.g., those that choose to direct resistance against the state, or to work within the state, or to create a drag on capital – will face recurrent problems. Instead, approaches that recognize the paradoxical workings of power may have more chances for success (although "success" becomes harder to define).

Our project suggests building a global response from the ground up, taking the pieces of radical projects that have been variously refracted by the paradoxes of neoliberalism and pulling them together to create a powerful response, even if that power is not built from a unified approach to practice. Placing gender and sexuality at the center of analysis opens new opportunities for understanding

Introduction **21**

political possibility. For example, the contribution made by queer theory and politics to this project is the possibility of turning the perversities induced by racial capitalism toward the project of producing alternative subjectivities, subjectivities that are not coherent in normative terms and can, thus, resist the terms of governmentality (Ferguson 2003).

Some of this possibility can be found in the collaborative projects among activists, artists, and academics that *Paradoxes of Neoliberalism* explores: queer political art in the Dominican Republic, women with HIV in Mexico who have developed peer-led networks to support one another in ways that both challenge and exceed biomedicalization, organizing amongst domestic workers as the newly paradigmatic global workers, and activists across the globe who continue to fight for gender justice across multiple different neoliberal transformations.[32]

These are not the sites usually understood as the engines for revolutionary change, but, as our analysis shows, movements that are unable to incorporate gender justice are also unlikely to be able to respond to the paradoxes of neoliberalism. In the end, our project seeks new paths for global justice that crisscross the globe in a network of connection, rather than containing all possibilities for justice within a singular frame. We suggest an approach which assembles justice – in its political-economic, racial, and gendered forms – from diverse sites and from the ground up.

When our collaborative research team held a meeting in Mexico City, hosted by Ana Amuchástegui, we also met with members of the sex workers' collaborative, Brigada Callejera, for example. As activists and advocates, Brigada Callejera has navigated some of the many paradoxes of neoliberalism in important and instructive ways. Sex work was decriminalized in Mexico City in 2019, but this move has been linked to efforts to *increase* anti-trafficking enforcement and attendant governmentality (Murray 2019). And sex workers still find themselves without workplace protections. Even the condoms available to them to purchase with their own money to prevent sexually transmitted disease have often been of poor quality. So, they decided to make their own. In doing so, they produced protection of such a high quality that it was soon in demand from other sex workers, customers, and pretty much anyone who heard about the effort. The collaborative then decided to develop their own factory and began producing their condoms for a broader market rather than just for their friends, colleagues, and contacts. The money produced by the sale of these condoms, in turn, went to sustain their collective members and support their activism and advocacy on behalf of sex workers.

The efforts of the Brigada Callejera, along with those of many activists and intellectuals, have been inspirational for our collaborative efforts to write about the paradoxes of neoliberalism and the ways in which these paradoxes might be engaged. The situation in which the Brigada Callejera members found themselves is paradigmatic of many of the problems, as well as the paradoxes of neoliberalism. One neoliberal policy that tends to run in parallel with the economic precarity faced by those working in survival economies is a lack of

22 Elizabeth Bernstein and Janet Jakobsen

government support even in the face of public health challenges like HIV/ AIDS, or now the COVID-19 pandemic. Without much support for safer sex practices and limited access to "public" healthcare, the workers of Brigada Callejera are left on their own to figure out how to protect themselves. And so they do. They move away from typical neoliberal practices, though, by banding together into a workers' cooperative. Acting cooperatively, rather than as individuals personally responsible only for themselves, Brigada Callejera was able to fashion (literally) a response to their precarious situation that made many people safer – themselves as workers, their customers, and eventually, a wider public, even as this public is mediated by the market. And, so, even as Brigada Callejera moves around neoliberalism, their efforts are brought back within its market logic.

In another turn, however, their cooperative decisions about how to distribute and deploy the profits of their factory have enabled them to move outside of neoliberal parameters in other ways. The traditional neoliberal (and, indeed, liberal) expectation would have been for Brigada Callejera members to renounce sex work and go "straight" as more respectable workers, as entrepreneurs even (one of the most respected positions in neoliberal lore). But, as a number of scholars have shown, among them Elizabeth Bernstein, Sealing Cheng, Kerwin Kaye, Sine Plambech, Mark Padilla, and Svati Shah from our collective, the respectable economic paths "out of" sex work rarely provide a livable life for those who are purportedly saved from making a living by doing sex work. Instead of acceding to the values of neoliberalism, Brigada Callejera decided to reinvest their income from condom sales in a series of activities that support their sex work and their lives as sex workers. Thus, their goal has not been to move from a survival economy to a straight economy, but to resist the precarity of neoliberal work and lives overall and to do so by banding together and sustaining their bond as a brigade.

Through our conversations with the Brigada Callejera, with each other, and with the activists our collective members work with, we have learned that movement amongst neoliberal policies and practices – refusing and resisting, but also sometimes reconfiguring the demands of neoliberal economics and sociality – can be a key to not being trapped in the paradoxes of neoliberalism. We explore this question in depth in our concluding chapter, "Political Power and Practices of Resistance," by looking further into cases in Mexico, Argentina, the Dominican Republic, and the US. And we do so by connecting the inventive and creative contributions of activists like Brigada Callejera to those of HIV-positive peer educators in Mexico City, to those of artists and intellectuals who are engaged in various forms of transformative practice.

Historian Joan Scott (1996) has argued that the modern political liberalism accompanying the development of capitalism has only paradoxes to offer. Neoliberalism intensifies these paradoxes by increasing precariousness and evacuating the formerly liberal public. But in the past several years of discussions with activist groups like Brigada Callejera and with one another, we have learned to analyze the current moment in ways that allow for movement around the apparent strictures of neoliberal policies and practices, suggesting a path toward change in precarious and paradoxical times.

Plan of the book

This book is organized thematically into six collaboratively written chapters, each of which, by design, spans different regions, institutions, policies, and practices. In Chapter 2, "Gender Justice, Economic Justice: Production, Reproduction, and Survival," co-authors Janet Jakobsen, Mark Padilla, and Maja Horn, draw from two distinct settings, the Dominican Republic and the US, to think about gendered labor in ways that blur the generally assumed boundaries within and among productive, reproductive, and survival economies. In the DR, work in the informal sector accounts for nearly one-half of non-agricultural employment and is, thus, incredibly important to the economy as a whole, facilitating economic survival for many people. In studying domestic work in the US, we similarly recognize the role of informal employment and the interstitial spaces of the workforce that are most open to migrants, in this case predominantly women of color. Informal labor in both the DR and US has been part of a larger expansion of the service sector in the neoliberal era, an expansion that is inter-related, not just with shifts in productive and reproductive relations, but also with shifts in migratory patterns and global economic structures. We thus argue that social movement action across sites of social difference, different economic sectors, and national boundaries can make a major difference in the effects of and the effectiveness of resistance to neoliberal policies and practices.[33] As such, this first substantive chapter in our book tracks the full and varied imbrication of gender justice and economic justice.[34] One is not possible without the other.

In Chapter 3, "Neoliberal Vulnerability and the Vulnerability of Neoliberalism," Kerwin Kaye, Ana Amuchástegui, Abosede George, and Tami Navarro together consider a central cultural and political paradox of neoliberalism, one with important implications for questions of sex and gender. On the one hand, shifts in the living and working conditions that people confront under neoliberalism, alongside new forms and distributions of gendered precarity, demand immediate attention and analysis. At the same time, shifts in representations of endangerment and the changing institutional mechanisms through which narratives of vulnerability and suffering are communicated have profoundly altered the terrain in which we think about exposure to harm. As a result, neoliberal discourses of vulnerability often work to shore up sexual and gendered inequalities, despite the fact that these same mechanisms can also be deployed "from below" to advance certain kinds of ameliorative claims. Utilizing a number of case studies, including women living with HIV in Mexico City, the #BringBackOurGirls movement in Nigeria, the rise of development programs within the US Virgin Islands, and street youth engaged in the San Francisco sex trade, the authors further demonstrate how a focus on gender and sexuality within neoliberalism yields fresh insights into conditions of precarity as well as their governance. They

24 Elizabeth Bernstein and Janet Jakobsen

argue that, under neoliberalism, the exceptionalizing discourse of vulnerability has transformed and delimited prior discussions of citizenship, social justice, and human rights.

Building upon this analysis, in Chapter 4, "The Productive Incoherence of 'Sex Trafficking,'" Elizabeth Bernstein, Sealing Cheng, Sine Plambech, and Mario Pecheny demonstrate how a specific and prominent instance of gendered neoliberal governance – burgeoning transnational campaigns against sex trafficking – has been shaped by both locally specific histories and broader political-economic trends. In this chapter, the authors resituate global feminist concerns about the threat of sex trafficking by tracking the travels of this discourse across national and international borders over the course of the past two decades. Despite significant evidence that the trafficking framework is neither descriptive nor ameliorative when it comes to the lived experiences of women, men, and transgendered people who engage in sexual labor, they argue that this political rubric does important work to shore up locally specific gender agendas, as well as broader neoliberal commitments to incarceration, border securitization, and capitalist exchange. Drawing upon fieldwork in the US, South Korea, Nigeria, and Argentina, they demonstrate the ways that global legal frames have interfaced with local debates around gender, sexuality, citizenship, and nationhood in the reconfiguration of state apparatuses. In so doing, the authors show the productive incoherence that has made trafficking a simultaneously durable and malleable framework for the contemporary governance of sex and gender. The combination of consistency and fungibility in the trafficking discourse allows it to be a mechanism by which the incoherence of neoliberalism becomes productive of new formations of gender and sexuality, as well as broader patterns of exclusion that pertain to marginalized populations.

In Chapter 5, "Borders and Boundaries: Thinking Migration, Sex, and Precarity in a Neoliberal Age," co-authors Sine Plambech, Mark Padilla, Sealing Cheng, and Svati Shah provide an in-depth analysis of the ways in which gender and sexuality are integral to structuring the patterns of migration and border control that are a core feature of precarity in the neoliberal age. Over the neoliberal period, migration has been the site of one of the most productively incoherent sets of policies and practices. The neoliberal period has been a time of increasing border regulation and rising nationalism, which is often interpreted in popular media and activist circles as an openness to the movement of capital but not of people.[35] Yet neoliberal political economies have depended on the movement of people and on the growth of both trans-border and nationally internal migration, as we argue throughout this volume. This chapter shows in detail how the paradoxes of neoliberalism work out in practice, leading to incoherent state interventions – often productively incoherent and producing double binds and resulting ambivalences for the people who are the objects of these policies. Within this context, sex and gender can paradoxically become both strategic resources for migrants to draw upon in shoring up economic and social capital, and sites of heightened political and moral regulation by the state.

Introduction **25**

In this chapter, the authors draw upon insights from long-term ethnographic studies conducted among four migrant groups: asylum-seekers in Hong Kong, deportees in the Dominican Republic, Nigerian migrant sex workers in Italy and Denmark, and rural-to-urban labor migrants in Mumbai in order to examine the ways in which migrancy, gender, and sexuality converge in migrants' negotiation of border regimes. For migrants who have circumscribed access to social and financial capital, their ability to deploy alternative forms of gendered, sexual, and racial capital serves as a means to mitigate the effects of border regimes premised upon exclusion and subordination, even as gender and sexuality are also part of regulatory interventions that intensify precarity and maintain inequality. Such are the paradoxical conditions of neoliberalism that in turn demand variegated and multifarious responses for both individual survival and social change.

In Chapter 6, "Political Power and Practices of Resistance," co-authors Mario Pecheny, Janet Jakobsen, Ana Amuchástegui, and Maja Horn consider the implications of the preceding analysis for collective action, creative expression, and informal practices of resistance, together weighing how we might best leverage and respond to the neoliberal paradoxes previously described. Focusing specifically on governmental power and the ways in which neoliberal policies and practices lead to an experience of "fractured state actions and institutions," the authors argue that the paradoxical features of neoliberalism identified in the above chapters may be harnessed either to intensify governmentality or to expand possibilities for resistance. To that end, we return to the example of the peer support groups of women living with HIV in Mexico, consider the forms of activism accomplished by workers in queer survival economies in the US, and engage the insights and actions offered by feminist and queer artists in the Dominican Republic. This chapter shows how variegated strategies, like those named by Chela Sandoval's (2000) idea of "differential consciousness," can allow people to move through and around the double binds of neoliberal paradox. The very unevenness of neoliberal policies and practices, the differences among and across locations, and the imbrication of social relations with political economy allows for the creation of networks of action and organizing, simultaneously engaging the state and realms well beyond the state and creating unexpected possibilities for justice despite paradoxical conditions.

Notes

1 See, e.g., Mitropoulos (2020); Powell (2020); Ray and Rojas (2020); Timmerman (2020); Nugent (2021).
2 See Inequality.org (2021); Romei (2020); Aljazeera (2021).
3 Federici (2021); Ozkazanc-Pan and Pullen (2020); Allen, Jenkins, and Howard (2020).
4 Mitropoulos (2020); Taub (2020); Laster Pirtle (2020).
5 See, for example, Ehrenreich and Hochschild (2004).
6 For an analysis of the pandemic as both the culmination and acceleration of neoliberal trends, see Miropolous (2020).
7 We have been deeply influenced by Stuart Hall's (1978) classic *Policing the Crisis: Mugging the State and Law and Order.* We expand feminist and queer aspects of this analysis to build on Hall's de-colonial, anti-racist materialism.

8 We are following the lead of Sasha Berger Bush (2017) here, although we use the phrase "nationalist neoliberalism" rather than Berger Bush's "national neoliberalism" so as to emphasize the connections within and among the history of US nationalism, the Trump movement, and contemporary nationalist movements in many parts of the world.

9 Jakobsen and Pellegrini (2009, 1227).

10 See, e.g., Connell and Dados (2014).

11 On the idea of a social body multiple, see Jakobsen (2020), especially Chapter 3, "Because the Social."

12 We lay out this analysis further in the Introduction to the journal issue that initiated this project, Bernstein and Jakobsen (2012/2013). Harvey (2007) provides the classic neo-Marxist account. For Foucaultian versions, see Foucault (2008); Brown (2005, 37–60); and Rose (1999). Social science perspectives focused upon state transformations include Wacquant (2009); Lewis and Mosse (2006); and Feher (2007); Gowan (2012/2013); Springer (2012); Wacquant (2012); Reddy (2011); and Ferguson and Hong (2012) provide helpful summaries of the above distinctions.

13 In addition to those characteristics that we consider in the body of the text, we could name many others as key components of neoliberal formations and we will, in fact, consider many of them in these pages, including privatization or the sense that many activities carried out by modern governments are better handled by private businesses, such as the privatization of public schooling. Privatization can also be understood as part of ongoing processes of primary accumulation in which value, that has been created outside of the market through government support, is appropriated into the market. Rupert Murdoch once famously said of public schools in the US that they represented a $500-billion-dollar industry open to being appropriated (Faux 2012). Privatization is part of a larger mechanism of marketization or the framework in which the only value that counts is market value – so, for example, university education only matters if it increases the earning power of students, not if it contributes to an educated (and politically engaged) public. One of the largest areas of marketization currently is that of Big Data, in which data collected for one purpose – such as healthcare or sharing with friends on social media – is collected and sold for market purposes, like advertising. Disaster capitalism is another important neoliberal mechanism, analyzed in depth by Naomi Klein (2007), in which disasters, like hurricanes or the COVID-19 pandemic, are mined for their market value.

14 For a helpful feminist reading of the 1997–98 and 2007–09 financial crises, see Kang (2012).

15 As Margaret Thatcher, an early institutor of neoliberalism, famously said, in an interview with Douglas Keay in *Woman's Own*, "There is no such thing as society, only individuals." Margaret Thatcher Foundation (1987).

16 Suddenly, the EU, which recently had been looking open to fracture, has taken an approach that looks more like that of states within a nation banding together than did the punitive responses to the 2008 crisis among lender and debtor EU member states. This, despite early criticisms from Spanish and Italian commentators that Germany's early successes in handling the virus occurred while Europe's southern states were left to founder. See, e.g., Adler (2020).

17 See also Cheng and Kim (2014).

18 Gayatri Spivak (1999) makes a similar point about the paradox of enlightenment-based rights – the critique of the colonialist and neoliberal aspects of rights discourse is well developed and persuasive, but to live without rights is also deeply dangerous. Spivak (1999, 172) uses a double-negative: one "can't not want" rights to describe the challenge of trying to live without access to any of the protections, however minimal that might be provided by rights.

19 For example, with a paradoxical analysis of sovereignty, Kauanui (2018, 21) is able to look to "Indigenous values that are not premised on capitalist exploitation, destructive land tenure practices, male domination, or sexual subordination in order to

suggest a new ethics of relationality that is life sustaining." Attending to the paradoxes of sovereignty also allows Kauanui (2018, 22) to attend to the fact that power does not come from a single sovereign source acting within a juridical model but is multiple in its enactments.

20 On ambivalence as a basis for political possibility, see Jakobsen (1998), especially pp. 93–7.

21 On kaleidoscopic common sense, see Jakobsen (2020).

22 On Trump's invocation of "honor crimes" as legitimation for his ban on travel from several predominantly Muslim countries, see Winston (2017), and on the invocation of sex trafficking in Mexico as legitimation for militarization of the border with Guatemala, see Leyva (2015).

23 On corporate-driven "equality" politics in the LGBT movement, see Duggan (2003); Joseph (2002); and Chasin (2000). On the corporate "pinking" of the breast cancer movement, see Sulik (2012); Ehrenreich (2009); and King (2006). The literature on the imbrication of seemingly progressive sexual agendas in nationalist projects is ample: Farris (2017); Fraser (2013); Ticktin (2008); and Puar (2007) provide some useful perspectives on these intersections in the US and Western European contexts. The mutual reinforcements between contemporary sexual and carceral politics have been less elaborated upon but see Bernstein (2018); Lancaster (2011); Bumilller (2008); and Gottschalk (2006) for some articulations of the connections.

24 In a comparative study of religious conservatism in the US and Iran, Martin Reisebrodt (1998) shows that commitments to patriarchal versions of Christianity and Islam are not the result of some other – more material concern – but are, in fact, sustained as a primary commitment even when such commitment is costly to other values and interests.

25 See Lugones (2007); Crenshaw (1989); McClintock (1995); and Federici (2012).

26 On Social Reproduction Theory see: Bhattacharya (2017); Bhattacharyya (2018); and Silvia Federici: *Revolution at Point Zero: Housework, Reproduction, and Feminist Struggle* (Oakland: PM Press, 2012). On racial capitalism, see: Gilmore (2007); Malamed (2011); Reddy (2011); and Johnson and Kelley (2017). The development of these different approaches as separate fields raises questions about their inter-relation. We have developed an analysis that maintains the specificity of categories of social difference – they are not all the same type of axis of oppression intersecting at various points – without the need to find a way to unify these different categories in their differences. Sustaining a focus on inter-relations, particularly *dynamic* inter-relation, allows for a recognition of persistent multiplicity as constitutive of the social body multiple.

27 Hortense J. Spillers (1987) argues that enslavement is a fundamentally de-gendering process that makes "flesh" of human beings who are enslaved, thus denying certain forms of gendered embodiment to them. This de-gendering also paradoxically makes enslaved people targets for sexualized violence that Spillers terms "pornotroping," thus creating the connections between racial domination, de-gendering, and the sexualization of economic activity that Davis and the Black Sexual Economies (BSE) Collective (2019) study.

28 Sanyal terms such activity "needs economies," and we follow Amber Hollibaugh (N.d.) by using the term "survival economies."

29 We thank one of the anonymous readers from Routledge Press for this succinct formulation.

30 See, e.g., Palumbo-Liu, Robbins, and Tanoukhi (2010).

31 See, e.g., Karim (2011); Lind (2005); and O'Neill and Thomas (2011).

32 In June 2020, for example, there was a major march with over 15,000 in support of Black Trans Lives in Brooklyn, New York. See, e.g., Maxwell (2020); and Patil (2020).

33 See, for example, Feng, Hu, and Li (2013).

34 Svati Shah (2017) articulated the value of conceptualizing social relations through the metaphor of imbrication at our project's final conference at the Danish Institute for International Studies.
35 See Fraser (2015) for a typical center-left articulation of this view.

References

Adler, Katya. 2020. "Coronavirus Outbreak Eats into EU Unity," BBC, 3 April. https://www.bbc.com/news/world-europe-52135816.

Aljazeera. 2021. "COVID has Worsened Inequality Even as the Rich Thrive," *Aljazeera*. 2021. https://www.aljazeera.com/economy/2021/1/25/covid-19-worsened-global-inequality-even-as-the-rich-bounced-back.

Allen, Juliet, Daniela Jenkins, and Marilyn Howard. 2020. "Crises Collide: Capitalism, Care, and COVID-19," *Feminist Studies* 46, no. 3, 583–595.

Alvarez, Sonia. 2010. "Advocating Feminism: The Latin American Feminist NGO 'Boom,'" *International Feminist Journal of Politics* 1(2): 181–209.

Amar, Paul. 2013. *The Security Archipelago: Human-Security States, Sexual Politics, and the End of Neoliberalism*. Durham, NC: Duke University Press.

Amar, Paul. 2016. "Thug Love: Sexuality and New Authoritarian Populism in Megarabia," Workshop on Global Attachments: Sexuality and the Changing State, Williams College, Williamstown, MA, 15 October.

Bedford, Kate. 2009. *Developing Partnerships: Gender, Sexuality, and the Reformed World Bank*. Minneapolis, MN: University of Minnesota Press.

Bernstein, Elizabeth. 2018. *Brokered Subjects: Sex, Trafficking and the Politics of Freedom*. Chicago. IL: University of Chicago Press.

Bernstein, Elizabeth and Janet R. Jakobsen. 2009. "U.S.A. Country Report: Religion, Politics and Gender Equality," United Nations Research Institute for Social Development. http://www.unrisd.org/unrisd/website/document.nsf/%28httpPublications%29/DA28E37EB9DA9259C12576580028C998?OpenDocument.

Bernstein, Elizabeth and Janet R. Jakobsen. 2012/2013. "Introduction: Gender, Justice, and Neoliberal Transformations," *Scholar & Feminist Online*, 11, no. 1–2, http://sfonline.barnard.edu/gender-justice-and-neoliberal-transformations.

Berger Bush, Sasha. 2017. "Trump and National Neoliberalism," *Dollars & Sense*, January/February. www.dollarsandsense.org.

Bhattacharya, Tithi, ed. 2017. *Social Reproduction Theory: Remapping Class, Recentering Oppression*. London: Pluto Press.

Bhattacharyya, Gargi. 2018. *Rethinking Racial Capitalism: Questions of Reproduction and Survival*. London: Rowman & Littlefield.

Brooks, Siobhan. 2012/2013. "Beyond Marriage and the Military: Race, Gender, and Radical Sexual Politics in the Age of Neoliberalism," *Scholar & Feminist Online*, 11, no. 1–2 (Fall/Spring): http://sfonline.barnard.edu/gender-justice-and-neoliberal-transformations/beyond-marriage-and-the-military-race-gender-and-radical-sexual-politics-in-the-age-of-neoliberalism/.

Brown, Wendy. 2005. *Edgework: Critical Essays on Knowledge and Politics*. Princeton, NJ: Princeton University Press.

Bumiller, Kristin. 2008. *In an Abusive State: How Neoliberalism Appropriated the Feminist Movement against Sexual Violence*. Durham, NC: Duke University Press.

Chasin, Alexandra. 2000. *Selling Out: The Gay and Lesbian Movement Goes to Market*. New York: Palgrave Macmillan.

Cheng, Sealing. 2012/2013. "Embodying the Sexual Limits of Neoliberalism" *The Scholar & Feminist Online*. Issue 11 no. 1-2; Fall 2012/Spring 2013. https://sfonline.barnard.edu/gender-justice-and-neoliberal-transformations/embodying-the-sexual-limits-of-neoliberalism/.

Cheng, Sealing, and Eunjung Kim. 2014. "The Paradoxes of Neoliberalism: Migrant Korean Sex Workers in the US and 'Sex Trafficking,'" *Social Politics: International Studies in Gender, State and Society* 21, no. 3: 355.

Cohen, Cathy. 2005. "Punks, Bulldaggers, and Welfare Queens: The Radical Potential of Queer Politics?" In *Black Queer Studies: A Critical Anthology*, edited by E. Patrick Johnson and Mae G. Henderson, 21–51. Durham, NC: Duke University Press.

Connell, Raewyn and Nour Dados. 2014. "Where in the World Does Neoliberalism Come From? The Market Agenda in Southern Perspective," *Theory and Society* 43, no. 2 (March): 117–38.

Crenshaw, Kimberlé. 1989. "Demarginalizing the Intersection of Race and Sex: A Black Feminist Critique of Antidiscrimination Doctrine, Feminist Theory, and Antiracist Politics," *University of Chicago Legal Forum*, 1989.1. http://chicagounbound.uchicago.edu/uclf/vol1989/iss1/8.

Crosby, Christina and Janet R. Jakobsen. 2020. "Disability, Debility, and Caring Queerly," *Social Text, Special Issue, "Left of Queer,"* 38(4(145)): 77–103.

Cypher, James M. 2019. "The Zigs and Zags of Neoliberalism in Latin America," *Dollars & Sense* 345, (November/December): 22–4.

Davis, Adrienne D. and the Black Sexual Economies Collective, ed. 2019. *Black Sexual Economies: Race and Sex in a Culture of Capital*. Champaign, IL: University of Illinois Press.

Duggan, Lisa. 2003. *The Twilight of Equality? Neoliberalism, Cultural Politics, and the Attack on Democracy*. Boston, MA: Beacon Press.

Ehrenreich, Barbara. 2009. *Bright-Sided: How Positive Thinking Is Undermining America*. New York: Picador.

Ehrenreich, Barbara and Arlie Hochschild, eds. 2004. *Global Woman: Nannies, Maids, and Sex Workers in the New Economy*. New York: MacMillan.

Farris, Sara R. 2017. "Femonationalism and the 'Regular' Army of Labor Called Migrant Women," *History of the Present* 2, no. 2: 184–99. https://doi.org/10.5406/historypresent.2.2.0184.

Faux, Jeff. 2012. "Education Profiteering: Wall Street's Next Big Thing?" Economic Policy Institute. epi.org/education-profiteering-wall-street/.

Federici, Silvia. 2012. *Revolution at Point Zero: Housework, Reproduction, and Feminist Struggle*. Oakland: PM Press.

Federici, Silvia. 2021. "COVID, Women's Work, and the Crisis of Social Reproduction," 21 April. The Center for Global Justice. https://globaljusticecenter.org/videos/covid-womens-work-and-crisis-social-reproduction.

Feher, Michel. 2009. "Self-Appreciation; or, The Aspirations of Human Capital," *Public Culture* 21, no. 1 (1 January): 21–41. https://doi.org/10.1215/08992363-2008-019.

Feng, Ling, Weijun Hu, and Zhiyuan Li. 2013. "The Effects of Globalisation on the US Labour Market: Service Sectors Considered," *The World Economy*, 36, no. 12 (24 June): 1542–65. https://doi-org.ezproxy.cul.columbia.edu/10.1111/twec.12088.

Ferguson, Roderick A. 2003. *Aberrations in Black: Toward a Queer of Color Critique*. Minneapolis, MN: University of Minnesota Press.

Ferguson, Roderick A. and Grace Kyungwon Hong. 2012. "The Sexual and Racial Contradictions of Neoliberalism," *Journal of Homosexuality* 59, no. 7: 1057–64.

Foucault, Michel. 2008. *The Birth of Biopolitics: Lectures at the Collège de France, 1978–1979*. Basingstoke, UK: Palgrave Macmillan.

Fraser, Nancy. 2013. *Fortunes of Feminism: From State-Managed Capitalism to Neoliberal Crisis*. London: Verso.

Fraser, Giles. 2015. "Money Isn't Restricted by Borders, So Why Are People?" *The Guardian*, 8 October. https://www.theguardian.com/commentisfree/2015/oct/08/money-isnt-restricted-by-borders-so-why-are-people.

Gilmore, Ruth Wilson. 2007. *Golden Gulag: Prisons, Surplus, Crisis, and Opposition in Globalizing California*. Berkeley, CA: University of California Press.

Gottschalk, Marie. 2006. *The Prison and the Gallows: The Politics of Mass Incarceration in America*. New York, Cambridge: Cambridge University Press.

Gowan, Teresa. 2012/2013. "Thinking Neoliberalism, Gender, Justice," *Scholar & Feminist Online*, 11, no. 1–2 (Fall/Spring). http:sfonline.barnard.edu/gender-justice-and-neo-lliberal-transformations/thinking-neoliberalism-gender-justice.

Hall, Stuart, et al. 1978. *Policing the Crisis: Mugging, The State, and Law and Order*. New York: The Macmillan Press Ltd.

Harvey, David. 2007. *A Brief History of Neoliberalism*. Oxford: Oxford University Press.

Ho, Josephine. 2008. "Is Global Governance Bad for East Asian Queers?" *GLQ: Journal of Lesbian and Gay Studies* 14, no. 4 (October): 457–79.

Hollibaugh, Amber. n.d. *Queer Survival Economies*, http://queersurvivaleconomies.com/.

Inequality.org. n.d. "Covid-19 and Inequality," https://inequality.org/facts/inequality-and-covid-19/#wealth-income-inequality-covid.

Jakobsen, Janet R. 1998. *Working Alliances and the Politics of Difference: Diversity and Feminist Ethics*. Bloomington, IN: Indiana University Press.

Jakobsen, Janet R. 2020. *The Sex Obsession: Perversity and Possibility in American Politics*. New York: NYU Press.

Jakobsen, Janet R. and Ann Pellegrini. 2009. "Obama's Neo-New Deal: Religion, Secularism, and Sex, in Political Debates Now," *Social Research* 76, no. 4 (Winter): 1227–54.

Johnson, Walter with Robin D.G. Kelley. 2017. "Race, Capitalism, Justice," *Boston Review*, Forum 1.

Joseph, Miranda. 2002. *Against the Romance of Community*. Minneapolis, MN: University of Minnesota Press.

Kang, Laura Hyun Yi. 2012. "The Uses of Asianization: Figuring Crises, 1997–98 and 2007-?" *American Quarterly* 64, no. 3 (September): 411–36.

Karim, Lamia. 2011. *Microfinance and Its Discontents: Women in Debt in Bangladesh*. Minneapolis, MN: University Of Minnesota Press,.

Kauanui, J. Kēhaulani. 2018. *Paradoxes of Hawaiian Sovereignty: Land, Sex, and the Colonial Politics of State Nationalism*. Durham, NC: Duke University Press.

Kempadoo, Kamala. 2017. Comments at "New World Disorder" Conference at Danish Institute for International Studies, Copenhagen, Denmark, June.

King, Samantha. 2006. *Pink Ribbons, Inc.: Breast Cancer and the Politics of Philanthropy*. Minneapolis, MN: University of Minnesota Press.

Klein, Naomi. 2007. *The Shock Doctrine: The Rise of Disaster Capitalism*. New York: Picador.

Lancaster, Roger N. 2011. *Sex Panic and the Punitive State*. Berkeley, CA: University of California Press.

Lancaster, Roger N. 2017. "The New Pariahs: Sex, Crime, and Punishment in America," In *The War on Sex*, edited by David M. Halperin and Trevor Hoppe, 65–125. Durham, NC: Duke University Press.

Laster Pirtle, Whitney N. 2020. "Racial Capitalism: A Fundamental Cause of Novel Coronavirus (COVID-19) Pandemic Inequities in the US," *Health Education & Behavior* 47, no. 4: 504–508.

LeBlanc, Paul. 2020. "GOP congressman says letting more Americans die of coronavirus is lesser of two evils compared to economy tanking," *CNN Politic.* CNN, 15 April. https://www.cnn.com/2020/04/14/politics/trey-hollingsworth-coronavirus/index .html.

Lewis, David, and David Mosse, eds. 2006. *Development Brokers and Translators: The Ethnography of Aid and Agencies.* Bloomfield, CT: Kumarian Press.

Leyva. 2015. "Aspectos de salud pública en el trabajo sexual: Estudio de caso de la frontera sur," Presentation at the forum Sexo, poder, y dinero: Perspectivas críticas sobre "la trata de mujeres," Universidad Nacional Autónoma de México, Mexico City, 19 May.

Lind, Amy. 2005. *Gendered Paradoxes: Women's Movements, State Restructuring, and Global Development in Ecuador.* University Park, PA: Penn State University Press.

Linthicum, Kate. 2020. "It took decades to build Mexico's middle class. The coronavirus could demolish it," *The Los Angeles Times,* 5 September. https://www.latimes.com/ world-nation/story/2020-09-05/it-took-decades-to-build-mexicos-middle-class-the-coronavirus-threatens-to-demolish-it-in-a-matter-of-months.

Lugones, Maria. 2007. "Heterosexualism and the Colonial/Modern Gender System," *Hypatia,* 22, no. 1 (Winter): 186–209.

Lugones, Maria. 2008. "The Coloniality of Gender," Worlds and Knowledges Otherwise, (Spring): 1–17.

Margaret Thatcher Foundation. 1987. "Interview for *Woman's Own*," margaretthatcher .org/document/106689.

Maxwell. 2020. "June Newsletter: Defund NYPD | New & Updated Resources | Upcoming Virtual Events," *Audre Lorde Project,* 18 June. https://alp.org/news/june-newsletter-defund-nypd-new-updated-resources-upcoming-virtual-events.

McClintock, Anne. 1995. *Imperial Leather: Race, Gender, and Sexuality in the Colonial Conquest.* New York: Routledge.

Melamed, Jodi. 2011. *Represent and Destroy: Rationalizing Violence in the New Racial Capitalism.* Minneapolis, MN: University of Minnesota Press.

Mitropoulos, Angela. 2020. *Pandemonium: Proliferating Borders of Capital and the Pandemic Swerve.* New York: Pluto Press.

Mol, Annemarie. 2002. *The Body Multiple: Ontology in Medical Practice.* Durham, NC: Duke University Press.

Muñoz, José Esteban. 2009. *Cruising Utopia: The Then and There of Queer Futurity.* New York: New York University Press.

Murray, Christine. 2019. "Mexico City to Decriminalize Sex Work, Eyes Steps to Cut Trafficking," *Reuters,* 2 June. https://www.reuters.com/article/us-mexico-sexwork-trafficking/mexico-city-to-decriminalize-sex-work-eyes-steps-to-cut-trafficking-idUSKCN1T30OM.

O'Neill, Kevin Lewis and Kendon Thomas, eds. 2011. *Securing the City: Neoliberalism, Space, and Insecurity in Postwar Guatemala.* Durham, NC: Duke University Press.

Ozkazanc-Pan, Banu and Alison Pullen. 2020. "Reimagining Value: A Feminist Commentary in the Midst of the COVID-19 Pandemic," *Gender, Work, and Organization* 28, no. 1: 1–7. https://www.ncbi.nlm.nih.gov/pmc/articles/PMC7753812/.

Palumbo-Liu, David, Bruce Robbins and Nirvana Tanoukhi. 2010. "'The Most Important Thing Happening': An Introduction," In *Immanuel Wallerstein and Problem of the World: System, Scale, Culture,* edited by Bruce Robbins and Nirvana Tanoukhi. Durham, NC: Duke University Press.

32 Elizabeth Bernstein and Janet Jakobsen

Patil, Anushka. 2020. "How a March for Black Trans Lives Became a Huge Event," *The New York Times*, 15 June. https://www.nytimes.com/2020/06/15/nyregion/brooklyn-black-trans-parade.html.

Pecheny, Mario. 2012/2013. "Sexual Politics and Post-Neoliberalism in Latin America" *Scholar & Feminist Online*, 11, no. 1–2, http://sfonline.barnard.edu/gender-justice-and-neoliberal-transformations/sexual-politics-and-post-neoliberalism-in-latin-america/.

Powell, Catherine. 2020. "The Color and Gender of COVID: Essential Workers, not Disposable People," *Think Global Health*. https://www.thinkglobalhealth.org/article/color-and-gender-covid-essential-workers-not-disposable-people.

Prieve, Judith. 2020. "East Bay politician under fire for saying let coronavirus kill the elderly, weak, and homeless," *East Bay Times*, 29 April. https://www.eastbaytimes.com/2020/04/29/east-bay-councilwoman-calls-for-commissioners-resignation-over-coronavirus-comments/.

Puar, Jasbir. 2007. *Terrorist Assemblages: Homonationalism in Queer Times*. Durham, NC: Duke University Press.

Ray, Rashawn and Fabio Rojas. 2020. "Inequality During the Coronavirus Pandemic," *Contexts: Sociology for the Public*, 16 April. https://inequality.org/facts/inequality-and-covid-19/#wealth-income-inequality-covid.

Reddy, Chandan. 2011. *Freedom with Violence: Race, Sexuality, and the US State*. Durham, NC: Duke University Press.

Riesebrodt, Martin. 1998. *Pious Passion: The Emergence of Modern Fundamentalism in the United States and Iran*. Berkeley, CA: University of California Press.

Romei, Valentina. 2020. "How the Pandemic is Worsening Inequality," *Financial Times*. 31 December. https://www.ft.com/content/cd075d91-fafa-47c8-a295-85bbd7a36b50.

Rose, Nikolas. 1999. *Powers of Freedom: Reframing Political Thought*. Cambridge: Cambridge University Press.

Sandoval, Chela. 2000. *Methodology of the Oppressed*. Minneapolis, MN: University of Minnesota Press.

Scott, David. 2004. *Conscripts of Modernity: The Tragedy of Colonial Enlightenment*. Durham, NC: Duke University Press.

Scott, Joan Wallach. 1996. *Only Paradoxes to Offer: French Feminists and the Rights of Man*. Cambridge, MA: Harvard University Press.

Shah, Svati P. 2015. "Queering Critiques of Neoliberalism in India: Urbanism and Inequality in the Era of Transnational 'LGBTQ' Rights," *Antipode* 47, no. 3 (June): 635–51. https://doi.org/10.1111/anti.12112.

Shah, Svati P. 2017. Comments at "New World Disorder," Conference at Danish Institute for International Studies. Copenhagen, Denmark, June.

Spillers, Hortense J. 1987. "Mama's Baby, Papa's Maybe: An American Grammar Book," *Diacritics* 17, no. 2 (Summer): 64–81.

Spivak, Gayatri Chakravorty. 1999. *A Critique of Postcolonial Reason: Toward a History of the Vanishing Present*. Cambridge, MA: Harvard University Press.

Springer, Simon. 2012. "Neoliberalism as Discourse: Between Foucauldian Political Economy and Marxian Poststructuralism," *Critical Discourse Studies* 9, no. 2 (1 May): 133–47. https://doi.org/10.1080/17405904.2012.656375.

Sulik, Gayle A. 2012. *Pink Ribbon Blues: How Breast Cancer Culture Undermines Women's Health*. Reprint edition. Oxford: Oxford University Press.

Tadiar, Neferti X.M. 2012/2013. "Uneven Times, Times of Inequity," *Scholar & Feminist Online*, 11, no. 1–2 (Fall/Spring): http://sfonline.barnard.edu/gender-justice-and-neoliberal-transformations/uneven-times-times-of-inequity/.

Taub, Amanda. 2020 "A New COVID-19 Crisis: Domestic Abuse Rises Worldwide," *The New York Times*, April 6. https://www.nytimes.com/2020/04/06/world/coronavirus-domestic-violence.html.

Ticktin, Miriam. 2008. "Sexual Violence as the Language of Border Control: Where French Feminist and Anti-immigrant Rhetoric Meet," *Signs* 33, no. 4: 863–89. https://doi.org/10.1086/528851.

Timmerman, Ruben. 2020. "Covid-19 Exposes the Realities of Europe's Neglected Essential Workers," *Border Criminologies*, December 2. https://www.law.ox.ac.uk/research-subject-groups/centre-criminology/centreborder-criminologies/blog/2020/12/covid-19-exposes.

Wacquant, Loïc. 2009. *Punishing the Poor: The Neoliberal Government of Social Insecurity*. First edition, Paperback issue edition. Durham, NC: Duke University Press Books.

Wacquant, Loïc. 2012. "Three Steps to a Historical Anthropology of Actually Existing Neoliberalism," *Social Anthropology/Anthropologie Sociale* 20, no. 1 (February): 66–79. https://doi.org/10.1111/j.1469-8676.2011.00189.x.

Wilson, Ara. 2004. *The Intimate Economies of Bangkok: Tomboys, Tycoons, and Avon Ladies in the Global City*. Berkeley, CA: University of California Press.

Winston, Kimberly. 2017. "Trump Travel Ban Orders a Report on 'Honor Killings,'" *Religious News Service*, 6 March. https://religionnews.com/2017/03/06/trump-travel-ban-orders-a-report-on-honor-killings/.

Wright, Melissa. 2006. *Disposable Women and Other Myths of Global Capitalism*. New York: Routledge.

Yong, Ed. 2020. "The U.K.'s Coronavirus 'Herd Immunity' Debacle," *The Atlantic*, 16 March. https://www.theatlantic.com/health/archive/2020/03/coronavirus-pandemic-herd-immunity-uk-boris-johnson/608065/.

2

GENDER JUSTICE AND ECONOMIC JUSTICE

Production, reproduction, and survival

Janet Jakobsen, Mark Padilla, and Maja Horn

Gender justice aspires to a world in which people of any gender can flourish.[1] Social justice feminism (Burnham 2008) demonstrates that questions of gender justice intersect with a wide range of issues, including nation, race, religion, economics, migration, policing, militarization, public health, and more. In the pages that follow, we demonstrate the broad range and imbrication of sexual politics,[2] and suggest the limitations of attempts to disarticulate gender and sexuality from other political, economic, and social concerns.

In *Paradoxes of Neoliberalism*, we are particularly interested in the ways in which gender justice is embedded in broader structures of political economy. Some of the main questions we consider are: To what extent is gender justice possible within the current political-economic order of things? If neoliberalism is itself a source of gender injustice, does justice, when it comes to gender and sexuality, also require radical changes in political economy? We also ask the correlative but obverse question: is economic or political justice possible without gender justice? If, as social justice feminism has long shown and as we will detail in the case studies that form the basis of our analysis, neoliberalism is inextricable from sexual politics – that is, from issues of gender and sexuality – then there is no social justice without gender justice, and gender justice must also hinge upon a wide array of reworked social relations.

When stated this directly, the point seems obvious. How could there be social justice without gender justice? But there are long traditions on both the political right and the political left that ignore sexual politics or claim it is a distraction from the real or important issues of the day, arguing, for example, that sexual politics is (or should be) a private matter. And on the other side of the analytic conundrum, there have also been those, both advocates of neoliberalism and conservative critics, who claim that neoliberalism is good for issues related to gender and sexuality, that neoliberal economic relations help women in the job

DOI: 10.4324/9781003252702-2

market or relax many forms of gender and sexual regulation, such as the regulation of transgender people and their movements or the regulation of gender and sex in relation to marriage and reproduction. Some on the left then respond to these arguments on behalf of neoliberalism with a dismissal of the importance of sexual politics, claiming that the politics of gender and sexuality deal only with issues of recognition and ignore crucial questions of redistribution.[3] Instead, we build an analysis based on the intertwining of recognition and redistribution. Economic distribution cannot be boiled down to some material essence in class divisions that is not also striated by the afterlives of colonialism and slavery, the ongoing international division of labor, transnational (and inequitable) flows of labor and capital, and regimes of racial and gender domination.

Gender does not fulfill a single function in capitalist formations like neoliberalism. First of all, gender is not a singular thing, but is rather a social relation. And as such, gender is variously dynamic, determined not by a binary biological division but by a range of interactions that create multiple possible gender identities – transgender and gender non-conforming identities among them. For example, Cinzia Aruzza (2015) provides a materialist reading of gender as a social temporality, analytically grounding Judith Butler's sense of gender as performance in a material and inter-relational context.[4] As a social relation, gender dynamically intersects with other social relations, creating matrices that are differentiated along multiple relational lines (race, gender, sex, religion, nation) even as those relations are variously imbricated.[5]

Second, this dynamic imbrication contributes constitutively to political economy, making political-economic formations like neoliberalism correlatively complex. To take just one instance that we pursue in detail below, in traditional liberal political economy, "the economy" is understood as being separated both from the political life of democratic governance and the intimate life of the private sphere. Or, in traditional Marxian theory, the productive political economy of wage labor and capital is separated from the sometimes-unpaid sphere of reproductive labor. But neither of these frameworks adequately account for the breadth of economic arrangements that have involved service labor. Even in nineteenth-century Britain, the putative home of industrial capitalism, being "in service" was one of the major routes to wage labor. Working in domestic service continued to be the largest sector of employment for women through the first half of the twentieth century, and the service sector as a whole remained significant throughout the industrial period.[6] The productive economy is intertwined with reproductive and service economies, and as we shall see, also with informal and survival economies.

In both classical economics and Marxian theory, it often seems as though human beings arrive in the world fully grown and ready to work. As Tithi Bhattacharya (2017, 2) observes, "Against this, social reproduction theorists perceive the relation between labor dispensed to produce commodities and labor dispensed to produce people as part of the systemic totality of capitalism. The framework thus seeks to make visible labor and work that are analytically hidden by classical economists and politically denied by policy makers."[7] Gayatri Chakravorty Spivak (1987) similarly denaturalizes the production of the worker, arguing that the Marxian understanding of the chain of value – from labor to labor-power to move from resources to commodities to market exchanges – should begin with the production of the worker, rather than with the work's production. Spivak's critique broadens the context to include all of the social and cultural relations – the full discursive, material context – that predicates both laborers and the structure of their labor. Indeed, she places labor in the geopolitical context that includes the international divisions and transnational flows that constitute domestic work as precarious and debilitating labor.

Spivak's reading suggests that denaturalizing the Marxian chain of value indicates many possible points of rupture. Each transition point, whether from use value to exchange value, goods to commodity, labor to labor power, or from labor power to exchange value, might be otherwise. Not all labor that keeps up everyday life is reproductive, nor is it all functionally supportive of capitalism. It may be variously queer, geared toward other timelines than that of remaking life as we know it, toward, for example, what José Esteban Muñoz (2009) suggests is the "then and there" of queer futurity. A queer reading of value challenges any idea of a natural sociality or of a naturalized use value and instead seeks to build a more just conceptualization of need and its relations.

Conversely, social reproduction is not fully removed from exchange value. Social reproduction is, instead, a *social space* suffused with commodities and often supported by waged service labor.

Attending to gender justice, then, actually requires a rethinking of not just neoliberalism but of political economy as a whole: what are the relations between production and reproduction? how best to conceptualize social need? how to develop an analysis of complexly imbricated social relations? Many schools of thought have pursued this type of rethinking over the past several decades, including post- and de-colonial thought, analyses of racial capitalism, social reproduction theory, feminist, and queer materialism.[8] All of these schools of thought are relevant to any analysis of gender justice and neoliberalism, even as they make differential contributions and do not produce a new singular and coherent framework, but are rather productively incoherent.

One of the questions repeatedly raised in our analysis of neoliberalism is whether neoliberalism is itself a new formation or simply another iteration of long-standing colonial relations. Kamala Kempadoo (2017) argued at the closing conference for our research group, held in 2017 at the Danish Institute for International Studies, that the structural adjustment and austerity measures associated with neoliberalism, which have been imposed by transnational institutions like the International Monetary Fund (IMF) and World Bank, were reiterations of colonial mechanisms for extracting value from colonized and formerly colonized countries in the Global South on behalf of political and economic powers in the Global North. Abosede George had made similar arguments in small group discussions at our initial symposium on gender justice and neoliberal

Gender justice and economic justice **37**

transformations.[9] Taking these arguments seriously, we thus begin our analysis of gender justice and neoliberalism by placing the advent of neoliberalism, which is usually traced back to the 1970s, into the context of colonialism and racial capitalism, a context that neoliberalism reiterates, restores, sustains, extends, and reconfigures.

The imbrication of social relations and political economy

In the final third of the twentieth century, a number of political conflicts amidst shifting economic conditions led, in different areas of the world, to the consolidation of neoliberal policies that favor market-based rather than state-based solutions to economic problems. The most obviously violent event was in Chile, when, in 1973, the CIA contributed to the violent overthrow of the recently elected President, the socialist Salvador Allende (Porpora et al. 2013). As Marcus Taylor (2006) and Naomi Klein (2007) have narrated, in a complex feedback loop, ideas incubated in the United States (US) became part of a policy experiment in Chile that was variously aided and abetted by the US and its security forces. The Chilean dictatorship of Augusto Pinochet then produced a set of practices and policies that helped to form neoliberalism in the US, a shift that intensified with the 1980 election of Ronald Reagan.

This reading of the coup in Chile places it in the context of the panoply of anti-colonial movements that spread across many areas of the world after World War II and picked up steam in the 1970s.[10] Lisa Duggan (2019) understands neoliberalism as in part a direct response to these movements as nations, international institutions, and transnational corporations from the Global North all worked to maintain their power despite anti-colonial movement. These efforts at retrenchment took place through both violent suppression and the imposition of neoliberal economic policies, like structural adjustment and indebtedness organized through the IMF and the World Bank. Jody Byrd et al. (2018, 4) have powerfully named this continuing coloniality as "an ongoing relation of theft, displacement, foreclosure, and violence" that sustains systems of primary accumulation.

For Ramón Grosfoguel, a decolonial perspective is thus concerned not just with an end to colonial administration but with an end to *coloniality*, the set of global practices that continue to sustain the dominance of the Global North and produce extraction of resources from the Global South to the Global North resulting with correlative inequalities. As Grosfoguel (2006, 176–7) summarizes, "'[C]oloniality' is entangled with, but is not reducible to, the international division of labor…. In these 'post-independence' times, the colonial axis between Europeans/Euro-Americans and non-Europeans is inscribed not only in relations of exploitation (between capital and labor) and relations of domination (between metropolitan and peripheral states), but also in the production of subjectivities and knowledge." In these terms, neoliberal practices and policies are very much a continuation of coloniality.[11]

Grosfoguel's (2006, 167) overall argument is that multiple perspectives are necessary to "decolonize political–economic paradigms." Instead of a single source of oppression, Grosfoguel argues for an analysis of what Aníbal Quijano (2000, 174) calls "[t]he 'colonial power matrix' [which] is an organizing principle involving exploitation and domination exercised in multiple dimensions of social life, from economic, sexual, or gender relations, to political organizations, structures of knowledge, state institutions, and households."[12] Racial capitalism is central to Grosfoguel's understanding of the colonial power matrix, and we follow feminists like Maria Lugones (2008) in adding to our analysis the import of both social reproduction theory and queer materialism.[13]

We thus take up an analytic approach organized, not as a description of a singular and coherent social body, but as what Janet Jakobsen (2020) has called "a social body multiple," following the idea of a "body multiple" as laid out by medical ethnographer Annemarie Mol (2003). In a study of the disease atherosclerosis, Mol delineates a method for analyzing the multiple realities of illness while also attending to the epistemological mechanisms by which discontinuous versions of disease are made to line up, so as to produce a sense of coherence. These same epistemological *practices* for producing coherence out of complexity in embodied life are also employed to produce analytic coherence out of the complexity of social relations.

In response to Grosfoguel's call for attention to a combination of multiplicity and inter-relation, the social body multiple method allows us to trace an interactive body of neoliberal policies and practices while recognizing political-economic differentiation in various ways – across gender, race, class, religion, and nation, among other social relations, and across different forms of economic activity, which are all part of the material practices (base) of political economy. By following this approach, which holds together a sense of an interactive and articulated world with the specificities of diverse systems, we are able to produce an analysis of neoliberalism that does not accept the usual – gendered – division between productive and reproductive labor, but instead analyzes various aspects of economic activity together in their dynamic inter-relation. Social reproduction is not just supportive of racial capitalism, but, rather, as Lisa Lowe (2015, 30) demonstrates in *The Intimacies of Four Continents*, this constitutive relation works in both directions. Social reproduction works to sustain racial capitalism, and racial capitalism also produces the intimacy of the bourgeois household.[14]

This multi-directionality is further compounded by the "ungendering" identified by Hortense Spillers (1987) as being at the heart of racial capitalism, which complicates both the analysis of gender segregation and stratification in productive economies and the relation between production and reproduction. Spillers (1987, 67) explains the conditions created by the fact that enslaved persons were not treated as persons with a "motive will": "Under these conditions, we lose at least gender difference in the outcome, and the female body and the male body become a territory of cultural and political maneuver, not at all gender-related, gender-specific."[15] Spillers (1987, 68) tracks the effects of ungendering along

Gender justice and economic justice **39**

different vectors of power that were wreaked upon enslaved persons, including (1) physical force and violence (regardless of gender, enslaved persons were subject to both the intimate violence of rape (usually associated with women) and the violence of discipline "that we imagine as the peculiar province of *male* brutality and torture inflicted by other males"); (2) labor (while some labor in plantation households was divided by gender, most work in agricultural fields was ungendered, and the distinction between the ungendered and gendered was often mediated by factors such as lightness of skin color); and (3) property relations (kinship relations through which property flowed under patriarchal capitalism for white people were for enslaved persons ubiquitously disrupted by those very property relations).

In Spillers's (1987, 67) analysis, slavery involves paradoxes, one of which is that the violent "ungendering" of enslavement is itself entwined with a discourse that attributes to enslaved people an "irresistible, destructive sensuality." Spillers names this project of violently projected sensuality, "pornotroping."[16] Amber Musser (2018) extends Spillers' argument, delineating how the sexual violence of "pornotroping" played a constitutive role in relation to both slavery and to regimes of variously enforced colonial labor across multiple continents, as documented by Lowe.[17] In articulating the connections between sexual violence and labor regimes, Musser (2018, 8) quotes Roderick Ferguson's reminder that "'[n]onwhite populations were racialized such that gender and sexual transgressions were not incidental to the production of nonwhite labor, but constitutive of it.'"

The continuing coloniality of pornotroping means that the people who do the "essential labor" of sustaining both reproductive and productive relations are persistently charged with perversion. Workers who do domestic work or sex work or labor in grocery stores or warehouses often work multiple jobs in both formal and informal economies but are nonetheless depicted in much public and political discourse as variously perverse: unconcerned with the disciplines of hard work, overly sensual, and even lazy. Ungendering was part of the dehumanization that allowed for the enforced labor that entwined ongoing coloniality with contemporary capitalist systems. Effective dehumanization has been sustained by the violence of pornotroping, with its projections of perversity onto those who do the work constitutive of colonial nations and capitalist systems.[18]

The projection of what Spillers (1987, 68) so clearly names as "destructive sensuality" onto the racialized others of capitalism also continues in the form of neoliberal narratives such as those about "personal responsibility." These narratives are reiterated at individual, national, and global scales when, for example, debtor nations are held "responsible" for bad loans (instead of the capitalists who make risky loans), and this sense of who is responsible for economic distress is reinforced through narratives about the supposed laziness of entire peoples.[19] For instance, in the US in the 1990s, as neoliberalism became the predominant economic approach for both major political parties, "personal responsibility" became the ideological basis for "welfare reform." This major change in the structure of the US welfare state was accomplished through narratives of racialized sexual perversity embodied in the trope of "teenage mothers" and "welfare queens." At that time, the majority of welfare recipients were white and, of course, poor and working-class people of all races often have multiple jobs and work more hours than more wealthy people simply to make a living wage. Yet Black and Brown people were positioned as sexually suspect and correlatively as suspect laborers, suspicions that could be rhetorically applied to workers and even to powerful people, like President Obama, or, during the 2020 campaign, Vice Presidential candidate Kamala Harris, who was deemed "insubstantial" and "frivolous" by conservatives simply for laughing and dancing.[20]

The disavowal of labor at the intersections of race, gender, and sexuality also complicates any analysis of the relationship between the formal economic activity of the productive economy, the often-unwaged labor of the reproductive economy, and the various forms of economic exchange that are actively criminalized and relegated to illicit economies. The entwined violences of ungendering and pornotroping place racialized and sexualized labor on both sides of the productive/reproductive paradigm and also outside of its frame.[21] Within the US institution of chattel slavery, for instance, reproductive relations were part of the productive economy not just in producing laborers but also in directly producing human beings as property, even as enslaved laborers produced profit for property owners without waged labor.[22] Thus, Adrienne Davis (2019) argues that racial capitalism can be understood as a "Black sexual economy," rather than an economy divided between production and reproduction, an understanding that Musser's argument persuasively extends to coloniality. Capitalist dependence on Black, Brown, and Indigenous labor was variously disavowed as labor, whether through claims of property (rather than the offering of wages) or through charges of perversion based on exclusion from the normative structures of reproductive kinship.

Those who work in these disavowed economies, whether in formal domestic work or informal service work, may, as Amber Hollibaugh (2015) has made clear in her project on queer survival economies, find themselves leading invisible economic lives, even as they may be simultaneously targeted by both corporate and state surveillance. As we noted in the Chapter 1, political scientist Cathy Cohen (1997, 37) has advocated a "left intersectional analysis" that attends to "the ways in which non-normative heterosexuality has been controlled and regulated through the state and systems of marginalization," arguing that this can be the basis for a queer materialism. Cohen names her essay after "Punks, Bulldaggers, and Welfare Queens" as just some of those whose lives should be included in the analytic attention of materialist analysis. We respond to Cohen's exhortation by also attending to all those who do non-normative labor, including sex workers, domestic workers, and many different kinds of informal workers in touristic economies. Our analysis shows how non-normative gender and sexuality produce disavowals, not just about gender identities and sexual practices, but also about labor.

Gender justice and economic justice **41**

To produce a full analysis of neoliberalism and of gender justice, then, it is necessary to attend to the work of those in survival economies as imbricated with the productive and reproductive economies. Gargi Bhattacharyya (2018, 16) draws upon the writing of Kalyan Sanyal to argue that "some populations are not hailed by capital as actual or potential sources of labor power but nevertheless are entwined in the money economy through other means." Informal economies persist and, in some places, expand under neoliberalism, indicating that informal sectors do not disappear with economic development, but are instead, "an outcome of processes of capitalist development" (Bhattacharyya 2018, 16). And, most importantly, although the informal sector is often theorized as "non-capitalist" or as an "other" to capitalist production, "accumulation under postco-lonial capitalism also relies on this parallel non-capitalist space" (Bhattacharyya 2018, 15). Bhattacharyya's line of analysis suggests that informal economies have long been entwined with (rather than being wholly separate from) the capitalist production of value. As the rise of neoliberal gig economies also makes clear, the boundaries between productive, reproductive, and informal economies are increasingly blurring as venture capitalists (such as those who turned "ride sharing" into transnational corporations like Uber) try to capture more and more profit from such spaces.[23] We will, in fact, argue in this chapter that workers who labor at the intersections of the formal and informal sectors, in service and/or survival economies, are central to neoliberal capitalism and its processes of accumulation.

Laboring at the intersections of race, gender, and sexuality

Sexual politics are part of every aspect of neoliberal political economies, part of the productive economy with its raced and gendered labor markets, and part of the very idea of a productive economy as distinct from reproductive or informal economies. Sexual politics are part of the service economies that operate at the boundary between productive and reproductive relations, and sexual politics are part of the various forms of labor, such as domestic labor or sex work, that people do to survive when excluded from or marginalized within the conventionally recognized boundaries of productive economies.

As a starting point to ground even a partial analysis of the extensive imbrications within and among gender, sex, and neoliberalism, in this chapter we offer two brief case studies from the Dominican Republic and the US. While these sites are geographically near one another, the labor sectors we focus on – sex work and domestic work – are positioned in divergent ways with respect to the underpinnings of neoliberal economies – a juxtaposition that we find analytically enlightening. Furthermore, the Dominican Republic benefits from the dynamics of racial capitalism, particularly in its relations to Haiti. Yet, as an economy that is heavily dependent on tourism, it is also an object of ongoing coloniality in relation to the US, which is itself a settler colonial society. In our case studies, we will attend to these complex relations as they are manifest in immigration law

42 Jakobsen, Padilla, and Horn

in the US and the Dominican Republic, and in both formal and informal labor markets in each of the two settings.

Despite the proliferation of sexual commerce in the Dominican Republic and other highly touristed regions, the precariousness of sex work is intensified because it is not understood to be a form of legitimate economic activity, crossing the border from the familial and reproductive sector that is presumed to link sex and romantic love into the world of economic activity and severing that link. Gender and sexuality also contribute to the construction of domestic work as a precarious sector of the informal economy, but for a different reason: the implicit assumption that domestic work is so central to gendered familial life as to be a "labor of love" (Polletta 2018). The contexts of colonialism, racial capitalism, and feminist and queer materialism also suggest that the usual analytic boundaries between productive, reproductive, and informal economies are both helpful heuristics and in need of more inter-related and dynamic analysis. A full analysis of the inter-relations among different economic sectors is beyond the scope of this – or any single – book. Our hope, however, is to contribute to this more complex analysis by attending to some of the sites that challenge both the usual analytic boundaries and the ways that each sector has been made to seem coherent unto itself.

As Sanyal and Bhattacharyya have suggested, for example, the informal economy is not just a pool of labor, a site for people waiting to be employed in the productive economy. What Sanyal (2007) calls the "need economy" is rather a set of relations in which people may well conduct all of their economic activity.[24] In the Dominican Republic, neoliberal strategies include the expansion of factory work through free trade zones, a twelve-fold increase in the tourism sector over three decades, and the redirection of agriculture toward support for tourism (Meyer 2020). The informal economy of the Dominican Republic has also expanded significantly since the 1980s, reaching sustained levels of nearly 50% of total non-agricultural employment in the 2000s (International Labour Organization 2014). In the US, the growth of finance capitalism has been accompanied by growth in both formal and informal service sectors, that break up reproductive labor into a series of service exchanges (daycare, restaurants, dry cleaners and laundries, home and office cleaning, etc.), some aspects of which are done formally through contracts and some informally through direct cash payment. In both the Dominican Republic and the US, much of the informal labor is undertaken by migrants, including Haitian migrants in the Dominican Republic and Dominican migrants in the US, as colonial and racial hierarchies continue to have effects in both countries (Fine and Petrozziello 2017).

Notably, whereas the economic particularities and the locations of the Dominican Republic and US are quite distinct geopolitically, in both cases neoliberal policies and their effects – austerity and tax incentives in the Dominican Republic and intensified inequality in the US – have been accepted and presented *prima facie* as being good (or, at least, the best possible) for the nation

Gender justice and economic justice **43**

and its people. In the 1980s and 1990s, former Dominican President Joaquín Balaguer advocated for neoliberal policies that favored investment from the Global North in free trade zones and tourism in the post-Trujillo era in the Dominican Republic.[25] Even though these policies were set to enrich investors in the Global North, they also promised to bring a new era of prosperity and freedom to the people of the Dominican Republic. In the same time period in the US, both Republicans and Democrats embraced neoliberal policies as the key to promised economic prosperity and freedom. This agreement across party lines was shared across Presidential administrations, including that of former US President Barack Obama, who argued that neoliberal economic policies were the best that could be achieved for people in the era of globalization (Sorkin 2016). President Trump campaigned against many of these policies in the 2016 presidential elections, but, once in office, he, too, embraced tax cuts and even his signature issue of criticizing free trade produced a new free trade agreement with Canada and Mexico with most of the same policies as its predecessor.[26] We term Trump's approach to economic policy *nationalist neoliberalism*, given that he did embrace intensified support for white Christian nationalism but could not or did not shift away from many of the neoliberal policies of his predecessors. Preliminary evidence suggests that less explicit forms of nationalist neoliberalism are likely to continue under the Biden administration, effectively countering Trumpism both by supporting US labor organizing and also appropriating an "America first" model of economic production.[27]

The promises of neoliberalism proffered by politicians have not just been about economic prosperity through greater market freedom; they have often included promises about greater freedom in social relations, like those of gender and sex. "Freedom" means something different in each case, but the linking of economic freedom to promises about, for example, the liberation of women, has been an important part of the package that holds together neoliberal policies and practices. Sometimes, the promises linking neoliberalism, gender, and sexuality are direct – i.e., the idea that neoliberal policies will lead to greater gender equality by, for example, opening up new opportunities for women in the workforce, a promise that has deeply informed Dominican economic policies. Sometimes the promises are more indirect – such as promises to "save" women from sex trafficking through policies that are compatible with neoliberal governmentality, as we discuss in Chapter 4 of this volume.

The paradoxes and contradictions of these promises are apparent almost immediately. The promise of economic freedom may expand markets even as newly free people become trapped by debt. And the promise of socio-economic mobility for women into the workforce may not in fact serve to destabilize gender hierarchies, for example. As research within the Dominican context illustrates, women who may have sought economic opportunities or independence from male providers are often integrated into the most exploited positions in service economies and free trade zones, limiting their ability to resist gender hierarchies in their daily lives. As Carla Freeman (2000) has noted, some women

44 Jakobsen, Padilla, and Horn

may benefit from the opening of opportunities, but multinationals are also able to appropriate the idea of "the working woman" to reap the benefits of women's conversion into devout pink-collar professionals.

One of the reasons neoliberal policies have such paradoxical effects is that they often do offer opportunities and economic resources to some people who need them, even as these resources are distributed within constricted limits and along the lines of existing social hierarchies. So, for example, Tami Navarro's (2021) study of financial services in the US Virgin Islands, *Virgin Capital: Race, Gender, and Financialization in the US Virgin Islands*, shows that the neoliberal expansion of this sector did offer new opportunities to many Black women in the Virgin Islands, but these opportunities also tended to reinforce existing racial and gender hierarchies, offering benefits to those who were deemed closest to dominant norms. Adding to the continued effects of race and gender hierarchies in productive economies, the neoliberal expansion of precarious or intermittent work reinforces existing hierarchies in the household and led many people to move back and forth within and among formal employment, informal employment, and unpaid reproductive work. These shifts can disempower workers over the full range of capitalist relations, as those who find themselves with formal, productive employment may nonetheless be willing to accept lower wages or higher precarity. Indeed, the structure of work in neoliberal economies has not been able to sustain an expansion of prosperity across the dividing lines of race, class, and gender, while gendered and racialized divisions of labor have persisted or even intensified.

For example, despite consistently high rates of economic growth over the neoliberal period, the Dominican Republic has one of the highest proportions (50.5%) of people living below the poverty line in the region (Bolivia, Honduras, and Guatemala have higher poverty rates, albeit with much smaller economic growth rates). The percentage of Dominicans with "vulnerable employment," defined by the World Bank (2013) in implicitly gendered terms as "unpaid family workers and own-account workers as a percentage of total employment," has hovered around 40%. The country also has the highest unemployment rate of all Latin American countries surveyed.

In the US, we see major corporations, including transnational corporations based in the US, also participating in a shift from an industrial/productive economy to a service/reproductive economy, along with a correlative shift that has many people working on the edge of formal service and informal survival economies. In part as a result of COVID-19, Amazon, a distribution rather than a manufacturing or finance corporation, is set to become the single largest employer in the world, even as the company has historically depended on the type of "disposable" workforce discussed by Tadiar (2013), where disposability is organized by race, gender, and national citizenship, as well as economics.[28] While seeking to expand its footprint in many areas, Amazon is organized mainly to deliver commodities for the purpose of social reproduction in households. The expansion of Amazon does involve some gendered shifts within the service economy, particularly in light of the pandemic. COVID-19 has led to shifts away from domestic work and food provision through restaurants, including many jobs that have historically been gendered female, and toward warehouse and delivery jobs that have traditionally been gendered male (Porter 2020).

As in the Dominican Republic, the effects of these shifts among intertwining sectors are to diminish labor rights and workers' wellbeing across the economy as a whole. Even beyond the warehouses and fulfillment centers, the organization of Amazon's workforce is best conceptualized as pertaining to the service sector or to the new "gig economy," rather than the industrial economy (Schor 2020). Amazon delivery drivers do not work for Amazon directly, but are independent contractors, working at the boundary between employment by service companies and gig workers (Weise 2020). Amazon pays its warehouse workers more than traditional retail service jobs but less than traditional warehouse work, pushing the paradigm of unskilled work away from that of the industrial sector and toward that of the service sector. In response, employees are pursuing newly invigorated unionization efforts, and activists are resisting the expansion of the company (Corkery and Weise 2021; Goodman 2019), even as these struggles take place within the context of a neoliberal political economy that has effectively undermined the labor movement over the past several decades. Meanwhile, Amazon is investing heavily in ensuring that its jobs are not organized as industrial jobs with unions but instead – like service jobs – without unions. Internal documents show that Amazon has been surveilling its employees globally to track even potential efforts at unionization, contracting with the infamously anti-union Pinkerton agency to surveil workers' organizing (Del Ray and Ghaffary 2020; Canales 2020). And Amazon is not the only corporation to be pushing the model of work in the neoliberal era toward a service economy and sometimes even further toward the boundary between service and survival economies. Walmart has also expanded its reach during the pandemic, and its business model actively positions workers on the border between service and survival economies, with wages that ensure workers will also need to depend on other sources of income, including state provisions like food stamps, to survive.[29]

In other words, any presumption that neoliberal policies will ultimately serve to mitigate social inequalities or to promote gender and sexual liberation must confront the fact that an ever-increasing pace of social change – in the structure of labor, in communications technologies, and in multiple forms of social relations – is entangled with the paradoxes of neoliberalism, ultimately reinforcing long-standing structures of domination alongside economic exploitation. By bringing together Grosfoguel's sense of continuing coloniality with the concept of a sexualized economy that entangles economics with raced and gendered social relations and intertwines productive, reproductive, service and survival economies, we can produce an analysis that tracks with the actual paradoxical effects of neoliberal policies and practices.

Coloniality, neoliberal restructuring, and sexual economies in the Dominican Republic

Policies commonly understood as the tangible sites of neoliberalism, such as structural adjustment, austerity, and the institution of free trade zones, began taking hold strongly in the Caribbean in the 1980s.[30] Overall, these neoliberal policies fit the pattern of ongoing coloniality in the Dominican Republic. Policies such as the austerity measures enforced by the World Bank and the IMF were instituted in ways that were mainly continuous with, rather than distinct from, long-standing inequalities. The poverty of state welfare programs and the growth of global capitalist interests and multinationals as dominant actors in domestic economies and trade relations were already entrenched early in the twentieth century. Indeed, one could argue that, in many parts of the Caribbean, entitlement programs never truly existed; thus analyses like that offered by David Harvey (2007, 3) that speak in terms of the withdrawal of these entitlements under neoliberalism are not fully applicable. For example, health expenditures have not plummeted as a result of neoliberalism *per se*, since the country has never enjoyed a thriving public healthcare system.[31] And, long-standing inequalities may well have shaped the effects of structural adjustment, ensuring that the benefits of IMF loans, for example, redounded to those with strong economic resources, such as landowners, whereas the costs were more likely to be borne by those on the margins.[32]

The later emergence of some of the hallmarks of neoliberalism, including free trade zones, does suture the Dominican Republic into broader logics related to neoliberalism, even if it does not mark an entirely new expression of economic and political order. Marion Werner (2016, 8) describes how the creation of free trade zones was inscribed within a broader Eurocentric developmentalist narrative, whereby "[t]he Dominican Republic apparently had progressed along a natural path from an agrarian to an industrial to a service-oriented (or post-industrial) economy." Specifically, these free trade zones emerged "[b]y the end of the 1980s, [when] Latin America's primary US creditors, together with multilateral development banks, implemented a series of policies that privileged so-called export-oriented industrialization, or the production of labor-intensive manufactured goods for Northern markets. This model, already in operation in a handful of experimental zones in regions such as the US–Mexico border and the Haitian capital Port-au-Prince, would soon become dominant" and are part of the "turn toward what is commonly called neoliberalism" (Werner 2016, 4).

Many scholars, including Werner and Steven Gregory (2007), have observed that free trade zones did little to alleviate precarious living conditions for the majority of people. According to Lauren Derby and Marion Werner, "[d]espite the trade zone boom, unemployment never dipped below 15% and underemployment remained stubbornly high. While offering jobs to women, poverty wages made trade zone work unsustainable for the vast majority of those with children."[33] Instead of improving economic opportunities, the institution of free trade led to the stagnation, if not regression, of hard-fought-for workers' rights, as Emelio Betances (2016) has documented in his important study of Dominican labor organizing.[34] Betances (2016, 254) concludes that "the Dominican state, in its eagerness to create optimal conditions for foreign capital, ignored the social rights of workers ... and the social rights of workers diminished."[35]

Consistent with the paradoxes of neoliberalism, even as factory work allowed some women to enter paid employment for the first time in their lives and attain greater financial status in the household, the persistence of gender disparities within both factory and household was facilitated by the barely subsistence-level wage for female employees, prohibiting any true independence or even capacity to leave an abusive or undesirable union.[36] In other words, the inter-relation between the gender hierarchy of the global factory and that of the intimate home persisted in the face of the institution of neoliberal "freedom."[37] Such paradoxes help explain why women's employment in new sectors of the productive economy instituted through neoliberal policies like free trade zones did not significantly disrupt gender hierarchies, or serve to unsettle hegemonic notions of femininity and masculinity.

Alongside the diminishing of labor rights, economic policies in the Dominican Republic since the 1980s have also led to another of the effects typically identified as part of neoliberalism: exponential growth in informal and intermittent employment. Taking into account this expansion of informal labor is crucial to understanding the effects of neoliberalism. The promise made by neoliberal politicians was that women could be liberated by movement from an unpaid reproductive sector into paid labor, thereby expanding economic wellbeing for both newly empowered women and society as a whole. Yet neoliberal promises such as these can only make sense within a traditional analysis that understands the productive economy as predominantly male and the reproductive economy as predominantly female and unpaid, while ignoring the more varied gender configurations and sexual circulations of informal economies.

Along with the exponential growth of free trade zones, the embrace of neoliberal policies resulted in a rapid expansion of the tourism industry in the Dominican Republic.[38] Various scholars, including Amalia Cabezas, Denise Brennan, and Mark Padilla have analyzed how Dominican formations of gender and sexuality interact with the neoliberal tourism industry, even as sites in the colonial history of places like the Dominican Republic are made into tourist attractions.[39] One way to think of tourism in the Dominican Republic is as a sexual economy in the context of ongoing coloniality, related to that described by Davis and the Black Sexual Economies Collective in the context of the afterlives of slavery. Overall, as Kempadoo (1999) has persuasively argued, the sexualization of the entire region of the Caribbean as a site of sun, sand, sex, and fun contributes to its attractiveness to tourists. Not surprisingly, tourism as a sexualized economy has included an informal service economy, with sexual labor made available alongside the services of the formal tourist economy. Steven Gregory (2007, 58–59) discusses, for example, how tourism is structured *via* gendered

48 Jakobsen, Padilla, and Horn

and racialized surveillance techniques, whereby "young women – in particular, women who were racially marked and poor – are routinely stopped by the POLITUR [the tourism police] during identity checks on the premise that they are *mujeres de la calle* (streetwalkers) and potential lawbreakers. The hierarchical landscape of the tourism zone is thus structured in gendered terms, since women are not only more likely than men to be viewed as being out of place there but are also more likely to be seen as exploiting their sexuality." Similarly, Denise Brennan has studied the "transnational social field" created by tourism, specifically sex tourism, and its interaction with gender norms in the Dominican Republic.

Analyzing the informal tourist sector as part of – rather than separate from – neoliberal transformations in the Dominican Republic, Mark Padilla (2007) has foregrounded the experiences and sexual labor of men as part of the overall gender dynamics of the tourism industry. Padilla's work (n.d.) in the "Syndemics Project" has documented the experiences of sexual labor and involvement in the drug economy among men employed in the tourism industry, examining the role that men's shifting labor in global economies has on household economies, gender relations, precarity, and health.[40] At the same time that many women have moved into economic roles traditionally defined as "masculine," like factory work, men's labor has become increasingly informal. Sexual commerce – sometimes glossed over, using gendered terms such as "romance tourism" – has become a more prominent strategy for survival.[41]

The informalization of Dominican men's labor represents another set of effects of neoliberal policies, one that is distinct from and yet works in conjunction with the effects of women's incorporation into free trade zones. Together, these gendered practices produce a neoliberal culture, even as the specific effects of the increased instability of men's labor have dramatically transformed men's patterns of migration and mobility.

Padilla has described the ways that the Dominican sex tourism market is oriented toward a particular construction of masculinity – one that emphasizes a nominally heterosexual, street-based *tigueraje*, a term used to describe a particular kind of Dominican man. The *tiguere*, in Dominican terms, is a figure who adapts to his circumstances, a chameleon-like being who is opportunistic and charismatic, who expresses a particularly keen ability for manipulating or taking advantage of others.[42] The growth of male informal sexual labor in tourism zones in the Dominican Republic stresses the paradoxical ways that the insertion of non-normative sexual practices into tourism economies can occur, while not demarcating these practices as "homosexual," but rather by marketing a particular notion of Dominican masculinity (Padilla 2007, 207). Here again, we see how neoliberalism both sustains the importance of gender and sexual norms to economic activity, and also reconfigures them in unpredictable ways.

The story of one tourism employee, Samuel, provides a useful illustration of the connections among gender, sexuality, and neoliberalism. Having been deported multiple times from the US and Puerto Rico, and having experienced problems related to drug addiction and to small-scale drug dealing in all of the countries where he has lived, Samuel spoke of the ways in which he had experienced both the positive and negative aspects of his pseudo-cosmopolitan life in the midst of global survival economies. "I've had a licentious life, to put it one way, But I've also done constructive things. Studied, and stuff like that." Samuel's migratory history expresses both trauma and joy; it highlights moments of pleasure and the joys of experiencing other cultures and ways of life, as well as experiences of intense discrimination, institutionalized violence, incarceration, and deportation (Padilla et al. 2018).

In Santo Domingo, after being deported from Puerto Rico, Samuel studied engineering, and struggled, unsuccessfully, to obtain a professional position. Ultimately, he was unable to obtain formal employment because of an exclusion that is institutionalized in Dominican policy through a deportee registry that functions to deny employment (for more on this registry, see Chapter 5 of this volume). In other words, rather than living in the zone of a reserve army of labor for the formal economy, Samuel was actively excluded from any prospect of professional employment now or in the future, making Samuel a permanent part of an expanding informal sector. When Padilla's project interviewed him at age 57, he was working in the drug and sex economy in Santo Domingo. His initial experience working in the global drug economy as a survival strategy while abroad provided the experience and skills he needed to continue making ends meet in the informal economy in the Dominican Republic. Furthermore, his linguistic skills in English allowed him to negotiate sexual services in an economy that relied fundamentally on the market for Dominican sexuality and masculinity.

As Samuel's experience indicates, the condition of statelessness that Dominican deportees experience places intense constraints on their possibilities for movement, employment, and community building. In response to these constraints, many men express a gendered agency in order to leverage opportunities to make a living through informal sexual labor and small-scale drug sales with tourists, from whom they received commissions as "middlemen" or direct payments as providers of sexual services. Sexuality had become for Samuel a resource for brokering contacts with tourists in the informal economy, and provided a means of, as these men often call it, *buscándose la vida* (looking for life) – a phrase that is used in the Dominican Republic to describe the multiple informal strategies that people use to make ends meet in the context of labor exclusion and a precarious informal economy. Men like Samuel have been able to insert themselves into a particularly Dominican landscape of neoliberalism, and crucially, sexuality and gender identity are essential resources in doing so.

It is difficult to grasp the evolution of the Dominican informal economy without reference to these dimensions of gender and sexuality – affecting men as deeply as women, but in distinct ways. The constraints on economic mobility are deeply imbricated with people's struggles to "look for life" in both the gendered economies of free trade zones and the sexual economies of tourism – outcomes

50 Jakobsen, Padilla, and Horn

that materialize the paradoxical promises of neoliberalism, and which nevertheless have become an essential part of the Dominican economic reality.

The meaning of value: domestic work
and neoliberal precarity in the US

As with the case of the Dominican Republic, coloniality, racial capitalism, and
sexual politics come together to structure neoliberalism in the US. This combination of forces is especially evident in fields like sex work and domestic work
that have, since colonial times, been organized by race and gender and that currently inhabit the afterlife of slavery and continuing coloniality. As we describe
below, domestic work, along with agricultural work, in the US is legally excluded
from significant portions of existing labor law because of the historical legacy of
these sectors in relation to slave economies and the post-emancipation political
power of states from the former Confederacy.[43] And this historical exclusion, in
conjunction with ongoing coloniality, has created these sectors of employment
as particularly precarious niches that are increasingly filled by immigrants from
the Global South.[44]

Premilla Nadasen and Tiffany Williams (2010) describe how neoliberal processes have led to immigrant women making up a large portion of the workforce for domestic labor in the US.[45] These workers face conditions that make
domestic work and farm work seem like the best of a bad set of options: "In the
1990s, the rising demand for domestic service was filled by growing numbers of
immigrant women. This was also a byproduct of the changes in global capitalism
and the US labor market over the past twenty years that led to greater reliance on
women's labor. The direct economic effects of globalization (e.g., debt reduction
programs that cut social service spending), along with the effects of armed conflict and political oppression, have provided the impetus for many women to look
for work outside their countries of origin. Today, women migrate in large numbers from poorer countries, often referred to as the 'Global South' (i.e., Southeast
Asia, Central America, and Africa), to the wealthy 'Global North' (i.e., western
Europe and North America) and in increasing numbers to wealthy Gulf states
(Indonesia to Saudi Arabia is a noted route). They work in the homes of the rich
and fill gaps in care left by the growing number of women who have recently
begun to work in the formal labor sector" (Nadasen and Williams 2010, 5).

Martin Manalansan furthers this analysis by arguing for a queer reading of
migrant domestic labor in which "reproduction is not the pivot for the mobilization of gender labor migration," biological motherhood and its naturalized
linkage to caring is decentered, and we bring "such queer creatures as gay men,
single and married women with no 'maternal instinct,' and transgendered persons into the mix." Such a reading, he suggests, would disrupt the heteronormative gender assumptions which undergird the chain of care paradigm, and allow
for the recognition of possibilities for self-cultivation and for moments of pleasure among some migrant care workers (such as those depicted in the striking

documentary film about Filipino gay and M-F transgender care workers, *Paper Dolls;* see Manalansan 2008: 2-3). Manalansan's argument makes clear that the burgeoning care work sector cannot be analyzed only through social reproduction while Nadasen's and Williams's analysis shows how the formal economy is intertwined with – and dependent upon – the informal economies in which many of these migrants work. And, indeed, domestic work in the US often takes place within an informal economy – workers are hired without contracts, are paid in cash, and cannot claim workplace rights. In both the Dominican Republic and the US, the activities of border enforcement and deportation also effectively ensure that many migrants only have access to informal labor markets. Thus, a full analysis of care work spans across productive, reproductive, and survival economies.

In the Dominican Republic, a pool of labor for the informal market in sex work is created by the forced registration of returning deportees, which denies them access to formal labor markets. Given that government policy not only supports but actively enforces people's need to do sex work, governmental powers must, therefore, see sex work as necessary for the tourist economy. Our sense of tourism as a sexualized economy organized by coloniality helps to explain the government's acceptance of the ways in which its deportation law supports a labor market for sex work. But this idea is of course also disavowed by the government – and by any social analysis that separates the operation of formal from informal markets or economic relations from gender and sexual relations. In the US, immigration laws also place constraints on migrants' access to markets, keeping many domestic workers without documents in informal jobs, rather than in jobs formalized through contracts or services (just as immigration enforcement often means that agricultural workers must move seasonally and will not settle in agricultural communities). And, of course, the economies of the Dominican Republic and the US are also connected by these governmental policies, as the largest percentage of Dominican immigrants to the US work in service industries, including domestic work, with remittances from the US to the Dominican Republic almost doubling between 2007 and 2017.[46]

These lines of entanglement show that, in both of these cases, sex work in the Dominican Republic and domestic work in the US, the broad matrix of relations we have been discussing in this chapter, including coloniality, racial capitalism, and sexual politics, are operative. Yet the specific mechanisms that produce the intertwining of gender, sex, and neoliberalism run in nearly the opposite direction in the two cases. The precariousness of sex work in the informal economy done by migrants recently repatriated to the Dominican Republic is intensified because it is understood as illicit work that divorces sex from familial love. Gender and sexuality also contribute to the construction of domestic work as an informal economy. But, in the case of domestic work, the informality of this sector of employment is constituted, in part, through claims that domestic work is so central to familial life as to be done from love, friendship, or feelings of kinship. The question of whether domestic work falls within the realm of

52 Jakobsen, Padilla, and Horn

"work" or of "family" is central to both economic structures and to individual experiences.[47]

Familialism, the sense that the family is a separate space of non-economic activity, powerfully contributes to the obfuscation of the articulations between production and reproduction. For example, the Trump Administration's nomination of US Representative Mick Mulvaney to be White House budget director ran into controversy when Mulvaney admitted that he had failed to pay federal payroll taxes when he employed a nanny. In response to critics' charges that this was a disqualifying violation of the law, Mulvaney claimed that the work done by the nanny hardly counted as labor.[48] Testifying before the Senate Budget Committee during his confirmation hearing, he said, "In 2000, we had triplets. When they came home, we hired someone to help my wife take care of the children. In our minds, she was a babysitter. She did not live with us. She did not spend the night there ... She did not cook. She did not clean. She did not educate the children, she helped my wife with the kids" (Weyl and Griffiths 2017). This labor of providing "help" for "[a man's] wife," even if paid, is treated as not worthy of being considered "employment." Nor did Mulvaney expect it to carry the implications of employment, like the payroll taxes he failed to pay. Adding to the gendering of domestic work as that done by women – specifically "wives" – is the location of domestic work within the private world of the home, rather than in the public world of economic activity. Caring labor, such as that done by nurses and certified nursing assistants, when done in institutional settings, rather than in the home, is still underpaid, but it is recognized as labor and sometimes unionized. The domestic location and its interpretation through the gendered division between public and private further emphasizes the idea that caring labor is not really work at all and, thus, does not have to be valued as work.[49]

The articulation of domestic work with immigration intensifies the status of domestic work as non-work done by people who are not recognized as workers. This articulation has shifted over the neoliberal period. The initial expansion of neoliberalism helped to create a relay in which structural adjustment and other neoliberal policies and practices, such as free trade deals, contributed to increased migration from the Global South to the Global North. In turn, this migration supported further structural adjustment in the Global North, such as allowing for the production of more low-wage non-union jobs in the US by providing a labor force that must take these jobs. As Jocelyn Campbell, a nanny in Westchester, New York, who migrated from Barbados, explains in a survey of domestic workers published by Domestic Workers United and the research group, DataCenter, "We have been forced here because US foreign policy has created poverty in our home countries. Once we are here in the US, searching for ways to survive, we are pushed into exploited jobs where our work is not recognized, respected, or protected" (Domestic Workers United 2006, 9).[50]

Zelem Guerrero (2009), a long-time domestic worker, clearly explains how the economics of "domestic work" not only extend beyond the intimate sphere of the home, but are part of the flows of money and labor that make for global capitalism, a reality highlighted by the global economic crisis in 2008:

> With the economic crisis, [my employers] fired me with no notice. No severance pay. We domestic workers earn our daily bread and pay our bills, doing long hours of undervalued back-breaking work. Our labor enables our employers to do other jobs as professionals and business owners in the city.... Our employers – the US government and the Philippine government – all benefit from our labor. The US government benefits when we are denied Social Security, Unemployment Insurance, and health care. The US government tolerates abuses through experience from bad employers; our exploitation is part of the system. The Philippine government remains silent when we are abused, deported, or denied our rights. But the Philippine government has no problem calling us national heroes when we need billions of dollars to sustain the Philippine economy.

A survey of domestic workers by the National Domestic Workers Alliance (NDWA Labs 2020) has shown a similar loss of jobs in response to the 2020 COVID-19 crisis. Over 90% of the workers surveyed had lost some or all of their work during the crisis, and, for those with any continuing employment, almost two-thirds did not have access to the most basic of personal protective equipment.

Despite the economic drivers of migration, Linda Green (2011) has shown in her study of migrants from Guatemala to the US how the increasingly common sense that immigrants are always already illegal reinforces the idea that they are not workers. Historian Mae Ngai has extensively documented the ways in which undocumented immigration to the US was not always categorized as "illegal," but was increasingly treated as such over the course of the twentieth century, with expanded and increasingly institutionalized systems of counting and controlling all immigration."[51] And, as with other aspects of the social relations that make up neoliberalism, gender and sexuality have played a crucial role in solidifying the regime of immigration and precarious labor that Green (2011) describes. Mary Pat Brady (2008) has pointed out that the widely popular mainstream association between migrants and illegality in the US was actively strengthened during the Clinton Administration as "perhaps the first emblem of the neoliberal structural adjustment programs that came home to the United States in the 1990s"[52] Brady (2008) also points out that the discourse of illegality as developed by Clinton and by initiatives in individual states, such as California's Proposition 187 from the same time period in the early 1990s, or Arizona's more recent SB 1070, which is central to Green's analysis, are deeply driven by discourses of gender and sexuality.[53] Together, Green's and Brady's analyses show how gender, sexuality, race, ethnicity, and national citizenship produce relays between the idea of domestic work as non-labor associated with women's roles in private social relations and broader neoliberal policies and practices, such as attacks on immigrants and on labor unions, and the expansion of precarious employment.

54 Jakobsen, Padilla, and Horn

Production and reproduction: gender, economics, and justice

Domestic work takes place at the points of articulation between productive and reproductive labor, as well as between service and survival economies. Is domestic work production? Part of the service sector, which is now the largest sector in the productive economy? Or is domestic work reproduction? Part of the informal, often unpaid, labor of reproducing social relations each and every day? The National Domestic Workers Alliance in the US, along with its allies in the International Labour Organization, are claiming the category of "worker" as their own and simultaneously remaking that very category.[54] Both work and worker are different from the imagination of a split between productive and reproductive labor and the imagined lunch-pail laborer of the past who brought home a "family wage." Tracing the ways in which domestic work is part of a broad sector of service work highlights the ways precarity and injustice are achieved through a fantasized split between public and private spheres. The presumption that caring labor is fundamentally "private" in nature hides the intertwining of public policy, economic exchange, and domestic life, just as it hides the intertwining of productive and reproductive economies.

Attending to the importance of domestic work clearly shows how these sectors are imbricated in ways that cannot be simply untangled. Before the pandemic, the professionals ensconced in gleaming glass towers were dependent on workers in service jobs, from low-paid clerical and cleaning staff to all manner of delivery services and workers in food trucks, coffee shops, and restaurants.[55] Yet, when bankers picked up their suits from the dry cleaners or when students picked up food from coffee shops, they rarely thought that they were depending on others to feed and clothe them, in part because the labor of cooking and doing the laundry has often been invisible *as work*. One of the major questions raised by the pandemic is how these relations will shift in a post-pandemic world. It seems likely many professionals may return to paying others for the labor of social reproduction, particularly in the form of domestic work and childcare at the same low rates that preceded the pandemic. For those countries, like the US, that experience a "K-shaped" economic recovery, professionals will benefit just as they did by being able to work from home during the pandemic, whereas workers depending solely on wages are likely to fall more deeply into debt. As such, even more service workers are likely to find themselves at the connecting points between formal and informal work, service, and survival economies, as they work in different sectors and undertake hazardous migration in order to contribute to their households through multiple jobs and remittances.

The discourse separating productive from reproductive labor creates certain blocks in organizing to address these issues. For decades, the labor movement in the US ignored or actively refused to organize rapidly growing sectors of the economy, particularly those like domestic work, in which women of color formed the majority of the workforce. Even in contemporary organizing, these divisions

Gender justice and economic justice **55**

can remain active. For example, although the drive to organize Amazon workers is very important in revitalizing a labor movement decimated by decades of neoliberalism, it tends to incorporate old divisions amongst types of workers within Amazon by focusing on warehouse workers. Amazon has made itself into a giant corporation in part by reconfiguring how profit can be made from domesticity by delivering domestic products. Many analyses of the company, however, tend to focus on the company as a "logistics" or "tech" company, rather than as a purveyor of domestic commodities.[56] And, as described above, Amazon has increased its profits by treating its workers in ways that are associated with the neoliberal service sector. Although Amazon's warehouse workers tend to resemble industrial workers in that they go to a single workplace and can be organized through traditional practices, Amazon also employs drivers who are dispersed and who work from their own households, and these workers are not included in this union drive. Notably, the National Domestic Workers Alliance (NDWA) suggests that contemporary labor organizing must include the dispersed workers who are associated with household labor as central to any social movement aimed at challenging neoliberal economic relations.

Revaluing domestic work and developing an analysis that does not reinforce the boundaries between productive and reproductive sectors of the economy would allow for new forms of political activism, as well as labor organizing. Currently, for example, activism about the environmental impact of industries tends to focus on corporations, whereas activism on the environmental impact of households tends to focus on individual actions and consumer efforts.

An analysis that refuses to split production from reproduction, however, could instead focus on the type of overarching reorganization of production and consumption that might provide the basis for climate justice, another profoundly urgent social need.

Conclusion: synthesizing case studies

Gender and sexuality in conjunction with race and nation are substantive parts of the apparatus of neoliberal precarity for many workers in the Dominican Republic and the US, whether they work in productive, reproductive, service, or survival economies (or some intermediate combination of these sectors). In both of the cases that we have described here, we see that sexual politics play a significant role in constituting neoliberal policies and practices. In political discourse, gender and sexuality are crucial to the idea that neoliberal forms of economic relations offer any promise, other than exploitation. Neoliberal promises of freedom often include promises of both gender and sexual freedom, even as gender and sexual regulation and the devaluing of gender and sexual labor are part and parcel of intensifying precarity. We have also demonstrated some of the ways that gender and sexuality come to be constitutive of particular economic arrangements within neoliberalism, as well as of underlying notions of value. The configuration of domestic work as women's work and of sexual labor as an illicit part of the tourist economy together constitute the service sector as a site of informal and questionably legal employment with few protections for people whose efforts to "look for life" are treated as insubstantial and unimportant, if not illegal.

In both the Dominican Republic and the US, gender and sexuality continue to constitute forms of labor that are non-labor, whether illicit, non-familial "sex work" or licit, familial "domestic work." Not only are sex work and domestic work part of the overall economies in both countries but they are both entwined with formal productive economies and governmental policies, if ambivalently and paradoxically so. The labor of connecting tourists to supposedly illicit activities is clearly valued by Dominican society to some extent, for instance, as the government creates the conditions to ensure that it is one of the only options for some people searching for economic survival. It does so in part through the unnecessary (and, therefore, overzealous) criminalization of returning migrants, even as criminal enforcement of sex and drug laws against tourists is markedly less frequent. The US similarly deploys criminalization and uneven enforcement as a means of managing labor relations across the economy, including a productive economy that depends on increasingly criminalized migrant labor. Undocumented migrants work extensively in urban service sectors, agricultural work, and in doing the reproductive work in individual households that allows men and women to participate in the formal economy. Recognizing the extent of migrant labor involved in these sectors would imply attending to the intertwining of productive, reproductive, and survival economies. Revaluing this labor would require rethinking the criminalization of a range of activities, including migration and sexual labor. Recognizing work *as work* across economic sectors would involve acknowledging the social needs and desires that give rise to it.

As Ai-jen Poo (2014) of the US National Domestic Workers Alliances has insisted: "Given the vast numbers of unorganized workers and the challenges and opportunities of our time … we need to be much, much more powerful, and strategic, and ambitious." Among the objectives that Poo outlines are enhanced social and economic supports for precarious workers, immigration relief for undocumented migrants, strengthened labor organizing by Black and Brown women, and "a whole new care infrastructure to support workers and families."

Moving away from a unified analysis of neoliberalism and toward a focus on the various paradoxes of neoliberal practices and policies opens conceptual space for articulating the different aspects of this new infrastructure and the more just social relations it would support. A focus on gender and sexuality shows some of the complex, even paradoxical, nature of what we might refer to as a global assemblage of neoliberal economic rationalities and technologies, on the one hand, and their associated gender and sexual logics within specific settings, on the other. This analysis becomes powerful when sexual politics are placed in the context of ongoing coloniality, racial capitalism, feminist activism, and queer materialism. Neoliberalism runs on a complex, shifting, and paradoxical set of relations between domination and exploitation, and on a set of obfuscations that hides relations among production and reproduction, formal and informal economics, wage labor and survival. Social change on behalf of justice requires an analysis and a politics that can address these interconnections.

Notes

1 In searching for an articulation of ethical values that might challenge colonial concepts of freedom and equality, Saba Mahmood (2005) turns, at the end of her path-breaking book, *The Politics of Piety*, to the concept of "human flourishing." What kind of social relations allow for human flourishing and how might that flourishing look different from the freedom and equity of autonomous individuals imagined by modern liberalism? We take up Mahmood's conceptualization of flourishing, now expanded to the world well beyond the human, as a means of conceptualizing gender justice otherwise from the strictures of modern liberalism.

2 On sexual politics see Cohen (1997); Case (2017); Jakobsen (2020); and Millet (1970).

3 See, for example, Thomas Frank's (2004; 2016) persistent argument that sexual politics actively contributes to what Harvey (2007, 42) terms, "the culture of neoliberalism," by pulling political attention away from material questions of redistribution. For a more complex reading of the relation between recognition and redistribution (that nonetheless still separates them), see Fraser and Honneth (2003).

4 Arruzza (2015, 50) writes that gender can be conceptualized as "the continuous, theatrical repetition over time of normative discursive acts and social practices ... [that] become part of the conceptual organization of time carried out by capital."

5 On the heterosexual matrix, for example, see Ferguson (2003).

6 There is some debate in the scholarly literature about the exact numbers of people employed in domestic work, in part, because domestic work is variously defined in different studies. There is little debate, however, about the import of domestic work in the nineteenth- and early twentieth-century British economy. Lucy Delap (2011) has convincingly debunked the "rise and fall" myth of domestic employment as disappearing by the 1890s, building on a scholarly genealogy that includes Leonore Davidoff (1976) and Pamela Horn (1987). For the service sector as a whole, in the 1840s, approximately one-third of workers were in the service sector and, by the 1880s, this proportion was more than one-half (Delap 2011).

7 This is work that reaches back to the campaign launched by the International Wages for Housework collective in the 1970s; they argued that the labor done by work in the home by women – bearing children, rearing them, cooking, cleaning, taking care of the men of the household, and so on – is expropriated labor. Silvia Federici is one of the original members of The Wages for Housework campaign, and her publications have continued to develop the analysis developed by the collective in the 1970s. One of her best-known books is *Caliban and the Witch: Women, the Body, and Primitive Accumulation* (Federici 2004), which argues that expropriation of women's labor was enforced by efforts to eradicate undomesticated women.

8 For an in-depth explanation of the epistemological method of moving dynamically among different analytic frameworks, see Medina (2013) and Jakobsen (2020).

9 These relations are refracted in a number of directions. For example, the shifting period from colonialism to neoliberal austerity overlaps with the Cold War, often understood as a bilateral conflict between the US and the Soviet Union, but which can instead be understood as a Global Cold War that shifted relations within and among multiple areas of the world. Petrus Liu (2015, 4) argues, for instance, that contemporary Chinese queer cultures should not be read as responses to neoliberalism but in relation to the Cold War division of China in 1949 into the People's Republic of China (PRC) and the Republic of China in Taiwan. This shift in perspective raises a new set of questions, about entangled phenomena, including "the incomplete

58 Jakobsen, Padilla, and Horn

decolonization in Asia, the achievements and failures of socialist democracy, the contradictory process of capitalist modernization, the uneven exchange of capital and goods" (Liu 2015, 7). Paul Amar (2013, 7) also raises questions about whether neoliberalism is the appropriate framework for analyzing social formations throughout the world and traces the development of a "security archipelago" with nodes in Egypt and Brazil in the 1990s and early twenty-first century as a means of articulating "intercontinental flows of security practices and protective discourses" imbricated with both morality and materialism, sexual and religious politics.

10 The literature on anticolonialism, postcolonialism, and decolonization is now vast. Some helpful summaries are provided by Odd Arne Westad (2005); Robert J. Young (2001); and George J. Sefa Dei and Meredith Lordan (2016).

11 "[P]eripheral nation-states and non-European people live today under the regime of 'global coloniality' imposed by the United States through the International Monetary Fund (IMF), the World Bank (WB), the Pentagon, and NATO. Peripheral zones inside and outside core zones remain in a colonial situation even though they are no longer under a colonial administration" (Grosfoguel 2006, 176).

12 Grosfoguel writes that the colonial power matrix is "a historical-heterogeneous structure (Quijano 2000, 174) ... that is, an entangled articulation of multiple hierarchies, in which subjectivity and the social imaginary is not derivative but constitutive of the structures of the world system. In this conceptualization, race and racism are not superstructural or instrumental to an overarching logic of capitalist accumulation; they are constitutive of capitalist accumulation on a world scale." Grosfoguel is pursuing what Walter Mignolo terms "diversality as a universal project." (Mignolo 2000 quoted in Grosfoguel 2006, 185).

13 Maria Lugones (2008) similarly emphasizes the ways in which race and gender are constitutive of this colonial power matrix.

14 Lowe (2015, 30) writes, "Bourgeois intimacy, derived from the private and public split that was the socio-spatial medium for both metropolitan and colonial hegemony, was produced by 'the intimacies of four continents' – both in the sense that settler colonial appropriation with enslaved and indentured labor founded the formative wealth of the European bourgeoisie, and ... in the sense that colonized workers produced the material comforts and commodities that furnished the bourgeois home."

15 The full passage in which Spillers (1987, 67) outlines the ungendering effects of the "socio-political order of the New World" reads as follows: "That order, with its human sequence written in blood, represents for its African and indigenous peoples a scene of actual mutilation, dismemberment, and exile. First of all, their New-World, diasporic plight marked a theft of the body – a willful and violent (and unimaginable from this distance) severing of the captive body from its motive will, its active desire. Under these conditions, we lose at least gender difference in the outcome, and the female body and the male body become a territory of cultural and political maneuver, not at all gender-related, gender-specific. But this body, at least from the point of view of the captive community, focuses on a private and particular space, at which point of convergence biological, sexual, social, cultural, linguistic, ritualistic, and psychological fortunes join. This profound intimacy of interlocking detail is disrupted, however, by externally imposed meanings and uses: (1) the captive body becomes the source of an irresistible, destructive sensuality; (2) at the same time – in stunning contradiction – the captive body reduces to a thing, becoming being for the captor; (3) in this absence from a subject position, the captured sexualities provide a physical and biological expression of "otherness;" (4) as a category of 'otherness,' the captive body translates into a potential for pornotroping and embodies sheer physical powerlessness that slides into a more general 'powerlessness,' resonating through various centers of human and social meaning. But I would make a distinction in this case between "body" and "flesh" and impose that distinction as the central one between captive and liberated subject-positions. In that sense, before the "body" there is the "flesh," that zero degree of social conceptualization that does

Gender justice and economic justice **59**

not escape concealment under the brush of discourse, or the reflexes of iconography. Even though the European hegemonies stole bodies – some of them female – out of West African communities in concert with the African "middleman," we regard this human and social irreparability as high crimes against the flesh, as the person of African females and African males registered the wounding."

16 We adopt the term "pornotroping" as fundamentally and dynamically tied to "ungendering" in Spillers's work and in creating some of the paradoxes of racialized sexuality. As Jennifer Nash explains in her brilliant analysis of depictions of Black anality (2014b), pornotroping describes "how race making is a sexual process that often hinges on fictions and fantasies about black women's bodies and pleasures" (Nash 2014b: 251). With theorists such as Nash, we resist reductive uses of the term by acknowledging the ways in which pornotroping extends well beyond what is called pornography, and note the multiplicity of meanings that pertain to racialized imagery even within mainstream pornographic genres (Nash 2014a, 2014b); see also Miller Young (2014). We also attend to the ways in which pornotroping often -- but not always -- involves projections onto women's bodies (Da Silva, Bradley, and Gossett 2015), as well as the expansive recent literature on Spillers's work, including Musser (2014 and 2018), Gumbs (2016), Holland (2012), Rivera (2015) and Weheliye (2014), to name just a few examples.

17 See also Amber Jamilla Musser (2014). For paradigmatic analyses of the role played by domination through racialized gender relations and what could be read as "ungendering" in colonialism, see Frantz Fanon (1968) and Edward Said (1979).

18 On the capitalist production of perversities, see also Roderick A. Ferguson (2003).

19 See also Matthew Karnitschnig (2017).

20 See Peggy Noonan (2020) and Robin Abacarian (2020).

21 " ... the 'reproduction of mothering' in this historic instance carries few of the benefits of a patriarchilized female gender" (Spillers 1987, 73); and "Even though we are not even talking about any of the matriarchal features of social production/reproduction – matrifocality, matrilinearity, matriarchy – when we speak of the enslaved person, we perceive that the dominant culture, in a fatal misunderstanding, assigns a matriarchist value where it does not belong; actually misnames the power of the female regarding the enslaved community. Such naming is false because the female could not, in fact, claim her child, and false, once again, because 'motherhood" is not perceived in the prevailing social climate as a legitimate procedure of cultural inheritance' (Spillers 1987, 80).

22 "If, as Meillassoux contends, "femininity loses its sacredness in slavery" (Spillers 1987, 64), then so does 'motherhood' as female blood-rite/right. To that extent, the captive female body locates precisely a moment of converging political and social vectors that mark the flesh as a prime commodity of exchange. While this proposition is open to further exploration, suffice it to say now that this open exchange of female bodies in the raw offers a kind of Ur-text to the dynamics of signification and representation that the gendered female would unravel" (Spillers 1987, 75).

23 For an economic history that locates the development of Uber in relation to the expansion of precarity, see V.B. Dubal or Veena B. Dubal (2017). And, for a further contextualization of this move to precarity with regard to differences and relations between the Global North and the Global South, see Sian Lazar and Andrew Sanchez (2019).
[24]See BCRW report on "Valuing Domestic Work."

24 For Sanyal's (2007) discussion of the "need economy," see especially Chapter 5, "Difference as Hegemony: Capital and the Need Economy."

25 Rafael Trujillo was the authoritarian president of the Dominican Republic who led a hardline and oppressive regime from 1930 to 1961. The post-Trujillo era coincided with political and economic opening to a broader global system, including greater multinational investment in tourism and free trade zones, both of which began to increase exponentially in the 1970s and 1980s.

26 See Adam Beshudi (2017). See also Ben White and Aubree Eliza Weaver (2018).

60 Jakobsen, Padilla, and Horn

27 Biden campaigned on economic policies that put America first, with a particular emphasis on manufacturing policy (see joebiden.com 2020) and in his first week in office signed an Executive Order to ensure that the federal government prioritize American products with its massive purchasing power (Lobosco 2021). While maintaining this form of nationalism, Biden countered Trumpism through support for labor, including organizing among Amazon employees and the PRO Act, which supports the rights of workers to organize (Concepcion 2021). And, of course, Biden's support for vaccination against COVID-19 protected the patents of US pharmaceutical companies over the need for worldwide vaccination.

28 With respect to the organization of Amazon's workforce as essentially disposable, Amazon's (2019) public data shows the clear inequities in race and class between managerial employees, predominantly white (72.5%) and male (50.3%) and all other employees. While scholarly studies of working conditions at Amazon are rare (but see Orrange (2020) for a helpful economic analysis of Amazon), these often depend on news reporting for documentation of working conditions within the company. Furthermore, reports on ongoing litigation against the company indicate that the demographic discrepancies correlate with an inequitable work environment, which has included retaliation against whistleblowers who have brought forward public claims about failures to protect workers during the pandemic (Greene 2015; Free and Fair Market Initiative 2018; Fung 2020; Athena For All 2020). During the pandemic, employees also brought lawsuits against the corporation for failing to protect warehouse workers, who are predominantly people of color, while providing better treatment and protections for management employees, who are predominantly white and male. On Amazon's global expansion, see Adam Beshudi (2017). The turnover rates at Amazon fulfillment centers in California also have far exceeded those in other warehouse companies (National Employment Law Project 2020). See also Ben White and Aubree Eliza Weaver (2018).

29 See Government Accounting Office (2020). See also Eli Rosenberg (2020). In some localities, like Washington state, Amazon is among the major employers whose workers depend on government programs for survival (*Mynorthwest.com* 2018).

30 "As a condition of debt renegotiation, circum-Caribbean countries acceded to structural adjustment policies designed and enforced by the International Monetary Fund (IMF) that radically restructured their regulatory regimes in line with the priorities of multinational capital. This set of policy prescriptions came to be known as the Washington Consensus … [which] included the strengthening of rights and protections for foreign investors, the devaluation of domestic currencies, and the loosening of protective rights" (Werner 2016, 35).

31 The Dominican state's health expenditures are one of the lowest in the region, 5.9% in 2009 (only Bolivia and Peru spent less) and the country had the lowest expenditures on education in Latin America, 2.3% in 2009 (Gordon 1994 and 1992).

32 See Greenberg (1997).

33 Derby and Werner (2013) and J R Sánchez-Fung (2000).

34 He highlights the difficulty of making labor movement gains in the free trade zones that were established by the state starting in the 1960s and that became especially economically significant from the 1980s onward.

35 As Betances (2016, 254) describes, salaries in the free trade zones were not sustainable but avenues for fighting for better compensation and working conditions were foreclosed, since "the companies … did not allow the freedom to unionize despite the fact that in 1992 this right had been affirmed in the country's Labor Code." "The companies … still did not allow freedom of association although in 1992 it had been approved in the Labor Code" (translation by authors).

36 In the productive sector in the Dominican Republic, garment factories made up three-quarters of free trade zone employment, and the predominance of women in the garment factories reflects how gender norms operate in the "global factory" and "serve as productive technologies that construct certain kinds of work as valuable or

Gender justice and economic justice **61**

valueless, on the one hand, and associate certain jobs with certain kinds of bodies, on the other hand." (Werner 2016, 37–56). See Betances (2016, 253) on women entering the labor force. Helen Safa (1995) shows that twice as many women were in consensual unions as in legal unions in this sample (national statistics at the time of Safa's study showed that 28.2% of Dominican unions were consensual), and women in consensual unions were considerably less dependent on the husband's household contributions than women in legal unions. Nevertheless, women in consensual unions were *more* likely to subscribe to patriarchal ideals, despite their lower economic dependence on men.

37 The Dominican sociologist Laura Faxas (2007, 225) suggests that "with...the incorporation of women into the work force...we can see the questioning of male authority in the household and a certain restructuration of male-female relations." She (Faxas 2007, 225) concludes, however, that, "even if an economically independent woman has achieved a greater autonomy and a new self-reappraisal and respect from others, she has not been able to erase the force of the machista tradition."

38 See T.G. Freitag (1994). As Steven Gregory (2007, 23) describes, "[b]eginning in the late 1960s and spurred by the aggressive promotion of tourism as an economic panacea by the World Bank, the Inter-American Development Bank (IDB), and other international agencies, the administration of President Joaquín Balaguer began an aggressive campaign to promote tourism." As a result, "whereas, in 1970, only 89,700 foreign tourists visited the Dominican Republic, by 1992 their number had grown to 1.6 million. Although tourism contributed only US $368.2 million in hard currency to the Dominican economy in 1985, that figure skyrocketed to US $1046.4 million by 1992" (Betances 1995 cited in Gregory 2007, 24). After the end of the Balaguer government in 1996, the new president Leonel Fernández (2000–4, 2004–2012) embraced neoliberal economic policies with new vigor, "advancing policies of trade liberalization, privatization, and fiscal and monetary discipline" (Gregory 2007, 28).

39 See Denise Brennan (2004). See also Amalia Cabezas (2009) and Mark Padilla (2007). Carrie Meyer (2020) documents the importance of the Colonial Zone of Santa Domingo to this expanding tourist industry. Although the economy in the Dominican Republic had diversified through neoliberalism, by 2018 tourism had become nearly 10% of the gross domestic product in the Dominican Republic, making the Dominican economy the most tourist-dependent economy in the Caribbean.

40 Since 2013, Padilla has led the "Syndemics Project," an interdisciplinary, collaborative research initiative aimed at understanding the social and structural factors contributing to health vulnerabilities among the growing population of tourism laborers in the Dominican Republic. Following on several years of ethnographic research examining informal sex work among men in the Dominican tourism economies, the project – involving researchers from the US, Dominican Republic, and Puerto Rico – was designed to explore how men's patterns of labor migration to tourism zones, as well as the social organization of these zones, are linked to vulnerabilities to HIV/AIDS and problematic drug use or drug addiction.

41 See Deborah Pruitt and Suzanne LaFont (1995).

42 See Padilla (2007). During conversations with him, Samuel related providing sexual services to male tourists in the past, a behavior which he found highly shameful and to which he hoped to never return. He expressed moral disgust at his need to resort to such behavior, as did other participants, but he has also been able to reconfigure himself as a masculine *tiguere* who is able to provide for himself and his family by any means necessary. More recently, Samuel had been working for small commissions from a brothel owner when he delivered male tourists to the locale.

43 "In the US, the racial politics of domestic work profoundly influenced its treatment in labor legislation in the first half of the twentieth century. When New Deal labor legislation was enacted in the 1930s, Southern Congressmen, concerned about maintaining control over the African-American labor force, insisted on the exclusion of

62 Jakobsen, Padilla, and Horn

domestic and agricultural workers from Social Security, minimum wage, and collective bargaining laws" (Nadasen and Williams 2010, 4–5). Sex work in the US has historically been criminalized *via* other racial logics, including those contained in the Chinese exclusion laws and campaigns against "white slavery" (for a fuller discussion, see Bernstein 2018).

44 A 2013 report by the Economic Policy Institute documents the demographics of domestic workers in the US (Sheirholz 2013). See also Linda Burnham and Nik Theodore (2012).

45 Amongst the many sociological studies of domestic workers in neoliberal capitalism, see especially Boris and Parreñas (2010); Hochschild and Ehrenreich (2003); Hondagneu-Sotelo (2001); Parreñas (2001); and Chang (2016).

46 The Migration Policy Institute (Zong and Batalova 2018) reports that 37% of Dominican immigrants to the US were employed in service industries while remittances back from the US to the Dominican Republic amounted to nearly 8% of the GDP in the DR. For additional demographic information on domestic workers in the US, see Wolfe et al. (2020) and for a qualitative sense of work in the US for Dominican immigrants see Brinkerhoff et al. (2019).

47 For some examples of the extensive literature on the complexities, see critiques of familialism in relation to paid caregiving by Evelyn Nakano Glenn (2010) and Pierrette Hondagneu-Stotelo (2001). And for documentation of the ways in which familialism affects not only paid caregivers, but also family members who do the work of care as a "labor of love," see Carol Levine, ed. (2000).

48 Senator Tom Daschle was forced in 2009 to withdraw from consideration as Secretary of Health and Human Services after failing to pay similar taxes for a driver and Zoe E. Baird and Kimba Wood both withdrew for similar failures to pay taxes for childcare workers after being nominated to be Attorney General by the Clinton Administration (Steinhauer 2017).

49 This report documents striking differences between the pay and benefits of institutional versus in-home caring labor and also major differences in the demographics of who does the work (Sheirholz 2013). Institutional caring labor is more likely to be done by white people, men and US citizens than is the lower-paid and more precarious work of providing in-home care.

50 For further explanation of how this large concatenation of neoliberal social relations is borne out in the experiences of domestic workers in the US, see the "Valuing Domestic Work" project, a research collaboration between the Barnard Center for Research on Women, New York's Domestic Workers United, and the US National Domestic Workers Alliance, which brought together domestic workers to produce an analysis for their organizing. The publications resulting from this project are: Nadasen and Williams (2010); and Fosado and Jakobsen (2009).

51 Immigrants did not need visas before arriving in the US, but simply arrived at points of entry (such as Ellis Island) where their entry was recorded, and they were generally allowed to enter. With expanded and increasingly institutionalized systems of counting and controlling all immigration, undocumented movement and "illegality" became conflated. See Mae Ngai (2004) especially, Part I, "The Regime of Quotas and Papers," and Chapter 7 on the ways that the supposedly liberal immigration reform act of 1965, which ended race-based exclusions, also permanently normalized quotas on immigration, even if these quotas were now supposed to be race-neutral. Whereas nineteenth-century immigration policy included major efforts to exclude certain populations, most notably the Chinese Exclusion Act of 1882, the counting and documentation of much immigration into the US only became regularized as passports and visas for entry into the country were standardized over the course of the twentieth century. The Immigration Act of 1924 first established quotas for entry into the US on the basis of national origin, and, although the Immigration Reform Act of 1965 ended the national basis for the quotas, numerical limits on immigration remained in force. Ngai argues that the maintenance of numerical caps in a law

that was supposed to be a liberalization of the 1924 Act effectively naturalized the idea that there must be "controls" on immigration, so that the only argument at the time was what the basis of those controls should be: national origin, sector of potential employment, or family reunification. For more on the sexual and racial politics related to immigration reform in the neoliberal era, especially through the Illegal Immigration and Immigrant Responsibility Act of 1996, see Reddy (2011).

52 Brady (2008) writes: "Clinton shifted the emphasis from what immigrants 'deserved' – emergency care, education, police protection – and what problems they caused or eliminated – depressed wages, labor shortages – to a rhetoric centered on their status as 'legal' or 'illegal.' He deployed his anti-immigrant policies and the development of Operation Gatekeeper by producing a new grid of intelligibility where legality became the central hermeneutic. The emphasis, Clinton repeatedly claimed, should not be on all immigrants, but rather on those who entered the country informally or stayed beyond their visa. By emphasizing such 'illegality' he shifted the focus in the US imaginary to immigrants' criminality, to their supposedly bad behavior, and away from issues of labor, wages, and poverty. And by emphasizing immigrants as criminals with a wanton disregard for the law, he transferred the anxiety of what immigrants might *want or demand* from the US (i.e., social services, protection from exploitation) and from what they might *contribute* to the country at large, to the utopian fantasy of a neutral criminal justice system. Under his guidance, new laws were passed that, as Jennifer Chacon (2007) argues, 'conflated illegal immigrants with crime' and also 'operated to reify the links between all immigrants and criminality.'"

53 Brady writes: "What tied [California's initiatives related to immigration and gay rights] together was in part the presumed assumption that both 'the gay agenda' and the 'immigrant agenda' took aim at the patriarchal white family, threatening to expose its homoerotic implications on the one hand, its vulnerability to multiple forms of desires, and on the other, its presumed status as a privileged, racialized site of consumption and protected locale for national reproduction." The connections between issues produced "a vibrant relay that derives from, even as it enhances, a nationalist erotic… [that] helps to structure national discourses about immigration and keeps nativism afloat in ever newer guises" (2008).

54 The International Labour Organization began developing a convention on domestic labor in 2010 and 2011, which was passed as Convention 189 and came into force in September 2013 (International Labour Organization 2013).

55 See Saskia Sassen (2001), see especially Part Two, "*The Economic Order of the Global City.*"

56 See, for example, MacGillis (2021), which provides both a helpful analysis of the shift from industrial production in the city of Baltimore to economic dependence on Amazon, while also showing a strong sense of nostalgia for industrial production and very little sense of the ways in which Amazon has reorganized broader economic relations.

References

Abacarian, Robin. 2020. "Column: Critics say Kamala Harris is a Giddy Lightweight. The Proof? She Likes to Dance and Laugh," *The Los Angeles Times*, 27 October. https://www.latimes.com/opinion/story/2020-10-27/column-kamala-harris-lightweight-dance-lau-gh.

Amar, Paul. 2013. *The Security Archipelago: Human-Security States, Sexuality Politics, and the End of Neoliberalism*. Durham, NC: Duke University Press, 2013. https://doi.org/10.1215/9780822397564.

Amazon.com. 2019. "Our Workforce Data," https://www.aboutamazon.com/news/workplace/our-workforce-data#:~:text=Here%20is%20our%20global%20gender,

as%20of%20December%2031%2C%202019.&text=Among%20Amazon's%20global
%20employees%2C%2042.7,and%2072.5%25%25%20identify%20as%20men.

Arruzza, Cinzia. 2015. "Gender as Social Temporality," *Historical Materialism* 23, no. 1: 27–52. https://doi.org/10.1163/1569206X-12341396.

Athena For All Action Network. 2020. "Stand with Hibaq," https://actionnetwork.org/petitions/stand-with-hibaq.

Bernstein, Elizabeth. 2018. *Brokered Subjects: Sex, Trafficking, and the Politics of Freedom.* Chicago, IL: University of Chicago Press.

Beshudi, Adam. 2017. "Trump's NAFTA Changes Aren't Much Different than Obama's," *Politico,* 30 March. https://www.politico.com/story/2017/03/donald-trump-nafta-changes-reality-236712.

Betances, Emelio. 2016. *En busca de la ciudadanía: los movimientos sociales y la democratización en la República Dominicana.* Santo Domingo: Archivo General de la Nación.

Bhattacharya, Tithi. 2017. "Introduction: Mapping Social Reproduction Theory." In *Social Reproduction Theory: Remapping Class, Recentering Oppression,* edited by Tithi Bhattacharya. London: Pluto Press.

Bhatttacharyya, Gargi. 2018. *Rethinking Racial Capitalism: Questions of Reproductive Survival.* Louisville: Rowman & Littlefield Publishing.

Boris, Eileen and Rhacel Salazar Parreñas, eds. 2010. *Intimate Labors: Cultures, Technologies, and the Politics of Care.* Stanford, CA: Stanford University Press.

Brady, Mary Pat. 2008. "The Homoerotics of Immigration Control," *Scholar and Feminist Online,* 6, no. 3 (Summer). http://sfonline.barnard.edu/immigration/brady_01.htm

Brennan, Denise. 2004. *What's Love Got to Do With It?: Transnational Desires and Sex Tourism in the Dominican Republic.* Durham, NC: Duke University Press, 131. https://doi.org/10.1215/9780822385400.

Brinkerhoff, et al. 2019. "'There You Enjoy Life, Here You Work': Brazilian and Dominican Immigrants' Views on Work and Health in the US," *International Journal of Environmental Research and Public Health* 16, no. 20, doi: 10.3390/ijerph16204025

Burnham, Linda. 2008. "The Absence of a Gender Justice Framework in Social Justice Organizing," Center for the Education of Women, University of Michigan, July. http://www.cew.umich.edu/PDFs/BurnhamFinalProject.pdf.

Burnham, Linda and Nik Theodore. 2012. "Home Economics: The Invisible and Unregulated World of Domestic Work," National Domestic Workers Alliance, Center for Urban Economic Development, University of Illinois, Chicago and DataCenter. https://community-wealth.org/sites/clone.community-wealth.org/files/downloads/report-burnham-theodore.pdf.

Byrd, Jodi A., et al. 2018. "Predatory Value: Economies of Dispossession and Disturbed Relationalities," *Social Text* 36, no. 2 (June): 1–18. https://doi.org/10.1215/01642472-4362325.

Cabezas, Amalia. 2009. *Economies of Desire: Sex and Tourism in Cuba and the Dominican Republic.* Philadelphia, PA: Temple University Press.

Canales, Katie. 2020. "Amazon Hires Pinkerton Spies to Monitor Unionization Efforts," *Business Insider,* 23 November. https://www.businessinsider.com/amazon-pinkerton-spies-worker-labor-unions-2020-11.

Case, Mary Anne. 2017. "Seeing the Sex and Justice Landscape through the Vatican's Eyes: The War on Gender and the Seamless Garment of Sexual Rights." In *The War on Sex,* edited by David Halperin and Trevor Hoppe, 211–25. Durham, NC: Duke University Press. https://doi.org/10.1215/9780822373148.

Chacon, Jennifer. 2007. "Unsecured Borders: Immigration Restrictions, Crime Control and National Security," *Connecticut Law Review,* 39, July.

Chang, Grace. 2016. *Disposable Domestics: Immigrant Women Workers in the Global Economy*. Chicago, IL: Haymarket Books.

Cohen, Cathy. 1997. "Punks, Bulldaggers, and Welfare Queens: The Radical Potential of Queer Politics," *GLQ: A Journal of Lesbian and Gay Studies* 3, no. 4: 437–65. https://doi.org/10.1215/10642684-3-4-437.

Concepcion, Summer. 2021. "Biden Takes His Support for Labor One Step Further with WH Endorsement of PRO Act," *Talking Points Memo*, March 8, https://talkingpointsmemo.com/news/biden-administration-omb-support-pro-act-passage.

Corkery, Michael and Karen Weise. 2021. "Amazon Workers' Union Drive Reaches Far Beyond Alabama," *The New York Times*, March 4, https://www.nytimes.com/2021/03/02/business/amazon-union-bessemer-alabama.html.

Davidoff, Leonore. 1976. *A Day in the Life of a Domestic Servant*. London: Allen & Unwin.

Da Silva, Denise Ferreira, Rizvana Bradley, and Che Gossett. 2015. "Speculative Planning Session." Conversations, New Museum. https://www.newmuseum.org/calendar/view/473/constantina-zavitsanos-speculative-planning-session-with-denise-ferreira-da-silva.

Davis, Adrienne D. and The Black Sexual Economies Collective. 2019. *Black Sexual Economies: Race and Sex in a Culture of Capital*. Champagne-Urbana, IL: University of Illinois Press.

Dei, George J. Sefa, and Meredith Lordan, eds. 2016. *Anti-Colonial Theory and Decolonial Praxis*. Bern, Switzerland: Peter Lang. https://doi.org/10.3726/978-1-4539-1857-9.

Del Ray, Jason and Shirin Ghaffary. 2020. "Leaked: Confidential Amazon Memo Reveals New Software to Track Unions," *Vox*, October 6, https://www.vox.com/recode/2020/10/6/21502639/amazon-union-busting-tracking-memo-spoc.

Delap, Lucy. 2011. *Knowing Their Place: Domestic Service in Twentieth Century Britain*. New York: Oxford University Press. 10.1093/acprof:oso/9780199572946.001.0001.

Derby, Lauren and Marion Werner. 2013. "The Devil Wears Dockers: Devil Pacts, Trade Zones, and Rural-Urban Ties in the Dominican Republic," *New West Indian Guide*, 87: 299–300. https://doi.org/10.1163/22134360-12340109.

Domestic Workers United & DataCenter. 2006. "Home is Where the Work Is: Inside New York's Domestic Work Industry," 14 (July): 9. http://www.datacenter.org/home-is-where-the-work-is/.

Dubal, V.B. 2017. "The Drive to Precarity: A Political History of Work, Regulation, and Labor Advocacy in San Francisco's Taxi & Uber Economies," *Berkeley Journal of Employment and Labor Law* 38, no. 1: 73–135. https://repository.uchastings.edu/faculty_scholarship/1589/.

Duggan, Lisa. 2019. *Mean Girl: Ayn Rand and the Culture of Greed*. Berkeley, CA: University of California Press.

Ehrenreich, Barbara and Arlie Russell Hochschild. 2003. *Global Woman: Nannies, Maids, and Sex Workers*. New York: Henry Holt.

Fanon, Frantz. 1968. *Black Skin, White Masks*. New York: New Grove Press. https://monoskop.org/images/a/a5/Fanon_Frantz_Black_Skin_White_Masks_1986.pdf.

Faxas, Laura. 2007. *El mito roto: Sistema político y movimiento popular en la República Dominicana, 1961–1990*. México City: Siglo XXI.

Federici, Silvia. 2004. *Caliban and the Witch: Women, the Body and Primitive Accumulation*. Brooklyn: Autonomedia.

Ferguson, Roderick A. 2003. *Aberrations in Black: Toward a Queer of Color Critique*. Minneapolis: University of Minnesota Press.

Fine, Janice and Allison Petrozziello. 2017. "Haitian Migrant Workers in the Dominican Republic: Organizing at the Intersection of Informality and Illegality." In *Informal*

Workers and Collective Action: A Global Perspective, edited by Adrienne E. Easton, Susan J. Schurman, and Martha Atler Chen, 71–95. Ithaca, NY: ILR Press of Cornell University Press.

Fosado, Gisela and Janet R. Jakobsen, eds. 2009. "Valuing Domestic Work," Special Issue of *Scholar and Feminist Online*, http://sfonline.barnard.edu/work/.

Frank, Thomas. 2004. *What's the Matter with Kansas?: How Conservatives Won the Heart of America*. New York: Henry Holt/Metropolitan Books.

Frank, Thomas. 2016. *Listen, Liberal, or What Ever Happened to the Party of the People?* New York: Metropolitan Books.

Fraser, Nancy and Axel Honneth, 2003. *Redistribution or Recognition?: A Political-Philosophical Exchange*. Translated by Joel Golb, James Ingram, and Christiane Wilke. New York: Verso.

Free and Fair Markets Initiative. 2018. "Amazon's Unfair Deal of the Day: Undercutting Women. and Their Wages," (October). https://freeandfairmarketsinitiative.org/wp-content/uploads/2018/09/FFMI-Amazons-Unfair-Deal-of-the-Day.pdf.

Freeman, Carla. 2000. *High Tech and High Heels in the Global Economy: Women, Work, and Pink-Collar Identities in the Caribbean*. Durham, NC: Duke University Press.

Freitag, T.G. 1994. "Enclave tourism development: for whom the benefits roll?," *Annals of Tourism Research* 21, no. 3: 538–554.

Fung, Brian. 2020. "Fired Amazon Worker Christian Smalls Sues Over Pandemic Working Conditions," *CNN*, November 12, https://www.cnn.com/2020/11/12/tech/amazon-worker-lawsuit/index.html.

Goodman, J. David. 2019. "Amazon Pulls Out of Planned New York City Headquarters," *The New York Times*, 14 February, https://www.nytimes.com/2019/02/14/nyregion/amazon-hq2-queens.html.

Gordon, Andrew J. 1992. "Influences on Biomedicine in Rural Dominican Republic: An Analysis of Process," *Medical Anthropology* 13: 315–336. https://doi.org/10.1080/01459740.1992.9966055.

Gordon, Andrew J. 1994. "Agrarian Transformation and Health Care in the Dominican Republic," *Human Organization* 53, no. 4: 352–357. https://www.jstor.org/stable/44127554.

Government Accounting Office. 2020. "Federal Social Safety Net Programs: Millions of Full Time Workers Rely on Federal Health Care and Food Assistance Programs," October. https://www.gao.gov/assets/720/710203.pdf.

Green, Linda. 2011. "The Nobodies: Neoliberalism, Violence, and Migration," *Medical Anthropology* 30, no. 4: 366–85. https://doi.org/10.1080/01459740.2011.576726.

Greenberg, James B. 1997. "A Political Ecology of Structural Adjustment Policies: The Case of the Dominican Republic," *Culture and Agriculture* 19, no. 3 (Fall): 85–93.

Greene, Jay. 2015. "Amazon Much More Diverse at Warehouses than in Professional Ranks," *Seattle Times*, August 14. https://www.seattletimes.com/business/amazon/amazon-more-diverse-at-its-warehouses-than-among-white-collar-ranks/.

Gregory, Steven. 2007. *The Devil Behind the Mirror: Globalization and Politics in the Dominican Republic*, Berkeley, CA: University of California Press.

Grosfoguel, Ramón. 2006. "World-Systems Analysis in the Context of Transmodernity, Border Thinking, and Global Coloniality," *Review* (Fernand Braudel Center), 29, no. 2: 167–87. https://www.jstor.org/stable/40241659.

Guerrero, Zelem. 2009. "Women and Work: A Panel Discussion," Published in "Valuing Domestic Work", edited by Gisela Fosado and Janet R. Jakobsen, *Scholar and Feminist Online*, 8, no. 1 (Fall). http://sfonline.barnard.edu/work/ndwa_01.htm.

Gumbs, Alexis Pauline. 2016. *Spill: Scenes of Black Feminist Fugitivity*. Durham, NC: Duke University Press.

Harvey, David. 2007. *A Brief History of Neoliberalism*. New York: Oxford University Press.

Holland, Sharon. 2012. *The Erotic Life of Racism*. Durham, NC: Duke University Press.

Hollibaugh, Amber. 2015. "Opening, Welcome and Overview of Queer Survival Economies," Invisible Lives, Targeted Bodies: Impacts of Economic Injustice on Vulnerable LGBTQ+ Communities Conference. Murphy Institute, 23–24 January. http://queersurvivaleconomies.com/conference/.

Hondagneu-Sotelo, Pierrette. 2001. *Doméstica: Immigrant Workers Cleaning and Caring in the Shadows of Affluence*. Berkeley, CA: University of California Press.

Horn, Pamela. 1987. *Life and Labor in Rural England*. New York: Palgrave.

International Labour Organization. 2013. "Landmark Treaty for Domestic Workers Comes into Force," 5 September. https://www.ilo.org/global/standards/information-resources-and-publications/news/WCMS_220793/lang--en/index.htm.

International Labour Organization. 2014. "Evolution of Informal Employment in the Dominican Republic," Regional Office for Latin America and the Caribbean, https://www.ilo.org/wcmsp5/groups/public/---americas/---ro-lima/documents/publication/wcms_245893.pdf.

Jakobsen, Janet. 2020. *The Sex Obsession: Perversity and Possibility in American Politics*. New York: NYU Press.

Karnitschnig, Matthew. 2017. 'Why Greece is Germany's 'de facto' colony," *Politico*, June 14. https://www.politico.eu/article/why-greece-is-germanys-de-facto-colony/.

Kempadoo, Kamala. 1999. *Sun, Sex, and Gold: Tourism and Sex Work in the Caribbean*. Oxford: Rowman and Littlefield.

Kempadoo, Kamala. 2017. "Neoliberalism and the Global South," Panel Discussion, Conference on Sex, Migration, and New World (Dis)Order, Danish Institute for International Studies, Copenhagen, Denmark, June.

Klein, Naomi. 2007. *The Shock Doctrine*. Toronto: Random House of Canada.

Lazar, Sian and Andrew Sanchez. 2019. "Understanding Labour Politics in an Age of Precarity," *Dialectical Anthropology* 43: 3–14. https://doi.org/10.1007/s10624-019-09544-7.

Levine, Carol ed. 2000. *Always on Call: When Illness Turns Families into Caregivers*. New York: United Hospital Fund.

Liu, Petrus. 2015. *Queer Marxism in China*. Durham, NC: Duke University Press. https://doi.org/10.1215/9780822375081.

Lobosco, Katie. 2021. "Biden Signs Executive Order Aimed at Strengthening American Manufacturing," *CNN*, 25 January, https://www.cnn.com/2021/01/25/politics/biden-executive-orders-manufacturing-buy-american/index.html.

Lowe, Lisa. 2015. *The Intimacies of Four Continents*. Durham, NC: Duke University Press. https://doi.org/10.1215/9780822375647.

Lugones, Maria. 2008. "The Coloniality of Gender," *Worlds and Knowledges Otherwise*, 2(2(Spring)): 1–17, https://globalstudies.trinity.duke.edu/projects/wko-gender.

MacGillis, Alec. 2021. "Amazon and the Breaking of Baltimore," *The New York Times*, 8 March. https://www.nytimes.com/2021/03/09/opinion/amazon-baltimore-dc.html.

Mahmood, Saba. 2005. *Politics of Piety: The Islamic Revival and the Feminist Subject*. Princeton, NJ: Princeton University Press.

Manalansan, Martin. 2008. "Queering the Chain of Care Paradigm." *Scholar and Feminist Online*. 6:3. http://sfonline.barnard.edu/immigration/manalansan_02.htm.

Medina, José. 2013. *The Epistemology of Resistance: Gender and Racial Oppression, Epistemic Injustice, and Resistant Imaginations*. New York: Oxford University Press.

Meyer, Carrie. 2020. "Tourism and Economic Growth in the Dominican Republic, 1985–2018," *GMU Working Paper in Economics*, 18 February, https://papers.ssrn.com/sol3/papers.cfm?abstract_id=3538902.

Mignolo, Walter D. 2000. *Local Histories/Global Designs: Coloniality, Subaltern Knowledges, And Border Thinking*. Princeton, NJ: Princeton University Press.

Miller-Young, Mireille. 2014. *A Taste for Brown Sugar: Black Women in Pornography*. Durham: Duke University Press.

Millett, Kate. 1970. *Sexual Politics*. New York: Doubleday.

Mol, Annemarie. 2003. *The Social Body Multiple: Ontology in Medical Practice*. Durham, NC: Duke University Press.

Muñoz, José Esteban. 2009. *Cruising Utopia: The Then and There of Queer Futurity*. New York: New York University Press.

Musser, Amber Jamilla. 2014. *Sensational Flesh: Race, Power, and Masochism*. New York: New York University Press.

Musser, Amber Jamilla. 2018. *Sensual Excess: Queer Femininity and Brown Jouissance*. New York: New York University Press.

Mynorthwest.com. 2018. "Amazon, Walmart Workers on Top List of Food Stamps Users," *KIRO*, 10 September. https://www.kiro7.com/news/local/report-amazon-walmart-workers-on-list-of-top-food-stamp-users/830854650/.

Nadasen, Premilla and Tiffany Williams. 2010. "Valuing Domestic Work," *New Feminist Solutions 5*. New York: Barnard Center for Research on Women. http://bcrw.barnard.edu/wp-content/nfs/reports/NFS5-Valuing-Domestic-Work.pdf.

Nakano Glenn, Evelyn. 2010. *Forced to Care: Coercion and Caregiving in America*. Cambridge, MA.: Harvard University Press.

Nash, Jennifer. 2014a. *The Black Body in Ecstasy: Reading Race, Reading Pornography*. Durham: Duke University Press.

Nash, Jennifer. 2014b. "Black Anality." *GLQ: A Journal of Lesbian and Gay Studies*, 20(4): 439–460.

National Employment Law Project. 2020. "Amazon's Disposable Workers: High Injury and Turnover Rates at Fulfillment Centers in California," March. https://s27147.pcdn.co/wp-content/uploads/Data-Brief-Amazon-Disposable-Workers-Injury-Turnover-Rates-California-Fulfillment-Centers3-20.pdf.

Navarro, Tami. 2021. *Virgin Capital: Race, Gender, and Financialization in the US Virgin Islands*. Albany, NY: State University of New York Press.

NDWA Labs. 2020. "6 Months in Crisis: The Impact of COVID-19 on Domestic Workers," National Domestic Workers Alliance October. https://domesticworkers.org/6-months-crisis-impact-covid-19-domestic-workers.

Ngai, Mae. 2004. *Impossible Subjects: Illegal Aliens and the Making of Modern America*. Princeton, NJ: Princeton University Press.

Noonan, Peggy. 2020. "A Good Debate, and It's Not Quite Over," *The Wall Street Journal*, 23 October. https://www.wsj.com/articles/a-good-debate-and-its-not-quite-over11603426466.

Orrange, Robert M. 2020. *The Corporate State: Technopoly, Privatization, and Corporate Predation*. London, New York: Routledge.

Padilla, Mark. 2007. *Caribbean Pleasure Industry: Tourism, Sexuality and AIDS in the Dominican Republic*. Chicago, IL: University of Chicago Press.

Padilla, Mark (PI). n.d. "Tourism, Migration, and the HIV/Drug use Syndemics in the Dominican Republic," NIDA Grant #1 R01 DA031581-01A1.

Padilla, Mark, Colón-Burgos, J. F., Varas-Díaz, N., Matiz-Reyes, A., and Parker, C. M. 2018. "Tourism Labor, Embodied Suffering, and the Deportation Regime in the Dominican Republic," *Medical Anthropology Quarterly*, 32(4) December: 498–519. https://doi.org/10.1111/maq.1244.

Parreñas, Rhacel Salazar. 2001. *Servants of Globalization: Women, Migration, and Domestic Work*. Stanford, CA: Stanford University Press.

Polletta, Francesca. 2018. "The Multiple Meanings of Familialism," *Law & Social Inquiry* 43, no. 1 (Winter): 230–7.

Poo, Ai-jen. 2014. "Justice in the Home Keynote," Barnard Center for Research on Women and National Domestic Workers Alliance Conference, 16 October. http://bcrw.barnard.edu/videos/ai-jen-poo-justice-in-the-home-keynote/.

Porpora, Douglas V., Alexander G. Nikolaev, Julia Hagemann May, and Alexander Jenkins. 2013. *Post-Ethical Society: The Iraq War, Abu Ghraib, and the Moral Failure of the Secular*, 244. Chicago, IL: University of Chicago Press.

Porter, Eduardo. 2020. "Reinventing Workers for the Post-Covid Economy," *The New York Times*, 1 December. https://www.nytimes.com/2020/12/01/business/economy/workers-jobs-training.html?smid=em-share.

Pruitt, Deborah, and Suzanne LaFont. 1995. "For Love and Money: Romance Tourism in Jamaica," *Annals of Tourism Research* 22, no. 2: 422–44. https://doi.org/10.1016/0160-7383(94)00084-0.

Quijano, Aníbal. 2000. "Coloniality of Power, Ethnocentrism, and Latin America," *NEPANTLA* I, no. 3: 533–80. https://doi.org/10.1177/0268580900015002005.

Reddy, Chandan. 2011. *Freedom with Violence: Race, Sexuality and the US State*. Durham, NC: Duke University Press. https://doi.org/10.1215/9780822394648.

Rivera, Mayra. 2015. *Poetics of the Flesh*. Durham, NC: Duke University Press.

Rosenberg, Eli. 2020. "Walmart and McDonald's Have the Most Workers on Food Stamps and Medicaid, New Study Shows," 18 November. https://www.washingtonpost.com/business/2020/11/18/food-stamps-medicaid-mcdonalds-walmart-bernie-sanders/.

Safa, Helen. 1995. *The Myth of the Male Breadwinner: Women and Industrialization in the Caribbean*. Boulder, CO: Westview Press.

Said, Edward. 1979. *Orientalism*. New York: Vintage Books.

Sánchez-Fung, J.R. 2000. "Empleo y mercados de trabajo en la República Dominicana: Una revisión de la literatura," *Revista de la CEPAL* 71 (Agosto): 163–175.

Sanyal, Kalyan. 2007. *Rethinking Capitalist Development: Primitive Accumulation Governmentality and Post-Colonial Capitalism*. New Delhi: Routledge.

Sassen, Saskia. 2001. *The Global City: New York, London, Tokyo*. Princeton, NJ: Princeton University Press.

Schor, Juliet. 2020. *After the Gig: How the Sharing Economy Got Hijacked and How to Win it Back*. Berkeley, CA: UC Press.

Sheirholz, Heidi. 2013. "Low Wages and Scant Benefits Leave Many In-Home Workers Unable to Make Ends Meet," Economic Policy Institute Briefing Paper #369, 26 November. https://www.epi.org/publication/in-home-workers/.

Sorkin, Andrew Ross. 2016. "President Obama Weighs his Economic Legacy," *The New York Times Magazine*, 28 April. https://www.nytimes.com/2016/05/01/magazine/president-obama-weighs-his-economic-legacy.html (Accessed July 2, 2018).

Spillers, Hortense. 1987. "Mama's Baby, Papa's Maybe: An American Grammar Book," *Diacritics*, 17, no. 2 (Summer): 64–81. https://doi.org/10.2307/464747.

Spivak, Gayatri Chakravorty. 1987. "Scattered Speculations on the Question of Value," In *In Other Worlds: Essays in Cultural Politics*, 154–75. New York: Methuen.

Steinhauer, Jennifer. 2017. "Trump Budget Nominee Did Not Pay Taxes for Employee," *The New York Times*, 18 January. https://www.nytimes.com/2017/01/18/us/politics/mick-mulvaney-taxes.html.

Tadiar, Neferti X.M. 2013. "Life-Times of Disposability with Global Neoliberalism," *Social Text* 31, no. 2: 19–48. https://doi.org/10.1215/01642472-2081112.

Taylor, Marcus. 2006. *From Pinochet to the "Third Way"*. London: Pluto Press. https://doi.org/10.2307/j.ctt18dztpr.

Weheliye, Alexander. 2014. *Habeas Viscous: Racializing Assemblages, Biopolitics, and Black Feminist Theories of the Human*. Durham, NC: Duke University Press.

Weise, Karen. 2020. "Pushed by Pandemic, Amazon Goes on a Hiring Spree Without Equal," *The New York Times*, 27 November. https://www.nytimes.com/2020/11/27/technology/pushed-by-pandemic-amazon-goes-on-a-hiring-spree-without-equal.html?smid=em-share.

Werner, Marion. 2016. *Global Displacements: The Making of Uneven Development in the Caribbean*. London: Wiley Blackwell.

Westad, Odd Arne. 2005. *The Global Cold War*. Cambridge: Cambridge University Press. https://doi.org/10.1017/CBO9780511817991.

Weyl, Ben and Brent Griffiths. 2017. "Mulvaney Defends Nanny Tax Lapse, Tangles with Democrats on Budget, *Politico*, 24 January. http://www.politico.com/story/2017/01/mick-mulvaney-tax-lapse-confirmation-hearing-234111.

White, Ben and Aubree Eliza Weaver. 2018. "Meet the New NAFTA," *Politico*, 2 October. https://www.politico.com/newsletters/morning-money/2018/10/02/meet-the-new-nafta-359219.

Wolfe, Julia, et al. 2020. "Domestic Workers Chartbook," Economic Policy Institute, 14 May. https://www.epi.org/publication/domestic-workers-chartbook-a-comprehensive-look-at-the-demographics-wages-benefits-and-poverty-rates-of-the-professionals-who-care-for-our-family-members-and-clean-our-homes/.

World Bank. 2013. "Table, 'Vulnerable Employment, Total.'" World Bank. 16 February: 224–25, (translation by authors). http://data.worldbank.org/indicator/SL.EMP.VULN.ZS.

Young, Robert J.C. 2001. *Postcolonialism: An Historical Introduction*. Oxford: Wiley Blackwell.

Zong, Jie and Jeanne Batalova. 2018. "Dominican Immigrants in the United States," Migration Policy Institute, 11 April. https://www.migrationpolicy.org/article/dominican-immigrants-united-states-2016#AgeEducationEmployment.

3

NEOLIBERAL VULNERABILITY AND THE VULNERABILITY OF NEOLIBERALISM

Kerwin Kaye, Ana Amuchástegui, Abosede George, and Tami Navarro

Rethinking questions of gender and political economy, as we have seen, yields fresh insights into both the social organization of neoliberalism and of capitalism more generally. Neoliberalism has also produced new modes of governance which similarly spur us to reassess our understandings of social belonging and of social marginality. In this chapter, we join with other recent social commentators in arguing that a language of vulnerability increasingly transforms and delimits discourses of rights and even justice in the neoliberal frame, significantly reworking the notion of citizenship in the process.[1] While transformations in political economy produce newly precarious populations at the material level, novel forms of social regulation simultaneously come to the fore, including ones which rely upon the discursive structure of vulnerability. At the same time, the frame of vulnerability offers its own distinctive grammar of resistance, generating new means by which people can make claims against hierarchically situated centers of power, sometimes successfully utilizing the paradoxical logic of neoliberal vulnerability to inhabit "victimization" and "powerlessness" in advancing their own agendas.

Speaking of vulnerability in the contemporary era raises immediate difficulties in that we seek to convey lived conditions which are themselves shaped by their descriptions. Yet the very meaning of the term "vulnerability" has been altered over recent decades by multiple levels of social change. On the one hand, shifts in the living and working conditions that people confront, and the rise of new forms and distributions of precarity, demand immediate attention and analysis. On the other hand, shifts in the ways in which various forms of endangerment are represented, and the changing institutional mechanisms and narrative structures through which vulnerability and suffering are communicated, profoundly alter the terrain in which we think about exposure to harm. The very ways through which people experience both the fear of vulnerability and the

DOI: 10.4324/9781003252702-3

actuality of suffering are shaped in part by these representations. How, then, does one point toward the institutional and conceptual limits of a given representation of vulnerability while acknowledging very real forms of harm, especially given that the nature of those harms is itself partly constituted by those (politically fraught) representations?

Questions of power are interwoven with these concerns. At an institutional level, we can observe how vulnerability and suffering have become entangled with governance, whether through state agents, non-governmental organizations (NGOs), or other actors acting in the name of reducing suffering as a matter of course. As Foucault (1978; 2008 [2004]) has shown, this link between power and the purported prevention of suffering is crystallized with the rise of the modern state and what he termed "biopower." The rise of biopower as a political logic marks a movement away from a system in which the sovereign governs by taking life (or threatening to do so) to one in which relations of rule operate through the administration and nurturance of (certain types of) life (Foucault 1978, 136–40).

The neoliberal focus upon "risk" marks a further turn in this biopolitical exercise and brings "vulnerability" – imagined threats to life – to the fore. Risk and vulnerability generate new forms through which both populations and individuals are governed through the mere potential (or alleged potential) for harm. Here, critical examination enables us to expose the ways that "vulnerability" works to oppress various groups. Alternatively, we can fruitfully read the forms of vulnerability that the state and its affiliated institutions identify through a reversed lens, learning to understand and decipher these, not so much as risks faced by individuals or populations, but as vulnerabilities that inhere within the governing structures of neoliberalism itself.

Yet the invocation of vulnerability and suffering does not just generate support for relations of domination. Indeed, as will be discussed below, there are numerous instances in which the representation of vulnerability functions as a *critique* of existing policy, and such portrayals can be powerful tools aimed at altering the existing forms of governmentality. Even here, these critiques remain entangled in differential, uneven, and hierarchical social relations, meaning that they will undoubtedly sometimes reinforce social domination. These complex and multifaceted effects challenge us to consider the possibility that there might be a good degree of overlap between counter-hegemonic representations of vulnerability and suffering and those that are used as tools of containment, exclusion, and domination, leading us into politically difficult terrain indeed.

The shifting nature of "vulnerability" in the contemporary period, combined with its increasing political prominence, has led to a number of academic studies of these issues. Indeed, "vulnerability," and variants thereof, has become key to the lexicons of a variety of academic fields including public health, environmental studies, and many others (Fuller and Pincetl 2015). A small field of "vulnerability studies" has also emerged within the humanities in relation to this trend, particularly in relation to feminist studies concerning sexual violence.[2] The work of Judith Butler (2004, 2009, and 2015) is perhaps most notable within this developing field of critical study, particularly her suggestion that vulnerability, as an existential condition faced by everyone, might provide the foundation for a much-needed corrective to a politics based on the liberal myth of the sovereignty of the isolated individual. While in no way guaranteeing a positive alternative to liberalism, Butler suggests that vulnerability can become a cornerstone for a new politics that places relationality and mutual dependencies at its core.[3]

Thus, we are left with an abundance of political and theoretical challenges. On the one hand, "vulnerability" is a term that references contrasting social trends. For instance, vulnerability can name both the expansion of precarity with the ascendance of neoliberalism and the narrowing scope of which harms are taken seriously, as will be discussed below. These domains significantly shape one another (in part, by defining the nature of "harm" itself).

We will argue that representations of "vulnerability" work to achieve both hegemonic and counter-hegemonic effects, and there may be no clear, bright line separating these usages. In what follows, we utilize a number of case studies related to each of our areas of expertise to detail the fluctuating terrain of "vulnerability" in terms of changes in lived conditions under neoliberalism (for which our preferred term is "precarity"), and in relation to shifting forms by which precarity is represented (for which we use terms such as "vulnerability" or "at risk").

After first detailing the key components of vulnerability discourse, we highlight a set of new fears and governmental logics that vulnerability establishes *via* disparate case studies from Mexico, Nigeria, the US Virgin Islands, and the continental United States (US). Questions of gender and sexuality animate and augment our examination, as do issues pertaining to class, race, and (post-) coloniality. We begin, however, not with the representation of vulnerability as such, but with representations of suffering. Suffering helps to ground the concept of vulnerability insofar as to be vulnerable is to be "at risk" of suffering. Vulnerability necessarily references the concept of suffering, whereas neoliberal rationalities of preemption have placed the emphasis on the presumed potential for suffering rather than upon (or in addition to) the experience of suffering. Narrative constraints that surround suffering – only certain forms of suffering are able to be represented in its current narrative form – thus govern the representation of vulnerability, even as neoliberalism increasingly uses the specter of future suffering as justification for action. In the constant invocation of dangers that must be avoided, however, neoliberal logics arguably instill new fears as much as they counter them.[4]

Suffering and vulnerability: narrative exigencies and exclusions

Images of suffering have assumed a new prominence within public discourse over the past several decades.[5] In some ways mirroring broader trends toward sensationalism within entertainment media, representations designed to evoke emotional reactions of sympathy (and, sometimes, of righteous anger against those causing that suffering) have become significant components of both news media and of campaigns designed to shape public policy. These images of suffering bodies have brought the affective dimensions of politics to the fore, particularly across mass media (such images are perhaps less prevalent within discussions held amongst governmental policy makers where *realpolitik* continues to predominate).

In some senses, these tropes are not new and can be said to arise in the formative moments of European modernity. Foucault famously argued, for example, that insofar as "modernity" is marked by the rise of biopower, fostering life through the administration of bodies problematized suffering in new ways. Although, for example, public spectacles of suffering within punishment diminished during this era, moralized displays reappeared within melodramatic literature (Foucault, 1978 [1975]).[6] Melodrama, as a genre, takes everyday life and invests its objects and persons with moral significance. It draws on what Peter Brooks (1976) calls "the moral occult," whereby moral values are materialized in everyday life and become signs to be deciphered by the audience. Virtue is most often personified in an attractive, unprotected, and innocent young woman, vice by a powerful, rich, older man who has designs on her that are often explicitly sexual. He was often a morally decadent aristocrat, who used his power to satisfy his own appetites or, alternatively, he might appear as a colonial or racial antagonist who threatened all that was virtuous and good within the existing (colonial/ white supremacist) social order. As the melodramatic story develops, the innocent victim is increasingly menaced by the villain, and her rescue depends on the efforts of the hero. His work to free the woman from the villain's clutches makes him representative of clearly drawn normative boundaries. In many cases, the melodrama further enacts romantic possibilities between the honorable hero and the virtuous "damsel in distress." A tripartite structure thus emerges within some versions of the melodrama, one featuring the stock characters of hero, villain, and victim.[7]

Although some critics have identified the origins of melodrama within Europe as occurring at the time of the French Revolution, as with so many European innovations, its roots can be found earlier, in colonial literatures, particularly "captivity narratives" in which white women narrated their ordeals – emphasized by a sense of both sexual and spiritual threat – after seizure by Native Americans.[8] Goodness within the melodramatic narrative came to be associated with the normative family, grounding a secular morality beyond the Church. Villains were often identified specifically by the threat they posed to familial innocence, and the vivid celebration of their defeat and punishment often constituted the melodramatic dénouement. The gendered and sexed virtue of the heroes and heroines of melodramatic literature contrasted sharply with the gendered and sexed perversity of the evil villains, a pattern that linked gender and sex to the formation of community identity: melodrama defined a group's champions, prized possessions, and adversaries.

Neoliberal vulnerability and the vulnerability of neoliberalism **75**

From its earliest days, melodramatic technique thus worked to establish national, race, and class boundaries, as melodramatic narrative became a critical tool in generating social hierarchies and in broadly distinguishing between the "barbarous Other" and the "cosmopolitan modern." Colonial writers made reference to a long list of practices including sati, foot binding, polygamy, veiling, or the harem, creating a colonial melodrama in which, as Gayatri Spivak (1988, 296) puts it, "White men are saving brown women from brown men." As Chandra Mohanty (1988) and others have observed, contemporary writers continue this tradition in the postcolonial period, using "exotic" issues such as dowry murders, female genital mutilation, honor killings, or the early marriage of girls to generate this narrative in its most conventionally gendered and raced form. As with its counterparts in the metropole, melodrama relies upon the evidence of the suffering or sexually threatened body in order to establish a Manichean view of morality, one which can generate passion within affective politics.

It is our argument that melodramatic narratives have proliferated in the contemporary moment through the identification of "vulnerable populations." Neoliberal vulnerability inherits the tripartite scheme of the melodramatic formula but with some key revisions. Perhaps most importantly for the study of social justice and neoliberalism, the contemporary language of "vulnerability" tends to highlight groups that are placed at the periphery of the biopolitical order, marking its subjects as socially abject others who are not members of the social whole. The expansion of a discourse of vulnerability has coincided with the rise of new forms of humanitarianism, such as those promoted by NGOs, over the neoliberal period. As Fassin (2011) (following Agamben) emphasizes in relation to the humanitarian gaze, in locating those who suffer outside of a social order, a "state of exception" exists in which the rule of law is suspended. Whereas emotion similarly played an exceptionalizing role in colonial forms of governmentality, vulnerability turns this into a more formalized *governmental organization of suffering* run by a state-NGO amalgam.[9]

We thus make a distinction between contemporary melodramatic representations that describe potential threats to victims who live at the heart of the social order and with the exceptionalizing discourse of "vulnerability" as such. As Oliviero (2018) points out in her book, *Vulnerability Politics*, there are numerous instances in which those at the center of social collectivities are portrayed as if they are in constant danger when their lives are actually actively protected by the social order. Much of the discourse on crime and policing in mainstream media in the US, for example, has traditionally focused on dangers to the predominantly white, wealthy communities actively protected by the police, while minimizing the dangers emanating from the police faced by Black and Brown people.[10] In response, protests against white supremacist police violence have invoked imagery highlighting Black and Brown innocence and vulnerability, as in the gesture and chant "Hands Up, Don't Shoot." The use of such counter-claims points toward ways in which the invocation of unjust exposure to

76 Kaye, Amuchástegui, George, and Navarro

harm can usefully shift attention away from the perspectives of the powerful and toward the concerns of those whose lives are variously precarious.

At the same time, however, because neoliberal vulnerability discourse can also position "at risk" communities as living in a state of exception, it is not possible to simply correct these discussions to focus on those who are most vulnerable. Neoliberal "vulnerability" has emerged in association with the emergence of a specifically humanitarian and technocratic gaze, one which reaches *outside* of the body politic. By oscillating between an inflated focus on the purported dangers faced by those at the center and a marginalizing attribution of vulnerability as a neoliberal state of exception for those living on the margins of society, the discourse of vulnerability can help to hold social hierarchies in place. As we will discuss below at greater length, counter-hegemonic efforts must often negotiate these differing meanings and effects of vulnerability discourse.

Neoliberal vulnerability takes place outside of the "normal" processes of the state, a place where charity and gifts are offered, but where no rights can be demanded. The gaze of vulnerability thus shapes social relations of power, even as it directs (voluntarily given) aid toward those deemed socially and morally worthy. The exceptionalizing quality of vulnerability intensifies a second feature of the discourse, namely the way in which vulnerability's "victims" can suddenly be transformed into "villains," as when "refugees" suddenly become "foreign invaders." As vulnerability relies upon a moral evaluation of those designated as "victims," an alternative assessment regarding their potential as a threat can rapidly turn the deserving other into a dangerous other. As Fassin (2011, 177) notes, in such cases "the victim can easily become a criminal." In positioning people outside of the biopolitically defined collectivity (race, nation, etc.), a state of exception applies to both deserving and dangerous others, with the line between the two governed by no rule other than that applied by those in power. This dynamic can perhaps be seen most clearly with groups deemed to be "at risk"; while "at-risk" populations are similarly identified as being vulnerable, in many cases, they are "at risk" of becoming "dangerous" (for men) or "dysfunctional" in a manner that burdens the state (for women). The term *at risk* thus identifies a space directly standing upon the line between these two types of biopolitical others; put differently, one is "at risk" of becoming the wrong type of social other, a category greatly expanded by neoliberal governance.

Narratives regarding vulnerability have proliferated and moved into new territories in recent decades due to a series of factors related to (1) the privatization of social assistance (*via* a neoliberal reduction in state support for social welfare programs and a correlative rise in humanitarian logics), (2) an increasingly securitized environment in which necropolitical action – interventions designed to eliminate or subordinate another group in the name of the wellbeing of the core collectivity – is justified in the name of protection, (3) the rise of humanitarian NGOs that rely upon emotive appeals in order to raise funds, and (4) a fracturing media environment that depends upon emotion to draw and maintain the attention of viewers. The political elasticity of vulnerability's tripartite formula

Neoliberal vulnerability and the vulnerability of neoliberalism **77**

helps to sustain its continued use, with a tremendous variety of actors generating vulnerability narratives for a wide range of political projects, ranging from humanitarian rescue to securitization against collective "villains" to revolutionary resistance.

While the melodramatic frame has pervaded many forms of both activism and state initiatives, it is with the neoliberal notion of vulnerability that the exceptionalizing formula becomes truly commonplace, arguably developing into a primary form through which political understanding operates at the mass level. In the neoliberal period, melodramatic modes of governance – humanitarian aid and securitization – have increasingly displaced prior narratives of citizenship, generating new forms of relationship with the state and making it more difficult to press claims of either social and economic rights or of structural oppression in their wake. The neoliberal deployment of vulnerability also marks a turn toward a new deployment of affect, particularly when a governmental organization of suffering is established. Whereas NGOs and news organizations often rely upon a version of vulnerability oriented toward publicity-seeking sensationalism, the fact that governments increasingly produce policy in the name of addressing vulnerability gives the term an official and technical-sounding status. Although vulnerability is linked to the intense emotionality of the melodrama, it can also be linked to the flattened affect associated with a bureaucratic sensibility, a tie that gives it the prestige of expertise while undergirding this purported neutrality with emotional intensity.

The bureaucratic sensibility that surrounds vulnerability seems to distance it from the most overt forms of gender stereotyping present in early melodramas. Women are enabled to become "heroes," and men can be framed as "vulnerable." Yet the formal equality achieved within vulnerability discourse is only partial: women generally achieve the hero role only by standing above the presumed vulnerability of more marginalized women (often differentiated by race and class). And the need for victims to be morally worthy often precludes men from assuming that "unmanly" role. While seeming to transcend sexual categories, vulnerability discourse in fact reinscribes many of the same norms of gendered worth that were present within classic melodramas. And as will be seen, the "threats" that vulnerability identifies often pertain not to suffering as such, but to hazards which imperil gendered ideals, rendering it a hindrance in identifying harms emanating from within the normative social order itself.

A final difference between melodrama and vulnerability is that, whereas the former created fully legible narratives, vulnerability often works through the effect produced in a single, disarticulated image. The meme-like quality of vulnerability enables it to operate in a more detached form – little needs be known about any given situation other than the person or group's alleged "vulnerability" – yet the melodramatic narrative can "trail behind" the image, enabling heroes and villains to appear from hidden corners off-stage.[11] The moralizing demands of the melodrama still remain, particularly in relation to the victim, who must be not only helpless and unable to advocate for themselves – a frame which privileges traditional notions of "womenandchildren" over "able-bodied men" – but also thoroughly "innocent" and virtuous, lest they risk losing whatever support audiences might give them (an issue that feminists have addressed at length in relation to representations of sexual violence; e.g., Madriz 1997a, 1997b). Overall, victims must be capable of motivating the hero's sacrifice lest melodramatic conventions place them on the outside of a narrowly circumscribed circle of care. Meanwhile, the form of vulnerability tends to maintain the extremities of melodramatic formulation, moving toward a totalizing denunciation of absolute "villains" and against a thorough analysis of complex issues that might require carefully crafted interventions rather than moralistic condemnation. The implicit melodrama of vulnerability has proven itself readily capable of mobilizing intense affect; however, it does so only by limiting the domain of concern to a well-regarded few and sharply restricting the possible range of political responses.

In the following sections, we turn toward the complex machinations of the discourse of vulnerability in specific cases, ones concerning women and HIV in Mexico, the #BringBackOurGirls campaign in Nigeria, economic development in the US Virgin Islands, and the general exclusion of men and boys from discussions of sex trafficking. While each case covers a range of issues, together they enable us to address four key domains within neoliberal governance: the medical apparatus (particularly public health), the security apparatus, the market itself, and the humanitarian sphere. Taken together, the cases demonstrate the ways in which vulnerability works to facilitate certain types of claims while making others less possible, thereby altering the terrain of neoliberal governance. Following these discussions, we discuss some ways to rethink the issue of vulnerability – as signaling structural weaknesses within neoliberalism itself – and offer an alternative to the language of vulnerability and its narrative foreclosures.

Vulnerability and HIV in Mexico: enabling and constraining agency

Mexico's response to the HIV epidemic has been shaped by vulnerability discourse, which is formative for institutional policies regarding prevention and medical care. Vulnerability as a governmental strategy works simultaneously as justification and as a constrained foundation for the action of feminist organizations and groups of women living with HIV, who sometimes appropriate this notion without an analysis of the framework that supports it – it is both the *raison d'etre* and a fenced-in enclosure for action. In this section, we discuss the capacities that vulnerability enables and the constraints that it imposes through an analysis of a peer-counseling research and intervention *dispositif*, carried out with and for women with HIV in two specialized public health services in Mexico.[12]

"Neoliberal governmentality has taken a new shape," João Biehl (2007) asserts in his ethnography on the response to the HIV/AIDS epidemic in Brazil. Not only has neoliberalism pressed for the privatization of the state and thereby given rise to a humanitarian logic of the gift, it also changes the terms under which state/civil society interaction occurs. Whereas social democratic states presume a direct relationship between a parental state and individual rights-holders, neoliberalism argues that individuals are better able to act through "their own" organizations, thereby creating a role for private organizations (which generally do not operate democratically) to "mediate" between the state and civil society, thereby altering the nature of civil society. As Biehl (2007, 11) argues:

> Rather than actively seeking areas in need to be addressed, the new market-oriented state selectively recognizes the claims of organized interest groups that "represent" civil society, leaving out broader public needs for life-sustaining assistance in the domains of housing, economic security, and so forth.

While a number of theorists have criticized the way in which social democratic forms of state governance enable technocratic forms of control and domination (e.g., Habermas 1973), the neoliberal reliance upon civil society organizations (NGOs of various sorts) has a number of its own problematic implications. Within Mexico's neoliberal regime, focalized programs and mechanisms of so-called "social participation" have become the dominant means through which the poor are governed. Thus, as welfare expenditure has been steadily reduced, civil society organizations have ironically come to play an important role. And with the institutionalization of "gender mainstreaming" in the 1990s, some women's organizations and/or feminist women have taken on this role.[13]

Biehl's description can here be used to look at current governance models regarding HIV/AIDS among women in Mexico, where a significant number of women's NGOs have worked with the frame of state policies. Yet, the organizational processes among these groups have not been homogenous. Since the HIV/AIDS epidemic in Mexico has been concentrated among men who have sex with men ("MSM"), HIV-positive women started their activism within gay men's organizations.[14] The disregard these organizations showed for women's specific needs, however, led them to later form their own groups. Unlike gay men, these women had typically not organized previously around either the recognition of gender inequality or sexual identity; rather, their main drive had been their common circumstances regarding the infection. On the other hand, some feminist groups – led mainly by HIV-negative, white-collar, middle-class women, who had been involved mainly in the struggle for sexual and reproductive rights – have taken HIV into their political agenda and have interacted with HIV-positive women more as beneficiaries than as partners or project leaders. These two kinds of organizations have established different relationships with the government: whereas the latter could be thought of as institutionalized feminist groups, the former frequently lack the specific skills and language required to deal with a governmental bureaucracy that professionalized NGOs have mastered since the implementation of gender mainstreaming. Predictably, the question as to who

80 Kaye, Amuchástegui, George, and Navarro

best represents HIV-positive women has become a frequent source of ongoing tension between these groups.

Mexico's acceptance of gender mainstreaming led to invitations to women's groups and certain feminist individuals "as gender experts … [for] the administration of projects targeted to women who were considered the most 'vulnerable' by globalized neoliberalism" (Álvarez 2013).[15] Thus, the procedure that Biehl describes, in which the "new market-oriented state" selectively partners with various NGOs in order to acknowledge the "claims of organized interest groups that 'represent' civil society," is expressed in the construction of a *vulnerability gradient* associated with specific communities, which can be equally applied to young people, people with disabilities, native groups, or women. Thus, a governmental organization of suffering works as a mechanism for distribution of both resources and interventions. Asserting that women face a greater vulnerability regarding HIV than has been previously recognized becomes a coherent lobbying strategy within the context of this governmental organization. Although constricting in some ways, this emphasis can result in their representation as victims, a rendering that grants them moral virtue, dignity, and even a certain type of authority (Pecheny 2010). By this logic, it is essential to emphasize the vulnerability that women face regarding HIV. One might question what kind of subjects are thus produced as "vulnerable," a label which allows them to receive benefits from these programs. Which processes seem to establish the condition of "vulnerability"?

In terms of sheer numbers, having unprotected sexual intercourse with a male partner within a "socially normative relationship" – such as marriage or cohabitation – has become the main way of transmission and situation of risk of HIV for Mexican women (Herrera et al. 2015). Already in 1994, the infection rate amongst women who were married or cohabitating – and who did not consider themselves as "at risk" – was seven times higher than the rate amongst female sex workers (Valdespino et al. 1994). In an interview conducted by Amuchástegui with Miriam, a 46-year-old schoolteacher who founded an organization for women's rights, she spelled out this dynamic as it had played out in her life. Some 18 years after her diagnosis with HIV, she described her experience:

> I didn't even know what HIV was. I knew that it existed, and that it gave you AIDS, but I kept thinking "It won't happen to me," because the flyers the government gave us said that you could get it *if you had many partners*, but not *if your partner had many partners*. If they don't spell it out, we can't see it! (emphasis added)

This differential denial of "risk" runs through the axis of the moral regulation of sexuality and the respectability of women. By producing subjects who are rendered "guilty" or "innocent" of their own infection – and equating gendered respectability with safety – the state helped generate a situation in which wives faced greater risk for HIV than non-married women who engaged in prostitution. The

Neoliberal vulnerability and the vulnerability of neoliberalism **81**

correlation of risk and respectability leaves the heteronormative regime untouched, including the unequal "structures of extramarital opportunity" that allow many men to have sex with other men without destabilizing their identities or marital relationships (Hirsch et al. 2007). As one of the male coordinators – who self-identifies as gay – said during a group session with women affected by HIV: "At least we knew we were looking for it, but you women didn't even see it coming!" This process has favored a division between women's HIV organizations: while sex workers and trans women's groups struggle for their independence and organize in order to increase their ability to *act*, wives tend to depend on feminist NGOs which, instead, highlight their *vulnerability*. Thus, in the case of organizational processes, respectability works as both a dividing axis and as a catalyst, one which generates diverse relationships with the state (as further discussed in Chapter 6).

Setting aside the smaller grassroots organizations, which root themselves in an activist orientation, one sees a paradox arising from within the vulnerability discourse promulgated by the larger and more mainstream organizations: while women are represented as *powerless subjects* who have no input on the conditions of their own sexual practices, they are still being targeted as the main recipients of HIV education and information. The focus upon "vulnerable women" may therefore be costing them their lives, inasmuch as it is ironically assumed that they can demand that their partners wear a condom. This is why some analysts argue that the real focus of attention should be men's sexual behavior, not women's vulnerability (e.g., Hirsch et al. 2002). In some sense, a desire to produce women as their own heroes here sits with a reluctance to challenge heterosexual men.

It may thus seem that the emphasis upon women's vulnerability is, in fact, not thorough enough. However, the focus upon "vulnerability" carries significant hazards of its own: a married woman who feels sexual desire and is sexually active does not fit into the moral distribution of risk we previously mentioned. Instead, an omnipresent assumption of "unwanted sex" underlies the discourse of governance. Vulnerability discourse here obscures the fact that, sometimes, married women do not use condoms, not because of the power their husbands exert over sexual intercourse, but because they themselves do not want to use them for reasons linked to notions of intimacy, trust, and pleasure (Hirsch et al. 2002). Isabela – one of the women interviewed during the course of research for this part of our project – confesses:

> Honestly, we never used to talk about condoms, it didn't make sense, did it? Once, I remember I was dating a bus driver and he was going to put on a condom and I told him, at the hotel, "Oh, are you wearing a condom?" I said it just like that. "But I'm not sick. Are you sick? If you want to be with me, you cannot wear a condom." Condoms hurt me, they irritated [her genitals].

The moralization of the victim within *vulnerability* here results in an almost complete denial of sexual desires of any sort.

Beyond this, the discursive "vulnerability" of partnered women not only depends upon this denial of sexual subjectivity, but it also places an emphasis on intimate partner violence, which has become the *via regia* through which many feminist organizations attract resources and attention to HIV. Recently, the head of infectology of a public health institution claimed that "the HIV epidemic goes hand in hand with a violence epidemic" (Volkow 2013). Yet, in a thorough analysis of official data regarding physical violence in domestic partnerships, Castro (2012, 31) argues that "on a national level, practically all women (97.8%) who were surveyed either experienced very low levels of physical violence or no physical violence at all. On the other side, only 0.2% at a national level who suffered physical violence reported the most severe level of physical violence." Accounts that emphasize women's agency are systematically neglected within these framings. Another woman interviewed for this project, Ema, a 60-year-old domestic worker, who says she got the virus from her last lover, shows how women's own narratives might navigate between the opposing shores of blame and virtue in novel ways: "It was only after my divorce that I knew what love was, so I got HIV because I wanted to live again." While not wishing to minimize actual precarity, Higgins, Hoffman, and Dworkin (2010) thus advise against over-reliance upon what they call a "paradigm of vulnerability" as the sole framework used to understand women's place in the epidemic.

The use of vulnerability discourse has other representational consequences as well. Although the economic, social, and cultural inequalities that women experience are sometimes acknowledged, the statistics used by mainstream feminist groups in order to attract attention to "vulnerable women" usually report episodes of *interactional* rather than *structural* violence. By ignoring and not specifying the relationship between these two levels, the indiscriminate use of the trope "violence against women" as a prominent factor in HIV risk individualizes and renders invisible the social, economic, and cultural conditions that produce this exposure. Thus, this form of melodramatic appeal generates a "depoliticization" process through which an "ideological eradication of structural conflicts" takes place (Pecheny 2010, 361).

Furthermore, while some feminist NGOs identify institutional violence within public services as a violation of women's rights, their approach to social and economic inequality involves a logic of the humanitarian gift that leaves the basic economic structure unchallenged: "aid" for transportation and meals are regarded as suitable to allow poor women to attend specialized services, and nurseries inside the clinics are described as "support" that makes treatment accessible to women. Though useful in specific moments, these assistance measures are regarded as "empowering" mechanisms for women, whereas little is said about their economic and social rights, such as well-paid jobs, education, social security, and housing. In this context, the invocation of rights for women with HIV works at a crossroads against neoliberal rationality; in neoliberalism, access to social services – which should be classed as a basic social right – constitutes an exception reserved only for those subjects who can prove a certain degree of both

Neoliberal vulnerability and the vulnerability of neoliberalism **83**

worthiness and damage: in other words, for *victims*. This is problematic in that the metaphor of the victim "sustains the 'logic of rescue' that permeates the marketing of efforts to combat HIV by corporate philanthropy" (Klot and Nguyen 2011). Within this logic, the rescue of the victim simultaneously generates the need for a hero – the feminist NGO or the philanthropic corporation – who is "better able" than the victims themselves to articulate damage and to provide for need. Structural forms of marginalization are thus left unaddressed, while new forms of social dependencies upon local NGOs or corporations are generated.

We have argued that the neoliberal paradigm of vulnerability asks women living with HIV to adopting an identity saturated by helplessness and powerlessness. Here, Judith Butler's deliberations invite us to "consider undoing the binary vulnerability-resistance as a feminist task," to stop thinking that vulnerability must be overcome by resistance, and that, on the contrary, can become a moving force (Butler 2016, 25). Our fieldwork shows that women's interest in counseling other women can produce a positive subjectifying effect – one could even call it *empowerment* – through the production of a *subject of the knowledge of experience* that can only arise from the intersection between HIV diagnosis and gender identity. In this process, vulnerability is not constructed as an essential and permanent attribute, but as an "enabling power" that outgrows the biographical condition in order to build a collective field of action (Butler 2004).

> I stopped being one of the many people who come to the clinic and became the eyes that see the needs of others, the mouth that asks information to the right person, and the presence that helps other users not to feel lost in their journey through the public health service. Being a counselor has given my experience as HIV positive a sense of purpose.

This is how Clara describes her experience as a peer counselor. Mariel – another peer counselor – defiantly asks: "If you can manage to be undetectable, you can have a completely normal life. Look at me! Do I look sick?" "Foucault locates the desire that informs the question, 'how not to be governed?' This desire, and the wonderment that follows from it, forms the central impetus of critique" (Butler 2002, 218). Mariel thus embodies a thorough critique of the use of the paradigm of vulnerability as the only framework for interpreting the HIV epidemic amongst women.

Nevertheless, her transformation and that of other women – from being helpless victims to working as empowered peer counselors – is dependent upon this initial moment of vulnerability. As an identity, vulnerability not only governs the context in which state funding is secured, it also acts as a point of reference for the newly empowered: they are empowered to help others who were vulnerable in the same way, even as aspects of their own narratives may, strictly speaking, push the foundations of "vulnerability" beyond their normative limits. Yet here we see the way in which vulnerability marks its "victims" in a way which Butler does not theorize. In the neoliberal context, previously "vulnerable" subjects

84 Kaye, Amuchástegui, George, and Navarro

are empowered to act, but only in the field of expertise that is defined by their prior vulnerability. Those who have lived through domestic violence can help only other victims of domestic violence; former drug addicts can counsel current addicts; and so on. Vulnerability freezes identity, branding the person with their vulnerability and making it a permanent attribute of self, never moving it fully into the past tense. One becomes a "survivor." Alternatively, a former victim might move into the market as a normative citizen, but only on the condition that their earlier "vulnerability" is discursively located entirely in the past and framed as essentially irrelevant to their present position. As the vulnerable subject is definitionally abject, there is no way to bring vulnerability into the "empowered" market without its lingering residues.[16]

As we have seen, the discourse of vulnerability facilitates other types of frameworks and actions as well. Thus, vulnerability can enable action in multiple ways: it can establish the terms for a governmental organization of suffering that is developed in association with local NGOs whose relationship with those they "represent" is frequently contested; it can create ways for women to come together as victims and to create conditions that facilitate the ultimate "empowerment" of those same individuals as they help other "victims"; and it can act as a form of moral regulation against those whose "indecency" or "social inferiority" (of whatever sort) challenges vulnerability discourse's implicit commitments to both respectability and normative measures of social esteem. Vulnerability, while identifying "victims" who purportedly lack all social power to act on their own behalf, is far from itself being socially inert.

Vulnerability as counter-hegemonic claims-making: #BringBackOurGirls

As a discourse, "vulnerability" thus does considerably more than simply extend the power of hegemonic norms. As noted above, new forms of governance are enacted using frameworks and discourses of vulnerability. The vulnerability framework here proliferates new taxonomies of the governed (endangered groups, most vulnerable populations, and so on) while shifting the dynamics of engagement between rulers and the ruled from that of citizens and the state to that of stakeholders and beneficiaries of charity. Where citizens were able to make demands of the state on the grounds that these might be of service to the larger nation, beneficiaries can receive gifts from the state and may occasionally shape the form of the gift by voicing strategically phrased vulnerability claims.

Yet these calls for "gifts" can be quite potent and can work to delegitimize actors who fail to become easily legible "heroes." The uses of vulnerability as a claims-making discourse are amply illustrated in the case of the Nigerian #BringBackOurGirls campaign. In April 2014, two hundred and seventy-six schoolgirls were abducted from the tiny town of Chibok, Nigeria. The federal government initially denied their abduction. Yet Nigerian activists who were steeped in the practices of humanitarian work were able to mobilize the twittersphere

Neoliberal vulnerability and the vulnerability of neoliberalism 85

FIGURE 3.1 An early image from the #BringBackOurGirls campaign (Chiluwa and Ifukor 2015)

for the cause of the girls' rescue by deploying a discourse of vulnerable girlhood. When the Bring Back Our Girls hashtag was first launched, the image that initially accompanied the slogan dramatized the theme of vulnerability. It featured a close-up black and white photo of an African girl staring directly at the camera. One of her hands seemed about to cover her mouth, while beneath her left eye, a single teardrop was edited onto her pristine complexion (see image above). The face of the campaign acted as a canvas upon which images of vulnerability, despair, stoicism, and salvation could be projected. With implicit narrative trailing behind the image, it invited an international audience of viewers to see themselves as saviors, whose demands might bring about a rescue of the abducted girls.

As seen in Mexico, one of the effects of the imposition of neoliberal economic policies on postcolonial governments was that the shrinkage of states provided opportunities for the ascent of NGOs in key sectors and the broad dissemination of NGO logics and discourses, which are rooted in humanitarianism and charity work. Where the independent state had citizens to whom it was bound by something like a contractual relationship, NGOs had recipients, beneficiaries, or stakeholders, who could be endowed with gifts. The gift in this dynamic travels unidirectionally, from the organization to the beneficiaries. The form and terms of the gift are also often unilaterally determined; contrary to a regime of social rights, citizen-stakeholders cannot enjoy the bare expectation that their needs are a concern of government. Structurally, then, citizen-stakeholders function as supplicants, who must conform to a vision of their role as articulated by the paternalist state, in order to entertain any hope of extracting needed goods.

In the #BBOG campaign, this translated into the construction of the abjectified modern girl. The abjectified modern African girl was internationally legible because she was a new iteration of an old figure whose roots lie in the high-point of European racial capitalism. Echoing Spivak's and Mohanty's observations regarding colonial narratives, historian Pamela Scully identified the figure of the "vulnerable African woman or woman of African descent" as a recurring trope in international human rights work from the abolitionist campaigns of eighteenth-century Britain to the transnational twenty-first-century campaigns against gender-based violence. In the early anti-slavery movement, Scully (2011, 21) writes, abolitionists frequently called up "the figure of the black woman vulnerable to terrible depredation on the plantations of the Caribbean" in order to buttress moral arguments for the abolition of slavery. During the colonial period, missionaries working in various parts of the continent combined ethical and economic justification for their labors by portraying the African woman as "a beast of burden who had to be rescued from the patriarchal grip of her husband and family." This, even as colonial labor and governance policies paradoxically emphasized the importance of preserving patriarchal power (Scully 2011, 24–5). Into the twenty-first century, human rights campaigns against gender-based violence continue to "achieve their sense of purpose and ethics through the figure of the abject and violated woman who needs the intervention of non-governmental organizations" (Scully 2011, 31). In short, from the era of Atlantic slavery to the colonial period and beyond, human rights campaigns have made use of African women by placing emphasis on African women as bodies, as bodies that face peculiar forms of sexual violation, and as bodies whose best chances for salvation lie in the benevolent hands of distant humanitarian actors.

Despite, or perhaps because of, the familiarity of the image of the vulnerable and violated African woman, the initial photographic campaign strategy worked. By the time the campaign logo had been changed to a simple crimson-red background featuring bold white or black text, the campaign image had done its job. The world had claimed the Chibok girls as OUR girls and the global attention pushed the Nigerian government to finally heed the cries of the Chibok parents and articulate some sort of official plan of rescue.

As seen above, Butler's (2016) reflections upon the discourse of vulnerability press us to consider whether it always and necessarily shores up paternalistic power. Are paternalism and victimization the only options within neoliberalism? This dichotomy seems insufficient to capture the dilemma of activists operating within the postcolony or, perhaps, anywhere. With regard to the postcolony, paternalism lurks on at least two registers: within the national melodrama involving citizens, the state, and a rotating cast of villains, and between the nation and the international community, read here as the Euro-American world. In the case of the Chibok girls, the discourse of vulnerability built around their abduction clearly loaned the girls a deep moral value for global audiences who almost immediately called for a transnational militarist rescue response. Yet, as the militarist potentialities of this development were unfolding, they were deftly contained by feminist activists who insisted on a rescue strategy that would be creditable to the Nigerian federal government in lieu of a transnational militarist intervention in Northeast Nigeria. In so doing, they foreclosed one layer of paternalism, preventing the interaction between the paternalist state and its citizen-stakeholders from being mirrored by an added layer, one mediated by the interaction between the Nigerian state and the "international community."

How were the paternalist underpinnings of the discourse of vulnerability deployed for claims-making against the state, ultimately forcing the performance of accountability to subjectified citizens? One must consider the role of neoliberalism in its globalized form as a factor in creating the possibility of this political alchemy. Neoliberal globalization is a system shaped out of networks of states, regions within states, or sometimes just cities, into relationships of unequal but shared benefit, and the vast outsider majority. Neoliberal networks, as Ferguson (2006) argued, skip over vast swathes of space and societies – indeed most places and people are redundant to its operations. These dynamics are mirrored within the spaces that are included in the networks, producing at each node a network of unequal but shared benefit framed by a backdrop of sheer waste. The inequalities inherent to neoliberalism in its globalized form mean that certain partners are always liable to exclusion from these nodal market systems. Due to their anxiousness about that structural precarity, individuals accept ever more self-annihilating conditionalities to membership within the system.

When neoliberalism came to African countries in the 1970s and 80's, it came as part of a package of ideologies that included democracy, human rights, and other ostensibly non-economic goods. The structuralist is tempted to argue that only the economic conditions were real and that the political ones were cosmetic, but we might think of the reality of the various conditions in a different way. Using the analogy of the performance review, with which most professionals are familiar, we find that most performance reviews have a number of boxes that must be ticked to indicate meritorious progress within the system. Some of those boxes are vital for advancement, but *all* of the boxes can be indicated for stagnation or worse. Thus, for nations that received neoliberalism as part of a neocolonial package of externally imposed requirements, economic liberalization was vital for participation in the neoliberal global system, whereas democracy and human rights could be cited *or ignored* as criteria for marginalization or exclusion.

The networked aspect of neoliberalism in its globalized form presents potential checks on states seeking a place in the neoliberal world that may be exploited by NGOs and humanitarians. To the extent that the theory of the market underlying neoliberalism flows from a theory of the individual that underlies liberalism, they both seek to maximize freedom of people or capital through minimal state intervention, a process that paradoxically requires strong state intervention to realize (strong in the dual sense of an intense level of – seemingly non-interventionist – intervention, conducted by a strong state that has the legal, economic, militarist ability to impose its will). Perhaps most strongly since the secessionist Biafran campaign of 1967–1970, the campaign for the rescue of the

88 Kaye, Amuchástegui, George, and Navarro

Chibok girls asked: Does Nigeria have the ability to impose its will? Can the state govern its subjects? By extension, can the state govern its markets? Can the state be a credible participant in the neoliberal global marketplace?[17]

The discourse of vulnerability worked in two ways in the #BBOG campaign. First, the image of the vulnerable schoolgirl was invoked to rally international attention to a girl-saving campaign in a small town in northeastern Nigeria. Second, the vulnerability of the state's position within global neoliberal networks provided an entrée for activists to shore up a kind of accountability, paternalist as it was, of the state toward its subjectified citizens.

Vulnerability appears as a strategy of governance of the neoliberal state for managing the conditions of precarity. When the expectation, or, more fundamentally, the ability to expect universal protections from precarity has been removed, the discourse of vulnerability may be introduced into the calculation about who might merit protection. Thus, the language of vulnerable persons and related categories come into use to particularize and taxonomize certain individuals. Because NGOs occupy so many roles in lieu of the state, and partly because they have been so successful in disseminating the language and logics of humanitarianism to broad audiences, NGOs have effectively shaped claims-making discourses ahead of the state. Claims-making discourse shifted from a language of contracts, in which there is mutual obligation and in which there is an obligation of the state to its citizens, to becoming a moral language reliant on appropriately vulnerable subjects and the brittleness of masculinist national honor.

From vulnerable subjects to precarious populations: the US Virgin Islands and neocolonial development

Although neoliberal discourses of vulnerability shape most narratives of social suffering, it is important to find other means to analyze the unequal ways in which people are made to suffer, and come to experience heightened precarity in their life chances. Such an examination must avoid the limitations of vulnerability discourse and generate alternative forms of affect in the course of offering expanded political possibilities. Here, we turn to a discussion of the relationship between the US and the US Virgin Islands in order to highlight some additional political consequences that follow from framing this suffering in terms of neoliberal vulnerability, to show the ways in which capital deploys this frame in its efforts at "development," and to begin to sketch what an alternative discursive approach to social suffering might look like. As noted above, we deploy the framework of *precarity* in order to highlight structural conditions as distinct from the exceptionalizing and moralistic frames which prevail in vulnerability discourse. While an exclusive focus on structure carries its own problems – making individual actors invisible – we argue that the concept of precarity offers a way of sustaining analytic focus on both the precarious experiences of individuals and the precarity of populations, thus offering an analysis that stresses a vision

Neoliberal vulnerability and the vulnerability of neoliberalism **89**

of collective politics and the contextualization of individual experience over a decontextualized and simplified sense of personal immorality.

The group of islands now known as the US Virgin Islands (USVI) was purchased by the US from Denmark in 1917. Since then, the US has struggled with ways to approach the disparate economic realities across the three islands of St. Thomas, St. John, and St. Croix. St. Thomas has long been the most economically successful of the three, featuring prominently on many cruise ship and tour group itineraries. For purposes of legislation and marketing, the twenty-square-mile island of St. John is often grouped together with St. Thomas as something of an awkward appendage, a relationship that has contributed to intra-territorial tensions around autonomy in the context of American imperialism.[18] St. Croix, however, the largest of the three islands, has long had difficulty penetrating tourist networks and has been the US Virgin Island most in need of economic intervention. After a number of unsuccessful attempts at economic development, including crude oil processing, aluminum manufacturing, and broader industrialization programs, the USVI exists today as a territory of the US with a struggling economy and very few viable options for economic advancement (Sheller 2014). For St. Croix in particular, given its lack of success entering the global tourist market and receiving the attendant service sector jobs in hotels, bars, and restaurants, there has been widespread economic precarity, conditions which have been experienced both by individuals and on a territory-wide basis.

This structural precarity has created opportunities for the US to further its economic interests with only limited benefits to the USVI. In the early 2000s, local and federal legislators worked together to implement the Economic Development Commission (EDC) program, a quintessentially neoliberal initiative that would make the American financial sector the driver of St. Croix's economy by offering dramatic tax cuts (including a 90% exemption for income taxes) to financial management companies willing to relocate to the island.[19] This program is demonstrative of a broader shift in development toward finance and information management (Freeman 2000).

The creation of the EDC program demonstrates the political, legislative, and economic reach of the US and its willingness to capitalize on its dominance in relation to its territory. In an earlier moment, the spaces that constituted "America's Backyard" served as areas of US experimentation.[20] Building on this history, the USVI continue to exist as spaces of exception for the US empire in the current moment, as evidenced through tax holiday programs like the EDC. The precarious position of these islands creates market opportunities for American capital to ebb and flow as needed – the territory serves as a port for capital in flush times and a site of exodus in leaner moments, as evidenced during the 2008 financial crisis, when the EDC program ground to a near-standstill.

In order to qualify for this program and receive the tax breaks it offers, companies are required to hire and train workers from St. Croix. As mentioned in Chapter 2, the overwhelming majority of these hires from the USVI are lighter-skinned young women from middle- to upper-middle-class backgrounds, referred

90 Kaye, Amuchástegui, George, and Navarro

to colloquially as "EDC girls" (Navarro 2010 and 2020). Building on a number of troubling histories, including the feminization of labor under industrialization in the region and the pigmentocracy of both slavery and colonialism (see, for instance, Douglass (1992) on the color/class category of "brown" in Jamaica), these hiring practices deepen existing hierarchies and increase stratification on the island.[21] Given that these workers are generally in their 20s or early 30s, it is of note that they are identified as EDC "girls," as scholars have marked neoliberalism's preoccupation with not just femininity, but particularly with "girls" as the agents most capable of neoliberalism's processes of self-transformation. This is evidenced, for instance, in the Nike Foundation's focus on "the girl" as point of entry for ending global poverty and marks a neoliberal shift toward humanitarian logics even within economic "development" (Murphy 2013). Beyond their classification as girls, Crucian women employed in the EDC sector are further positioned for inclusion in this neoliberal project by their middle- and upper-middle-class backgrounds, a positionality which has produced an aspiration for the neoliberal, consuming subject (Ringrose and Walkerdine 2008).

Whereas the discourse of economic development positions the USVI and "the EDC girls" as "vulnerable," "at-risk" recipients of aid, those who take advantage of the tax programs are seen to be "risk-takers" in a masculinist, positive sense. Ho (2009), for example, has detailed the ways in which the notion of taking financial risks among Wall Street bankers has been encouraged and rewarded both within and outside of this sector. Yet, while the idea of "taking risks" and being "at risk" might seem to be closely related, in fact they pertain to narrative structures that are extremely different in terms of both gender and moral status. While those who invest in the market are expected to "take risks"; they are expected to never become "vulnerable." Capitalist financiers are here situated within a conventionally masculine narrative concerning conquest and competition with other similarly situated subjects. They become heroes within the developmentalist narrative. Meanwhile, those who are marginalized within the market are narrated as either "risky" and dangerous ("criminals," "terrorists") or as needy ("vulnerable" and "at risk").[22] The terminology of being "at risk"/"vulnerable" here signals a need for "humanitarian" efforts at development. For instance, a space such as the USVI being deemed "at risk" for an economic crisis provides a logic for intervention by capital-rich individuals and nations (as with the EDC program).

The implications of neoliberalism in the USVI thus stretch far beyond simply the centering of capital. As in the Dominican Republic (discussed in Chapter 2), we see that neoliberalism results in profound consequences for those who are relatively excluded from the formal sphere of market exchange. As distinct from rights-bearing citizens, these abject figures oscillate between victims and villains, a dual positioning that helps to facilitate policy consequences that differ greatly from those that can be justified under a rubric of citizenship. Setting aside the presumptive need for a security apparatus to counter "villains," those who find themselves in need of services and opportunities outside of the market are positioned as "vulnerable" and "in need" of a (voluntary) humanitarian response in order to help them realize their appropriate, market-based personhood.[23]

Neoliberalism thus enacts a reorientation of belonging, shifting away from a state within which one might make claims and toward a market in which one must compete. That is, no longer can those deemed "citizens" reasonably expect to be endowed with rights and understand themselves to exist in some relationship of reciprocity with the state. Instead, individuals are required to maximize their human capital in order to earn basic protections. Thus, demands for services on St. Croix are noticeably not directed at either US or local government officials, but are instead directed toward the private sector, particularly those organizations involved in the EDC program. The emptying out of state responsibilities repositions wealthy individuals as generous patrons, and citizens who are marginalized within the market as "needy" and "vulnerable." An example: the wives of a number of EDC beneficiaries formed a nonprofit organization, the VI Ladies League, that functioned as a charitable organization and tasked itself with donating necessary items such as textbooks and toilet paper to schools and schoolchildren on St. Croix. This shift led to schools competing to be the most *deserving* of these donations and undermined attempts by local nonprofit organizations to hold the local government accountable for these required items. In this way, a voluntary relationship of patronage develops from the language of "vulnerability," creating a logic that can undermine efforts to instantiate "rights."[24]

The shift away from state-based rights toward market-determined possibilities has necessarily transformed claims-making and the entities toward which claims are directed. The new forms of governance heralded by neoliberalism have led to the positioning of individual donors and NGOs as the arbiters of claims.[25] Carrie Meyer (1999, 2–4) writes, "as participants in a changing balance among states, markets, and civil society, NGOs have both responded to and catalyzed change in a newly globalizing world order ... [while] states, in contrast, have retreated as economic powers and have looked for private-sector alternatives to provide public services." Vulnerability has thus emerged as a strategy of governance such that economic stagnation has become an invitation for intervention by either multinational corporations or supranational organizations, such as the International Monetary Fund (IMF) or the World Bank. The responses to economic need, now positioned as "vulnerability," include requirements of increased privatization of services and the implementation of structural adjustment and austerity packages – packages which have long disproportionately affected women in the region.[26] Thus, the response to economic marginality is a reassertion of the centrality of the market *via* policies that in fact penalize local economies and increase economic stratification.

The conditions of precarity that the EDC and the long history of (post-) colonialism foster, as well as the discursive positioning of the most marginalized as "vulnerable," is experienced on both an individual and a territory-wide level. In other words, beyond actual conditions of material harm that are experienced by individually positioned actors – e.g., the loss of a job because of more amenable conditions elsewhere – collective harms also ensue.[27] For instance, as a result of the race/color/gender histories and hierarchies outlined above, the lighter-skinned and moderately class-privileged women known as "EDC girls" are viewed by EDC businesses as ideal employees for this sector. Many locals thus see the EDC program as (re)inscribing a system of (neo)coloniality, insofar as (a) EDC companies are seen as having little interest in the island beyond profit, and (b) the hiring practices of EDC companies recreate some of the class and color hierarchies present during that colonial period (in which lighter-skinned slaves – often the offspring of slaveowners – were viewed as better suited for indoor labor, while darker-skinned slaves were seen as bestial and often performed the devastating work of cultivating crops in the fields). Many locals receive little benefit from the EDC program and criticize it as a return to the "slave days," viewing its effects partly in terms of its overall impacts on race, color, and gender. Neoliberal economic development attempts, such as the EDC, depend heavily on these histories and hierarchies, generating a need for a more expansive approach to social justice than the vulnerability frame enables.

Vulnerability discourse deflects attention away from structural hierarchies and the effects of governmental power. Demanding that neoliberal projects address their grounded effects strips such initiatives of the mask that they somehow operate at a supra-individual level. Political activity is necessary in order to constitute and maintain an organized market and other social structures. At the same time, however, structural analysis on its own carries attendant risks, and so we place individual narratives into a context that identifies and connects to these larger patterns. Doing so helps to create a narrative capable of moving beyond the limitations of vulnerability, a narrative capable of seeing the deployment of vulnerability as being itself a technique that facilitates the establishment and extension of local and transnational hierarchies, turning, for example, capital investment into a "gift" that benefits the precariously situated "EDC girls."

The gendered tropes of "sex trafficking" and the anti-drama of male rape

Vulnerability obfuscates social relations not only by displacing structural factors; its moralizing lens also excludes many from its gaze, and systematically misidentifies the challenges faced even by those individuals who are identified as being "vulnerable" (Vance 2011). The case of sex trafficking is illustrative. While the vision of the kidnapped young woman or girl who is forced into prostitution has gained currency since the early 2000s, numerous academics have criticized the trend, noting that the discourse presents an inaccurate and sensationalist vision of sex work that promotes counter-productive interventions, such as heightened border control measures and police raids against brothels and street-based sex workers (we elaborate upon these arguments in Chapter 4 of this volume). Although the narrative of "sexual slavery" abides faithfully to the tripartite structure of vulnerability – heroic NGO workers and police fight against villainous traffickers who threaten innocent girls and young women with sexual ruin – the reality is that anti-trafficking policies fail to engage the real issues faced by the vast majority of sex workers, including both underage participants and those facing other forms of extremely abusive situations. The imagined scenario of a "sexual innocent" who is forced to engage in prostitution through violence, fraud, or coercion also ignores the far more common scenario in which those already engaged in sex work find themselves in abusive situations (Doezema 1999).

Within this context, the discussion of sex trafficking has also been notable for the ways in which it has generally excluded significant mention of male, trans, or gender-nonconforming victims. Of 1,043 *New York Times* stories published over a ten-year period (2010–2019), in which the term "sex trafficking" appeared, only 16 mentioned boys as victims, three mentioned men, three mentioned transgender individuals, and there was no mention of gender-nonconforming or non-binary people.[28] A US survey of organizations offering services for trafficking victims likewise found that only two of the 37 residential programs in the country would accept male-identified victims (Reichert and Sylwestrzak 2013). Popular culture is similarly skewed: films and TV shows about sex trafficking – whether semi- or fully fictionalized, such as *Taken* (2008), *The Whistleblower* (2010), and *Trafficked* (2017), or documentaries, such as *Born into Brothels* (2004), *Very Young Girls* (2007), and *Tricked* (2013) – simply ignore victims who might not be female. When the far less common story of male sexual victimization is told, it rarely uses the language of "sex trafficking."[29]

Commentators on this issue have generally focused upon the exclusion of cis-males, and, while here building on these critiques, we further note that parallel omissions concerning transgender and other victims are also significant. Through such absences, presumptions about who is a proper "victim" are reaffirmed, coupled with affective currents of contempt and disgust toward those whose gender is seen as improperly enacted.[30] Critical commentary thus far has focused on the idea that men are perceived as "invulnerable beings" who "have total control over their destinies," and that these stereotypes render male victims "conceptually invisible" (Jones 2010, 1180–1). Willis et al. (2013, 11) similarly argues that commercially sexually exploited boys "are surrounded by a culture that is both hetero-centric and homophobic; it is a culture that portrays girls as vulnerable, weak, and victims, and men as strong, powerful, and perpetrators."[31] Although a gendered, conceptual dichotomization and heterosexist prejudices are important, these factors do not sufficiently explain the absence of even cis-men and boys from sex trafficking discourses, nor do they begin to challenge the problematic construction of female victimization.

Depending upon the gender of the victim, mainstream representations of sex trafficking tap into two entirely different "structures of feeling," generating pity for women and girls while generating discomfort and disgust in relation to men and boys (Williams 1977). The incompatibility between these two emotional structures, more than a strictly conceptual invisibility (or any disparity in actual circumstance), renders it difficult to frame boys or men as victims within conventional accounts. Boys and adult men are understood as sex slaves only after undergoing significant narrative contortions that alter the meanings associated with "sex slavery" and the emotions this idea provokes. One therefore cannot simply "add men and stir" without extensive transformations in the emotive structure of the narrative. Thus, speaking of men and boys as victims of sex trafficking simply does not *feel* right.

None of the sexualized gender tropes that pertain to women and girls operate in the same way in relation to men or boys. The difficulty of including the latter as victims of sex trafficking comes not only from the novelty of the suggestion that men might be raped, but also because an alternate narrative regarding sexual contact between males already exists. This pre-existing narrative invokes a set of emotions that disrupt the narrative conventions of vulnerability discourse. While the abuse of women and girls is positioned as a horrifying enactment of power against a helpless and morally worthy victim, sexual violence against men or boys is generally seen as (a) perhaps deserved (as when child molesters are raped in prison), (b) signaling a victim who cannot defend himself and is therefore morally unworthy, and/or (c) tainting the victim *via* homosexual contact (when the rapist is male). Male rape by other men may thus raise uncomfortable fears regarding both male failure and male pleasures, whereas sexual violence by women against men or boys is taken to be either impossible or as pleasurable for the victim. Given this affective context, it is not surprising that, in most circumstances, the sexual abuse of adult men in particular simply does not make for good theater. Any attempt at a detailed portrayal is undercut by mainstream disgust at the sexual acts, all of which makes the tale an "anti-drama," a story better left untold.[32]

Although men and boys are still mostly ignored as sex trafficking victims, over the past few years there has been an increasing trend to identify young men engaged in prostitution as victims of sex trafficking. The US State Department's 2013 *Trafficking in Persons Report* for the first time mentioned male victims of sex trafficking, devoting an entire section to the topic. A small number of anti-trafficking organizations have similarly begun to include boys (and, less frequently, men) as victims of sex trafficking in their service programs and publicity campaigns (Willis et al. 2013). At the same time, however, sex trafficking's relative openness to the victimization of "boys" (rather than "men") taps into the long history of anti-gay panic regarding the "seduction" of young men, stories advanced in repetitive cycles since the late 1800s (Lancaster 2011). Thus, even as "respectable" middle-class gay men now fall under less suspicion than in years prior concerning pedophilia, the familiarity of this villainous image lends a certain credibility to the idea of "traffickers" who take advantage of young, helpless boys.

Yet, it is important to ask what political effects identifying young men engaged in prostitution as "trafficking victims" will have at a concrete level. In previous ethnographic work conducted in San Francisco from 1999 to 2001,

Neoliberal vulnerability and the vulnerability of neoliberalism **95**

young men working on the street generally rejected "victim" identities as well as the strict rules of the rescue shelters provided by local service agencies.[33] Indeed, these young men overwhelmingly despised the local service organizations that purported to serve them. Tightly enforced curfews, prohibitions against drugs and prostitution, and requirements to notify one's parents of their whereabouts made life on the street seem more attractive to many. At the same time, they knew what services they could obtain from each agency, and sometimes created stories of their own victimization in order to obtain them. In effect, the service agencies created a market for tales of vulnerability and victimization. Whereas the young men had plenty of material to work with in creating these narratives, they told very different tales when not in need of goods from these agencies. Tales told away from the service agencies might indeed involve feeling deeply disturbed by the prostitution they engaged in, but this distress did not necessarily follow presumed patterns (e.g., one 16-year-old interviewed for this research felt he had let himself down because he started to enjoy sex with his clients and was now not sure he was straight). Meanwhile, other young men seemed to psychically adapt to the realities of paid sex and were not much troubled by it, or, alternatively, they had concerns that they saw as being far greater than those posed by prostitution.

In making sex trafficking the greatest evil, anti-trafficking NGOs minimize the impact of familial abuse, hunger, homelessness, pervasive violence on the street, or the possibility of getting HIV through a shared needle. In trafficking discourse, the series of problems faced by a young person on the street are reduced to a single motif – dangerous sex. Ultimately, vulnerability enacts a language in which the threats it envisions are spiritual, a frame which gives primacy to sexual morality. The threat posed to the young man's heterosexuality due to the pleasure he experienced, for example, is impossible to imagine, while the other dangers he faced recede into invisibility. Permeated by vulnerability, the sex trafficking frame thus focuses a myopic lens upon the dangers of commercial sex while ignoring the problem-filled context in which prostitution takes place, severely distorting the panoply of circumstances and needs that young men engaged in street-based prostitution confront.

A focus upon this larger context – in which youth may embrace prostitution as a problematic *solution* rather than seeing it as *the* problem in and of itself – helps to explain young people's decision-making around prostitution and the efforts they make to exercise greater control over their lives.[34] On the streets of San Francisco, a narrow focus upon the extreme danger represented by sex trafficking inevitably steered NGO interventions toward "rescue," often facilitated by police and arrest. Yet, these young men generally reacted with great hostility when humanitarian "helpers" attempted to coercively impose their vision of aid. Discourses that speak of survival strategies on the street as forms of sexual abuse may indeed speak to the experiences of some youth, but for others these frameworks may hide the ways in which "rescue" can become another force aimed at discipline and normalization.[35]

96 Kaye, Amuchástegui, George, and Navarro

Beyond these concerns, the narrow focus on sex trafficking has worked to foreclose attention to many individuals experiencing untenable situations that do not meet the legal definition of "trafficking." For example, approximately one-half of the young men working on the street in San Francisco were just *over* the age of consent. Although their circumstances were essentially identical to those who were a year or two younger, their legal standing was completely different. The state now defined them as "offenders" rather than as "victims." Or consider the Latin American day laborers who also stood on the streets of San Francisco, hoping for work in lawn care or construction, but who occasionally accepted offers of paid sex.[36] Though their stories shared certain similarities with sex trafficking narratives, they did not readily fit either legal or cultural definitions of "sexual slavery." The challenges these groups of men faced were not readily addressed by programming and policy focused upon sex trafficking, and many of the approaches taken in the name of the abolition of trafficking (such as increasing police efforts against undocumented migrants) actively made their situation worse.

There are a wide variety of alternative political and service approaches that might benefit groups engaged in that portion of prostitution better termed "survival sex" than "sex work." Policies favoring free movement across borders, the decriminalization of sex work, public health approaches to drug use, greater funding for affordable housing, support for low-wage laborers, service interventions focused on harm reduction, shelters that do not require drug abstinence, and the elimination of requirements that agencies contact a runaway youth's parents prior to offering services are all conceivable, though not within a frame that identifies need only in terms of "rescue" (including against that person's will, if necessary).

In order to advance these alternative approaches, however, a new cultural script is needed. Vulnerability discourse tends to oversell particular types of harms pertaining to a small subset of situations, generating simplistic "solutions" that create gendered and racialized scapegoats as a means of addressing a single, narrowly defined problem ("sexual slavery"). A new template for understanding is warranted, one that not only identifies a multiplicity of harms and needs, but that recognizes the complexity of confronting multiple difficulties simultaneously. Whereas the high-volume melodrama of "sexual slavery" easily captures attention, the reality of most sex work is decidedly mundane, and even the desperate situations that may incline one to engage in survival sex are not easily subsumed by "vulnerability."

The vulnerability of neoliberalism

Neoliberalism marks a shift in the institutional structures and governing logics of the state, as well as the broader social field. Under neoliberalism, the experience of precarity is both extended in range and intensified in depth for those who suffer not only from the lack of state supports but also from novel applications of the security apparatus. A masculinist sense of "citizenship" is radically delimited and transformed in the process, coming to refer only to those who successfully participate in the market "on their own" (ignoring all of the structural advantages and forms of socially reproductive labor that produce this success) or to those who enforce neoliberalism's security needs. The sense of citizenship as a form of social inclusion with accompanying rights and entitlements is replaced by a new "independent" citizen who makes fewer and fewer claims upon the state.

Meanwhile, those who are marginalized within the neoliberal structure are addressed through a language of vulnerability which positions them as either victims or villains. Those who are identified as *proper* victims are given some limited opportunities to collect the "gifts" from those above them, but only if they can successfully present moving stories that capture the attention of those (reproducing normative visions of worthiness in the process). Vulnerability thus generates new types of power dynamics, forcing "needy" groups and individuals to compete with one another, generating the conditions which produce what Martínez (1993) has termed an "oppression Olympics." Despite this, the logic of vulnerability can empower at least some individuals to act as heroes in their local communities, though only within a specified niche created by an overall governmental organization of suffering.

"Vulnerability" can also place some obligations upon the state, particularly in relation to the need to provide security and to defeat the designated "villains," and these obligations can be taken advantage of in campaigns from those below (as seen with #BBOG). Even as the discourse of vulnerability arises from a neoliberal turn that greatly advantages those who have power within the market, it does not leave those living precarious lives absolutely powerless (although, ironically, one mode of action involves making precisely such a claim).

Yet if the discourse of vulnerability generates possibilities for some, it brings new dangers to others. Those living in neoliberalism's heightened terrain of precarity, who are deemed unworthy of the charitably bestowed gift, become "villains" themselves: welfare cheats, addicts, and "social parasites" of other forms. As a representation of the abject, the vulnerable other constantly risks becoming a securitized other should they prove undeserving. Vulnerability's status as a moral language further works against a more complete recognition of precarity, both because it reduces the frame to decontextualized individuals (failing to see structural context and a more complete picture of need) and because it negatively judges many who suffer within neoliberal regimes, responding through a punitive moralism and the violence of securitization. A biopolitical selection is thus made, regarding which forms of life have value and which threaten that valued life. Not only are individuals moralized, but the type of aid they are seen as needing is similarly gauged by implicitly moral standards: certain types of "dangerous sex" stand as a threat to the soul in ways in which mere homelessness and hunger cannot. Biopolitics thus further determines which specific threats to life are to be recognized, and which are to be normalized, accepted, and largely rendered invisible.

The limited guarantees offered by the neoliberal state – offering only security for a supposedly "free" market (perhaps the only two "rights" which "citizens" can continue to insist upon) – hails citizens in new ways. "Heroism" awaits not only those who achieve market success, but a different sort of heroic narrative becomes possible through humanitarian benevolence. As seen above, however, the move toward humanitarianism involves judgment over which causes are worthy and which are not. Neoliberal governance thus calls upon citizens to judge the abject, rendering decisions not only in terms of privatized care, but also in terms of a new form of security. The line between the worthy and the unworthy abject – between deserving others and dangerous others – is thus subject to lobbying by those empowered as "citizens," and can therefore be thin indeed.

With rising economic insecurity among "citizens," some seek to buttress their position by turning toward one of the few "legitimate" demands they can place on the state: security. And when the state nevertheless fails to secure the collective/racial/moral purity required to keep the abject at bay, a newly "active citizenry" – distinguished from "passive" recipients of social insurance, and perhaps themselves at the margins of social respectability within the terms of the market – can take it upon themselves to enforce lines of demarcation from the abject through an advancement of direct vigilante violence (as seen with waves of anti-*dalit* violence in India, violence against drug users in the Philippines, the rise of the Proud Boys in the US, or individual acts of violence, such as the murder of Trayvon Martin by George Zimmerman or of Joseph Rosenbaum and Anthony Huber by Kyle Rittenhouse).[37] Such acts of "aggrieved entitlement" arise from the same structures which produce "vulnerability" (Kalish and Kimmel 2010). In displacing a prior language of citizenship, one which included social and economic rights, the neoliberal discourse of vulnerability – with its implicit normalization of the market, and its moralization of the abject as either worthy or unworthy – simultaneously becomes a discourse of violence against marginalized others.

But as noted at the beginning of this chapter, the discourse of vulnerability can be read in yet another direction, as a guidepost pointing toward the precarious locations within neoliberalism itself. The "villains" identified by the neoliberal state mark points against which it has been forced to mobilize. In challenging the idea that official enemies pose a "threat," one challenges the ability of the neoliberal state to function. In like manner, the discourse of vulnerability works to obscure the structural issues which produce precariousness, replacing them with a sensibility that frames solutions in individualist and moralized terms, often in the process mischaracterizing the needs that individuals have named as important to their survival. In working to counter these larger structures – including but not limited to the rule of the market – and in offering solutions which presuppose a different kind of sociality and, thus an alternative ethics, one undermines the favorable account of its own beneficence which neoliberalism offers.

Lastly, the discourse of vulnerability makes neoliberalism vulnerable insofar as it makes it difficult for the neoliberal state to address structural issues which threaten its own stability or even its own existence, as seen with the recent COVID-19 pandemic, or with the existential threat to human life currently posed by climate change. More generally, the neoliberal state is not well suited to respond to any sort of dysfunctionality of the market, no matter how much social rebelliousness it might provoke. Vulnerability gives it a limited set of tools – humanitarian charity and securitized policing – and this limitation gives it a rigid structure, one that is incapable of addressing its own defects.

Pressing for an end to neoliberalism, however, requires us to transcend its logics, including the narrative of vulnerability. As seen in the case of #BBOG, vulnerability can indeed be used as a tool against the established order, yet the tactic also carries a problematic invocation of a frame that ultimately reinforces preexisting social hierarchies.[38] Resisting neoliberal narratives of vulnerability also requires upending the moralizing, raced, gendered, and sexed frames that undergird its operations. Analyses that do not rely upon absolute victimization, but which instead recognize both the structural nature of precarity and the sheer complexity of power relationships, and which further do not demand that victims be morally pure and socially valuable in conventional terms, need to form the basis for this more complex understanding.

The need to identify harm remains a strong one for those seeking to upend the neoliberal order in favor of a more just social organization, but doing so in terms of vulnerability all too often leads to a troubling re-inscription of neoliberal frames. Setting aside vulnerability discourse may move one away from the intensely emotive and motivational aspects that inhere within that discourse, and a new economy of affect created through a frame centered on *precarity* may work to generate capacities for more flexible and nuanced approaches to political change.

Notes

1 See, e.g., Fassin (2011). Fassin's analysis revolves around the presentation of suffering within humanitarian discourse. We seek to extend his analysis in suggesting that vulnerability derives from a preemptive logic within neoliberalism: vulnerability identifies a territory that is marked for governmental intervention due to the risk that suffering may occur at some point in the future. Samuel Moyn (2010, 220) also notes that "rights" have been transformed and "humanized" in the neoliberal period, increasingly following the logic of what we are terming "vulnerability."

   On a parallel trend toward the "humanization" of international law, see also Meron (2000) and Meron (2006) (both cited in Moyn 2010).
2 BCRW (2012); Butler et al. (2016); Bergoffen (2003, 2009, and 2011); and Gilson (2011, 2014, 2015, and 2016).
3 See also Fineman (2008).
4 Foucault argues that the security apparatuses of the state have always staged a "fear game" in order to justify its own interventions (Lemke 2014, 66). Many scholars have argued that this dynamic has only accelerated within recent decades as "risk" became an increasingly common social logic and form of governmentality (Beck 1992; Castel 1991; O'Malley 1992 and 1996; Petersen et al. 1997; Lupton 1999).

100 Kaye, Amuchástegui, George, and Navarro

5 See Hesford (2011); Ticktin (2011); and Fassin (2011).

6 Work concerning the genre of "sentimentalism" and its rise during this period is also relevant (e.g., Reddy 2001; Ellis 2004; Strick 2014). On the emotional politics of compassion more generally, see also Haskell (1985a, 1985b); Clark (1995); Kleinman et al. (1997); Rai (2002); Berlant (2004); Anker (2014); and Jensen and Ronsbo (2014).

7 The boundaries of melodrama as a genre are, of course, contested, and sometimes feature additional stock characters, such as the malicious and immoral woman who either attempts to seduce the hero or oppresses the female heroine. Many melodramas also came to focus on domestic scenes where the heroine's spiritual wellbeing was placed in jeopardy. In terms of political emotionalities and the emergence of vulnerability in the neoliberal period, however, the tripartite structure delineated above seems key (for a useful overview of the genre as a whole, see Hayward 2018, 243–53). We thank Christina Crosby for her assistance in crafting this section.

8 On the history of melodrama, see Brooks (1976); Clark (1995); Williams (2001); Singer (2001); and Hayward (2018).

   On captivity narratives, see Strong (1999) and Snader (2000).

9 See Rai (2002) on the "rule of sympathy."

10 When privileged groups are at the center of these discourses, the language of "vulnerability" is not typically deployed, and the melodrama often focuses upon securitization, with the sense of harm more of a necessary passing point than a final destination.

11 The idea of narrative "trailing behind" effect comes from Talha İşsevenler (personal communication *via* Patricia Clough).

12 Following Deleuze's (1988, 160) discussion of Foucault's work, we use *dispositif* to reference "machines which make one see and speak" certain regimes of enunciation in relation to the knowledge, power, and subjectivity that are present in this field. The two public health centers in focus are Clínica Especializada Condesa, Mexico City, and Centro Ambulatorio de Prevención y Atención en SIDA e ITS, Oaxaca City.

13 In 1997, the United Nations (UN) and the World Bank began to require that governments consider factors which reproduce social inequality between women and men when proposing new projects and public policies. The UN (1997) defines this policy of *gender mainstreaming* as "The process of assessing the implications for women and men of any planned action, including legislation, policies, or programmes, in all areas and at all levels."

14 In 1985, there were 11 men for each woman living with the virus. HIV-positive women thus started their activism within gay men's organizations such as the *Frente Nacional de Personas Afectadas por el VIH/SIDA* (National Front for Affected with HIV/AIDS) (FrenpaVIH), which was constituted in 1996. By 2015, the ratio of men to women living with HIV had decreased to 5 to 1, with more than 95% of these women becoming infected through heterosexual intercourse.

15 Fraser (2013) has described this type of collaboration as a "dangerous liason" between certain feminisms and the neoliberal state.

16 Butler, Gambetti, and Sabsay (2016) seek a new formulation of vulnerability in order to challenge precisely this difficulty; however, this remains the challenge within more conventional deployments of the term.

17 In 1967, the region of Biafra in eastern Nigeria declared its independence. While Biafran troops met with some initial success, the Nigerian army – aided by both the UK and the USSR – eventually began to prevail, ultimately defeating the Biafran regime in 1970. It is estimated that some 2 million people (50% or more being children) in the Biafra region lost their lives due to either starvation or disease caused by a Nigerian blockade of the area during the conflict.

18 See Roopnarine (2011).

Neoliberal vulnerability and the vulnerability of neoliberalism **101**

19 For an in-depth analysis of the EDC program, see Navarro (2010).
20 For instance, see Briggs (2002) on experimental birth control methods implemented in Puerto Rico.
21 See, for instance, Abraham-Van der Mark (1983); Anderson (1986); Barrow (1995 and 1998); Bolles (1983); and Ellis (2004); Kempadoo (2004); Leo-Rhynie et al. (1997); Mohammed (2002); Mohammed and Shepherd (1988); Safa (1995); Momsen (1993); Yelvington (1995); Enloe (1989); Freeman (2000).
22 This framing also has implications for spaces/markets which carry with them the possibility of contagion and loss.
    In general, island-nations in the Caribbean are seen as potentially risky spaces for capital investment, given the possibility of political change/unrest, natural disasters, and so on. In contrast, investment in the US Virgin Islands is positioned as "safe," given its status as a possession of the US. A 2002 issue of the *Virgin Islands Investment Analysis*, an investment newsletter printed on the mainland for Americans interested in relocating to the USVI, makes clear the importance of this stability afforded by the USVI's status as a US territory, warning:

> Do Not Invest Outside the United States. Even seemingly stable island governments, such as those associated with Great Britain, for example, have established a history of turning possessions over to completely new forms of governments as short-term expediencies take precedence. In addition, investing outside the United States endows one with a whole new set of legal and cultural barriers that are often discovered only by painful firsthand exposure (*Virgin Islands Investment Analysis* 2002, 1).

23 See, for example, Ong (2006).
24 See also Fassin (2011), who notes that a similarly voluntary relationship develops in relation to "humanitarian reason."
25 See Quan (2005).
26 See, for example, Bolles (1983); Harrison (1997).
27 See Safa (1981) on "runaway shops."
28 A methodological caveat must be added, however, as the figures are not exactly comparable. A query for the term "sex trafficking" on 27 December 2020, using *The New York Times*' search engine revealed 1043 instances, a tally which included feature stories and opinion pieces directly addressing the issue, as well as brief mentions in other news articles. When the term "boy" was added, the search engine revealed 79 occurrences; however, these included instances in which boys were discussed in other terms (e.g., as when boyfriends were said to act as "pimps"). Going through these 79 individually revealed 15 in which "boys" were mentioned as victims. The same method was used in relation to the terms "men," LGBT," "L.G.B.T.," "trans," "gender nonconforming," and "non-binary" in order to derive the other figures.
29 Of films with a wider distribution, only *Trade* (2007) included a brief scene featuring an underage boy; see Steele (2007, 32).
30 For instance, the "Survived and Punished" project run by Mariame Kaba (2017) has documented that the police told rape survivor Ky Peterson when arresting him for killing his attacker in self-defense that Ky "did not look like a victim."
31 See also Dennis (2008).
32 The most notable exceptions being either films set in prison (which almost invariably feature black men as rapists and white men as victims; see Kaye (2018) or *Deliverance* (1972), Black which is notable both for its Othering of impoverished rural men, but also for the way in which it was *not* copied, despite its commercial success.
33 See Kaye (2007).
34 See also Montgomery (2001); O'Connell Davidson (2005); Kaye (2007); Curtis et al. (2008); Mai (2012); and Marcus et al. (2012).

35 See also Dank et al. (2015); Lutnick (2016); Musto (2016); Baker (2018).
36 Various researchers and journalists writing about this issue and suggest that approximately 10% of these workers sometimes also accept offers for paid sex (Gonzáles-López 2006; Abram 2006; Núñez 2007; Galvan et al. 2008).
37 On the murder of Trayvon Martin in 2012, see Yancy and Jones (2013); Johnson et al. (2015); and Oliviero (2016). On the murder of Joseph Rosenbaum and Anthony Huber in 2020, see Liberman (2020).
38 On this point, see also Anker's (2014, 203–204) comments on what she terms "left melodrama."

References

Abraham-Van der Mark, Eva. 1983. "The Impact of Industrialization on Women: A Caribbean Case." In *Women, Men, and the International Division of Labor*, edited by June Nash and María Fernandez-Kelly, 374–86. Albany, NY: State University of New York Press.

Abram, Susan. 2006. "Solicitation Just Part of Day Laborers' Lives." *Los Angeles Daily News*. 2 July. http://www.dailynews.com/general-news/20060702/solicitation-just-part-of-day-laborerslives.

Álvarez, Sonia. 2013. "Neoliberalismos y trayectorias de los feminismos Latinoamericanos," *América Latina en Movimiento*, 489 (October). http://www.alai net.org/es/active/68593.

Anderson, Patricia. 1986. "Conclusion: Women in the Caribbean," *Social and Economic Studies*, 35(2): 291–324.

Anker, E. R. 2014. *Orgies of Feeling: Melodrama and the Politics of Freedom*. Durham, NC: Duke University Press Books.

Baker, Carrie N. 2018. "Moving Beyond 'Slaves, Sinners, and Saviors': An Intersectional Feminist Analysis of US Sex-Trafficking Discourses, Law and Policy," *Journal of Feminist Scholarship*, 4 (Spring): 1–23. https://digitalcommons.uri.edu/jfs/vol4/iss4/2.

Barnard Center for Research on Women (BCRW). 2012. "The Scholar & Feminist 2012: Theorizing Vulnerability Studies," *Dare to Use The F-Word: Podcasts*. http://bcrw .barnard.edu/podcasts/the-scholar-feminist-2012-theorizing-vulnerability-studies/.

Barrow, Christine. 1995. *And I Remember Many Things: Folklore of the Caribbean*. Kinston, Jamaica: Ian Randle.

Barrow, Christine, ed. 1998. *Caribbean Portraits: Essays in Gender Ideologies and Identities*. Kingston, Jamaica: Ian Randle.

Beck, Ulrich. 1992. *Risk Society: Towards a New Modernity*. First edition. Newbury Park, CA: SAGE Publications Ltd.

Bergoffen, Debra. 2003. "February 22, 2001: Toward a Politics of the Vulnerable Body," *Hypatia*, 18 no. 1: 116–134. DOI: 10.1111/j.1527-2001.2003.tb00782.

Bergoffen, Debra. 2009. "Exploiting the Dignity of the Vulnerable Body: Rape as a Weapon of War," *Philosophical Papers*, 38 no. 3: 307–325. DOI: 10.1080/05568640903420889

Bergoffen, Debra. 2011. *Contesting the Politics of Genocidal Rape: Affirming the Dignity of the Vulnerable Body*. London: Routledge.

Berlant, Lauren, ed. 2004. *Compassion: The Culture and Politics of an Emotion*. London: Routledge.

Biehl, João. 2007. *Will to Live: AIDS Therapies and the Politics of Survival*. Princeton, NJ: Princeton University Press.

Bolles, Lynn. 1983. "Kitchens Hit by Priorities: Employed Working-Class Jamaican Women Confront the IMF." In *Women, Men and the International Division of Labor*, edited by June Nash and María Patricia Fernandez-Kelly, 138–60. Albany, NY: State University of New York Press.

Briggs, Laura. 2002. *Reproducing Empire: Race, Sex, Science, and U.S. Imperialism in Puerto Rico.* First edition. Berkeley, CA: University of California Press.

Brooks, Peter. 1976. *The Melodramatic Imagination: Balzac, Henry James, Melodrama, and the Mode of Excess.* New Haven: Yale University Press.

Butler, Judith. 2002. "What is Critique? An Essay on Foucault's Virtue." In David Ingram edited by *The Political*, 212–228. Malden, MA: Blackwell Publishers.

Butler, Judith. 2004. *Undoing Gender.* London: Routledge. https://selforganizedseminar. files.wordpress.com/2011/07/butler-undoing_gender.pdf.

Butler, Judith. 2009. *Frames of War: When is Life Grievable?* New York: Verso. https://edisciplinas.usp.br/pluginfile.php/4098884/mod_resource/content/1/Butler%20%282009%29%20Precarious%20life%20-%20grievable%20life.pdf.

Butler, Judith. 2015. *Notes Toward a Performative Theory of Assembly.* Cambridge: Harvard University Press.

Butler, Judith. 2016. "Rethinking Vulnerability and Resistance," In *Vulnerability in Resistance*, edited by Judith Butler, Zeynep Gambetti, and Leticia Sabsay, Reprint edition, 12–25. Durham, NC: Duke University Press Books. https://doi.org/10.1215/9780822373490.

Castel, Robert. 1991. "From Dangerousness to Risk." In *The Foucault Effect: Studies in Governmentality*, edited by Graham Burchell, Colin Gordon, and Peter Miller. Chicago, IL: University of Chicago Press.

Castro, Roberto. 2012. "Problemas conceptuales en el estudio de la violencia de género. Controversias y debates a tomar en cuenta," In Norma Baca Tavira and Graciela Vélez Bautista (coords.), *Violencia, género y la persistencia de la desigualdad en el Estado de México.* Buenos Aires: Ed. Mnemosyne.

Chiluwa, Innocent and Presely Ifukor. 2015. "'War Against Our Children': Stance and Evaluation in #BringBackOurGirls Campaign Discourse on Twitter and Facebook," *Discourse & Society*, 26(3): 267–296.

Clark, Elizabeth. 1995. "'The Sacred Rights of the Weak': Pain, Sympathy, and the Culture of Individual Rights in Antebellum America," *Journal of American History*, 82 no. 2 (September): 463–493.

Curtis, Ric, Karen Terry, Meredith Dank, Kirk Dombrowski, Bilal Khan, Amy Muslim, Melissa Labriola, and Michael Rempel. 2008. "The Commercial Sexual Exploitation of Children in New York City, Executive Summary." NCJ 225082. New York: National Institute of Justice/Center for Court Innovation. https://www.courtinnovation.org/sites/default/files/CSEC_NYC_Executive_Summary.pdf.

Dank, Meredith, Jennifer Yahner, Kuniko Madden, Isela Banuelos, Lilly Yu, Andrea Ritchie, Mitchyll Mora, and Brendan Conner. 2015. "Surviving the Streets of New York." Washington DC: Urban Institute, (February). https://www.urban.org/research/publication/surviving-streets-new-york-experiences-lgbtq-youth-ymsm-and-ywsw-engaged-survival-sex/view/full_report.

Deleuze, Gilles. 1988. *Foucault.* Translated by Sean Hand. 1st edition. Minneapolis, MN: University of Minnesota Press.

Dennis, Jeffery P. 2008. "Women Are Victims, Men Make Choices: The Invisibility of Men and Boys in the Global Sex Trade," *Gender Issues*, 25 no. 1 (1 March): 11–25. https://doi.org/10.1007/s12147-008-9051-y.

Doezema, Jo. 1999. "Loose Women or Lost Women? The Re-Emergence of the Myth of White Slavery in Contemporary Discourses of Trafficking in Women," *Gender Issues*, 18 no. 1 (1 December): 23–50. https://doi.org/10.1007/s12147-999-0021-9.

Douglass, Lisa. 1992. *The Power of Sentiment: Love, Hierarchy, And The Jamaican Family Elite*. Boulder, CO: Westview.

Ellis, Markman. 2004. *The Politics of Sensibility: Race, Gender and Commerce in the Sentimental Novel*. Cambridge: Cambridge University Press.

Enloe, Cynthia H. 1989. *Bananas, Beaches & Bases: Making Feminist Sense of International Politics*. London: Pandora.

Fassin, Didier. 2011. *Humanitarian Reason: A Moral History of the Present*. First edition. Berkeley, CA: University of California Press.

Ferguson, James. 2006. *Global Shadows: Africa in the Neoliberal World Order*. Durham, NC: Duke University Press

Fineman, Martha Albertson. 2008. "The Vulnerable Subject: Anchoring Equality in the Human Condition," *Yale Journal of Law and Feminism*, 20 no. 2: 1–24. https://digitalcommons.law.yale.edu/cgi/viewcontent.cgi?article=1277&context=yjlf&httpsredir=1&referer=.

Foucault, Michel. 1975. *Discipline and Punish: the Birth of the Prison*. New York: Vintage Books.

Foucault, Michel. 1978. *The History of Sexuality*. New York: Pantheon Books. https://suplaney.files.wordpress.com/2010/09/foucault-the-history-of-sexuality-volume1.pdf.

Foucault, Michel. 2008 [2004]. *The Birth of Biopolitics: Lectures at the Collège de France, 1978–1979*. Translated by Graham Burchell. New York: Palgrave Macmillan.

Fraser, N.. 2013. *Fortunes of Feminism: From State-Managed Capitalism to Neoliberal Crisis*. First edition. New York: Verso.

Freeman, Carla. 2000. *High Tech and High Heels in the Global Economy: Women, Work, and Pink-Collar Identities in the Caribbean*. Durham, NC: Duke University Press.

Fuller, A.T. and Stephanie Pincetl. 2015. "Vulnerability Studies: A Bibliometric Review," *The Professional Geographer*, 67 no. 3: 319–329. https://doi.org/10.1080/00330124.2014.970835.

Galvan, Frank H., Daniel J. Ortiz, Victor Martinez, and Eric G. Bing. 2008. "Sexual Solicitation of Latino Male Day Laborers by Other Men," *Salud Publica de Mexico*, 50 no. 6: 439. https://www.ncbi.nlm.nih.gov/pmc/articles/PMC2821784/.

Gilson, Erinn. 2011. "Vulnerability, Ignorance, and Oppression" *Hypatia*, 26 no. 2: 308–332. https://doi.org/10.1111/j.1527-2001.2010.01158.x.

Gilson, Erinn. 2014. *The Ethics of Vulnerability*. London: Routledge.

Gilson, Erinn. 2015. "Vulnerability, Relationality, and Dependency: Feminist Conceptual Resources for Food Justice," *International Journal of Feminist Approaches to Bioethics*, 8 no. 2: 10–46. https://doi.org/10.3138/ijfab.8.2.10.

Gilson, Erinn. 2016. "Vulnerability and Victimization: Rethinking Key Concepts in Feminist Discourses on Sexual Violence," *Signs*, 42 no. 1: 71–95. https://doi.org/10.1086/686753.

González-López, Gloria. 2006. "Heterosexual Fronteras: Immigrant Mexicanos, Sexual Vulnerabilities, and Survival," *Sexuality Research and Social Policy*, 3: 67–81. https://doi.org/10.1525/srsp.2006.3.3.67.

Habermas, Jürgen. 1973. *Theory and Practice*. Boston, MA: Beacon Press.

Harrison, Faye V. 1997. "The Gendered Politics and Violence of Structural Adjustment: A View from Jamaica." In *Situated Lives: Gender and Culture in Everyday Life*, edited by Louise Lamphere, Helena Ragoné, and Patricia Zavella, 451–68. New York: Routledge.

Haskel, T.L.. 1985a. "Capitalism and the origins of the humanitarian sensibility, Part 1," *The American Historical Review*, 90 no. 2: 339–361. https://doi.org/10.2307/1852669.

Haskel, T.L.. 1985b. "Capitalism and the origins of the humanitarian sensibility, Part 2," *The American Historical Review*, 90 no. 3: 547–566. https://doi.org/10.2307/18 60956.

Hayward, Susan. 2018. *Cinema Studies: The Key Concepts*. 5th edition. New York: Routledge.

Herrera, Christina, Kendall Tamil, and Lourdes Campero. 2015. *Vivir con VIH en México. Experiencias de mujeres y hombres desde un enfoque de género*. Ciudad de Méjico: El Colegio de Méjico.

Hesford, Wendy S. 2011. "Human Rights Rhetoric of Recognition," *Rhetoric Society Quarterly*, 41 no.3: 282–289. DOI: 10.1080/02773945.2011.575331.

Higgins, Jenny A., Susie Hoffman, and Shari L. Dworkin. 2010. "Rethinking Gender, Heterosexual Men, and Women's Vulnerability to HIV/AIDS," *American Journal of Public Health; Washington*, 100 no. 3 (March): 435–45. http://search.proquest.com/docview/215089263/abstract/429925485DAD4BFDPQ/1.

Hirsch, Jennifer S., Jennifer Higgins, Margaret E. Bentley, and Constance A. Nathanson. 2002. "The Social Constructions of Sexuality: Marital Infidelity and Sexually Transmitted Disease–HIV Risk in a Mexican Migrant Community," *American Journal of Public Health*, 92 no. 8 (August): 1227–37. https://www.ncbi.nlm.nih.gov/pmc/articles/PMC1447220/.

Hirsch, Jennifer S., Sergio Meneses, Brenda Thompson, and Mirka Negroni. 2007. "The Inevitability of Infidelity: Sexual Reputation, Social Geographies, and Marital HIV Risk in Rural Mexico," *American Journal of Public Health*, 97 no. 6: 986–96. DOI: 10.2105/AJPH.2006.088492.

Ho, Karen. 2009. "Disciplining Investment Bankers, Disciplining the Economy: Wall Street's Institutional Culture of Crisis and the Downsizing of 'Corporate America'," *American Anthropologist*, 111 no. 2 (21 May): 177–189. https://doi.org/10.1111/j.1548-1433.2009.01111.x.

Islands News. 2002. "Virgin Islands Investment Analysis," May.

Jensen, S., & Ronsbo, H. eds. 2014. *Histories of Victimhood*. Philadelphia, PA: University of Pennsylvania Press. http://www.jstor.org/stable/j.ctt5vkd7x.

Johnson, Devon, Amy Farrell, and Patricia Y. Warren, eds. 2015. *Deadly Injustice: Trayvon Martin, Race, and the Criminal Justice System*. New York: NYU Press.

Jones, Samuel Vincent. 2010. "The Invisible Man: The Conscious Neglect of Men and Boys in the War on Human Trafficking." *Utah Law Review*, 4 (November): 1143–88.

Kaba, Mariame, Alisa Bierria, Hyejin Shim, and Stacy Suh, eds. 2017. *#SurvivedAndPunished: Survivor Defense as Abolitionist Praxis*. https://survivedandpunished.org/wp-content/uploads/2018/06/survivedandpunished_toolkitbw.pdf.

Kalish, Rachel and Michael Kimmel. 2010. "Suicide by Mass Murder: Masculinity, aggrieved Entitlement, and rampage school shootings," *Health Sociology Review*, 19 no.4: 451–464. DOI: 10.5172/hesr.2010.19.4.451.

Kaye, Kerwin. 2007. "Sex and the Unspoken in Male Street Prostitution." *Journal of Homosexuality*, 53 no. 1–2: 37–73. doi: 10.1300/J082v53n01_03. PMID: 18019069.

Kaye, Kerwin. 2018."The Gender of Trafficking, Or, Why Can't Men Be Sex Slaves?" In *Understanding Sex for Sale*, edited by May-Len Skillbrel and Marlene Spanger. London: Routledge.

Kempadoo, Kamala. 2004. *Sexing the Caribbean: Gender, Race, and Sexual Labor*. London: Psychology Press.

Kleinman, Arthur, Veena Das, and Margaret M. Lock. eds. 1997. *Social Suffering*. Berkeley, CA: University of California Press.

Klot, Jennifer F., and Vinh-Kim Nguyen, eds. 2011. *The Fourth Wave: Violence, Gender, Culture & HIV in the 21st Century.* Paris: UNESCO.

Lancaster, Roger N. 2011. *Sex Panic and the Punitive State.* Berkeley, CA: University of California Press.

Lemke, Thomas. 2014. "The Risks of Security: Liberalism, Biopolitics, and Fear." In *The Government of Life: Foucault, Biopolitics, and Neoliberalism,* edited by Vanessa Lemm and Miguel Vatter. New York: Fordham University Press. http://ebookcentral.proquest.com/lib/columbia/detail.action?docID=3239890.

Leo-Rhynie, Elsa, Barbara Bailey, and Christine Barrow, eds. 1997. *Gender: A Caribbean Multi-Disciplinary Perspective.* Kingston, Oxford: James Currey.

Liberman, Alida. 2020. "Summer of Protest." *The Philosophers Magazine,* 91 (4th quarter): 33–39. https://doi.org/10.5840/tpm20209190.

Lupton, Deborah. 1999. *Risk.* 1st edition. London; New York: Routledge.

Lutnick, Alexandra. 2016. *Domestic Minor Sex Trafficking: Beyond Victims and Villains.* New York: Columbia University Press.

Madriz, Esther. 1997a. "Images of Criminals and Victims: A Study on Women's Fear and Social Control," *Gender & Society,* 11 no. 3 (June): 342 –56. https://doi.org/10.1177/089124397011003005.

Madriz, Esther. 1997b. *Nothing Bad Happens to Good Girls: Fear of Crime in Women's Lives.* Berkeley, CA: University of California Press.

Mai, Nick. 2012. "The Fractal Queerness of Non-Heteronormative Migrants Working in the UK Sex Industry." *Sexualities,* 15 no. 5–6 (1 September): 570–85. https://doi.org/10.1177/1363460712445981.

Marcus, Anthony, Robert Riggs, Amber Horning, Sarah Rivera, Ric Curtis, and Efram Thompson. 2012. "Is Child to Adult as Victim Is to Criminal?" *Sexuality Research and Social Policy,* 9 no. 2 (1 June): 153–66. https://doi.org/10.1007/s13178-011-0070-1.

Martínez, Elizabeth and Angela Y. Davis. 1993. "Coalition Building of People of Color," University of California, San Diego, (12 May). https://culturalstudies.ucsc.edu/inscriptions/volume-7/angela-y-davis-elizabeth-martinez/.

Meron, Theodore. 2000. "The Humanization of Humanitarian Law," *American Journal of International Law,* 94 no.2 (April): 239–278. DOI: https://doi.org/10.2307/2555292.

Meron, Theodor. 2006. *The Humanization of International Law.* Dordrecht: Martinus Nijhoff Publishers.

Meyer, Carrie. 1999. *The Economics and Politics of NGOs in Latin America.* Santa Barbara: Praeger.

Mohammed, Patricia. 2002. *Gendered Realities: Essays in Caribbean Feminist Thought.* Barbardos: University of the West Indies Press.

Mohammed, Patricia, and Catherine Shepherd, eds. 1988. *Gender in Caribbean Development.* Mona, Jamaica: The University of the West Indies, Women and Development Studies Project.

Mohanty, Chandra Talpade. 1988. "Under Western Eyes: Feminist Scholarship and Colonial Discourses." *Feminist Review,* 30: 61–88. https://doi.org/10.2307/1395054.

Momsen, Janet, ed. 1993. *Women and Change in the Caribbean.* Bloomington, IN: Indiana University Press.

Montgomery, Heather. 2001. *Modern Babylon?: Prostituting Children in Thailand.* New York: Berghahn Books.

Moyn, Samuel. 2010. *The Last Utopia: Human Rights in History.* Cambridge: Harvard University Press. https://doi.org/10.2307/j.ctvjk2vkf.

Murphy, Michelle. 2013. "The Girl: Mergers of Feminism and Finance in Neoliberal Times," *The Scholar & Feminist Online,* 11.1/11.2 (Fall 2012/Spring 2013). https://

sfonline.barnard.edu/gender-justice-and-neoliberal-transformations/the-girl-mergers-of-feminism-and-finance-in-neoliberal-times/.

Musto, Jennifer. 2016. *Control and Protect: Collaboration, Carceral Protection, and Domestic Sex Trafficking in United States.* Berkeley, CA: University of California Press.

Navarro, Tamisha. 2010. "Virgin Capital: Foreign Investment and Local Stratification in the US Virgin Islands." Ph.D., Duke University. http://search.proquest.com/docview/193508766/abstract/9B6166886FE841EBPQ/1.

Navarro, Tamisha. 2020. "'EDC girls' and women's work: Race, gender and labor in the financial services sector in the US Virgin Islands," *Feminist Anthropology*, 1 no. 2 (November): 165–175. https://doi.org/10.1002/fea2.12015.

Núñez, C. (2007). "Male Day Laborers Turn to Prostitution," *La Opinion*, trans. Elena Shore, 22 December.

O'Connell Davidson, Julia. 2005. "Child Trafficking: Known Unknowns and Unknown Knowns," In *Thatcher's Grandchildren?: Politics and Childhood in the Twenty-First Century*, edited by Stephen Wagg and Jane Pilcher. London: Palgrave Macmillan. https://link.springer.com/chapter/10.1057/9781137281555_4.

Oliviero, Katie. 2016. "Vulnerability's Ambivalent Political Life: Trayvon Martin and the Racialized and Gendered Politics of Protection," *Feminist Formations*, 28 no.1 (Spring): 1–32. DOI: 10.1353/ff.2016.0013.

Oliviero, Katie. 2018. *Vulnerability Politics: The Uses and Abuses of Precarity in Political Debate*. New York: NYU Press.

O'Malley, Pat. 1992. "Risk, power and crime prevention," *Economy and Society*, 21 no. 3: 252–275. DOI: 10.1080/03085149200000013.

O'Malley, Pat. 1996. "Risk and Responsibility." In *Foucault and Political Reason: Liberalism, Neo-Liberalism, and Rationalities of Government*, edited by Andrew Barry, Thomas Osborne, and Nikolas S. Rose. Chicago, IL: University of Chicago Press.

Ong, Aihwa. 2006. *Neoliberalism as Exception: Mutations in Citizenship and Sovereignty.* First edition. Durham NC: Duke University Press Books. https://doi.org/10.1215/9780822387879.

Pecheny, M. 2010. "Political Agents or Vulnerable Victims? Framing Sexual Rights as Sexual Health in Argentina," In *Routledge Handbook of Sexuality, Health and Rights*, edited by P. Aggleton and R. Parker. London: Routledge.

Petersen, Alan R. 1997. "Risk, Governance and the New Public Health," In *Foucault, Health and Medicine*, edited by Robin Bunton, and Alan R. Peterson. London: Psychology Press.

Quan, Adan. 2005. "Through the Looking Glass: U.S. Aid to El Salvador and the Politics of National Identity," *American Ethnologist*, 32 no. 2: 276–293.

Rai, Amit. 2002. *Rule of Sympathy: Sentiment, Race, and Power, 1750–1850.* New York: Palgrave.

Reddy, W. 2001. *The Navigation of Feeling: A Framework for the History of Emotions.* Cambridge: Cambridge University Press. doi:10.1017/CBO9780511512001

Reichert, Jessica, and Amy Sylwestrzak. 2013. "National Survey of Residential Programs for Victims of Sex Trafficking," Chicago, IL: The Illinois Criminal Justice Information Authority. http://www.icjia.state.il.us/assets/pdf/ResearchReports/NSRHVST_101813.pdf.

Ringrose, Jessica, and Valerie Walkerdine. 2008. "Regulating the Abject," *Feminist Media Studies*, 8 no. 3 (1 September): 227–46. https://doi.org/10.1080/14680770802217279.

Roopnarine, Lomarsh. 2011. "St. Croix's Secession Movement in the United States Virgin Islands: Sentimental or Serious." *Journal of Eastern Caribbean Studies; Cave*

Hill, 36 no. 1 (March): 43–66, 81. http://search.proquest.com/docview/881647758/abstract/32C3A060D8104716PQ/1.

Safa, Helen I. 1981. "Runaway Shops and Female Employment: The Search for Cheap Labor," *Signs: Journal of Women in Culture and Society*, 7 no. 2 (1 December): 418–33. https://doi.org/10.1086/493889.

Safa, Helen I. 1995. *The Myth of the Male Breadwinner: Women and Industrialization in the Caribbean*. 1st edition. Boulder, CO: Westview Press.

Scully, Pamela. 2011. "Gender, History, and Human Rights,." In *Gender and Culture at the Limit of Rights*, edited by Dorothy Louise Hodgson, First edition, 17–31. Philadelphia, PA: University of Pennsylvania Press.

Sheller, Mimi. 2014. "Caribbeans in Motion: Transoceanic, Transnational, Tidalectic," Paper presented at the American Historical Association Annual Meeting, Washington, DC.

Singer, Ben. 2001. *Melodrama and Modernity: Early Sensational Cinema and its Contexts*. New York: Columbia University Press.

Snader, Joe. 2000. *Caught Between Worlds: British Captivity Narratives in Fact and Fiction*. Lexington: University of Kentucky Press.

Spivak, Gayatri Chakravorty. 1988. "Can the Subaltern Speak?" In *Marxism and the Interpretation of Culture*, edited by Cary Nelson, Lawrence Grossberg, Henri Lefebvre, Chantal Mouffe, Catharine A. MacKinnon, Etienne Balibar, Gajo Petrovic, Simon Frith, Terry Eagleton, and Jean Franco. Reprint edition. Urbana, IL: University of Illinois Press.

Steele, Bruce. 2007. "Sex for sale," *Out Magazine*, (April): 32.

Strick, S. 2014. *American Dolorologies: Pain, Sentimentalism, Biopolitics*. Albany, NY: State University of New York Press.

Strong, Pauline Turner. 1999. *Captive Selves, Captivating Others: The Politics and Poetics of Colonial American Captivity Narratives*. London: Routledge.

Ticktin, Miriam I. 2011. *Casualties of Care: Immigration and the Politics of Humanitarianism in France*. Berkeley, CA: University of California Press.

United Nations. 1997. "Gender Integration," United Nations Human Rights Office of the High Commissioner. https://www.ohchr.org/EN/Issues/Women/Pages/GenderIntegration.aspx.

Valdespino, J. L., Garcia, M. L., Magis-Rodriguez., C., Salcedo, A., Gonazalez, G., and Sepulveda, J. 1994. "Increase Among Rural Cases in Mexico," International Conference on AIDS. Yokohama, Japan.

Vance, Carole. 2011. "Thinking Trafficking, Thinking Sex," *GLQ*, 17 no. 1: 135–143.

Volkow N.D. and Normand J. 2013. "The international HIV/AIDS pandemic has been closely intertwined with drug abuse and addiction from the time it began. Preface," *Drug Alcohol Dependence*, 132 no. 1 (November): S1. DOI: 10.1016/j.drugalcdep.2013.07.019

Williams, Raymond. *Marxism and Literature*. Oxford: Oxford University Press, 1977.

Williams, Linda. 2001. *Playing the Race Card: Melodramas of Black and White from Uncle Tom to O. J. Simpson*. Princeton, NJ: Princeton University Press.

Willis, Brian, Sara Ann Friedman, and Norene Robert. 2013. "And Boys Too: An ECPAT-USA Discussion Paper about the Lack of Recognition of the Commercial Sexual Exploitation of Boys in the United States." Brooklyn, NY: ECPAT-USA. http://www.zontayakima.org/advocacy/AndBoysToo_TraffickingofBoys.pdf.

Yancy, George and Janine Jones, eds. 2013. *Pursuing Trayvon Martin: Historical Context and Contemporary Manifestations of Racial Dynamics*. Louisville: Rowman and Littlefield.

Yelvington, Kevin. 1995. *Producing Power: Ethnicity, Gender, and Class in a Caribbean Workplace*. Philadelphia, PA: Temple University Press.

4

THE PRODUCTIVE INCOHERENCE OF "SEX TRAFFICKING"

Elizabeth Bernstein, Sealing Cheng,
Sine Plambech, and Mario Pecheny

In the late 1990s and early 2000s, the specter of global sex trafficking swept across the globe, transforming social policy and public discourse at local, national, and transnational levels. Spurred by growing concerns about accelerated cross-border migration, within a short span of time governments and governmental agencies were soon drawing up political commitments to "fighting trafficking" to justify a wide array of agendas: from crackdowns on labor migration to border control and surveillance to the erection of a protective wall on the southern border between the United States (US) and Mexico. Why did the rubric of "sex trafficking" travel so well across national and international borders, despite gathering evidence that this framework was neither descriptive nor ameliorative in terms of the lived experiences of women, men, transgender and gender-nonconforming people who engage in sexual labor?[1] What work has this framework done in different national contexts to shore up specific gender agendas, as well as neoliberal commitments to privatization, incarceration, border control, and surveillance? And how have global legal frames and language interfaced with local debates around gender, sexuality, citizenship, and nationhood in the configuration of state apparatuses of control?

In this chapter, we take up these questions through explorations of the work that the discourse of sex trafficking has accomplished across disparate regional settings. We focus, in particular, upon four differently situated case studies: the US, which, from the 1990s through the early 2000s, played a guiding role in disseminating and enforcing the trafficking framework on a global scale; South Korea, where the state, in conjunction with women's NGOs, launched a well-publicized effort to combat sex trafficking in the new millennium; Nigeria, which succumbed to pressures from the US and the anti-migration policies of the European Union (EU) in order to develop new policies targeting the undocumented migration of Nigerian women into the European sex industry;

DOI: 10.4324/9781003252702-4

110 Bernstein, Cheng, Plambech, and Pecheny

and Argentina, a more recent national context in which anti-trafficking policies have surged both in response to international pressures and *via* an unexpected "post-neoliberal" coalition of feminists, religious actors, and the secular left.

By juxtaposing these cases, which consider the discourse's travels through four continents over the course of two decades, we are able to gain a better sense of the "productive incoherence" that has made trafficking a simultaneously durable and malleable framework for the contemporary governance of sex and gender.[2] Political scientist Ilene Grabel (2015) takes up the concept of "productive incoherence" as a way of shifting understandings of overarching frameworks like the concept of neoliberalism. Productive incoherence can explain, for example, how major global events like the 2008 financial crisis induced change and also allowed major aspects of neoliberalism to continue: "Instead of comprehensive change, the global crisis [of 2008] has induced ambiguous, uneven, modest, and cross-cutting initiatives that reflect continuities and discontinuities" (Grabel 2015, 392).[3] In particular, this chapter is concerned with the ways in which the uneven and cross-cutting initiatives that Grabel identifies as productively incoherent are productive of neoliberalism.

If we connect Grabel's approach to a Gramscian understanding of hegemony, we can see how anti-trafficking discourses contribute to hegemonic social relations, like those of neoliberal political economy. Deploying this perspective, we can see how hegemony is produced through a series of discursive slippages and articulations. Human rights discourse can easily slip into the discourse of social justice, particularly when the critique of capitalism is barred.[4] In matters of global and local governance, trafficking is configured as a human rights issue that is rendered the same as – in other words, slips into – an imagination of gender justice. And, as we reveal in the case studies that follow, it is an issue that can be agreed upon by both evangelical Christians and by secular feminists. Christianity articulates moralism to capitalism, an articulation that is built on the link between Christian and corporate opposition to sex trafficking. Rather than distracting from political economy, sex trafficking discourse articulates a particular idea of political economy: that capitalism is redemptive rather than destructive. Below, we trace these slippages and articulations as they move through different areas of the world and in relation to one other. By following these traces, we endeavor to show how anti-trafficking discourses and the ideas of gender justice which they offer become crucial articulations in the social fabric of neoliberalism.

The combination of consistency and fungibility in the trafficking discourse allows it to be a mechanism by which the incoherence of neoliberalism becomes productive of new formations of gender, sexuality, exclusion, and belonging. It is thus our contention that tracking the contemporary trafficking discourse can provide a critical window into the operations of neoliberal governance more generally, in which neoliberalism is understood, not as a single or coherent set of policies and practices, but rather as a loose concatenation, such that trafficking may in fact do different work in disparate places and times.

The productive incoherence of "sex trafficking"   **111**

The intertwined genealogies of sex trafficking

Conventional genealogies of sex trafficking have narrated the (re)ascendance of this political framework by tracing its progression through a series of United Nations (UN) accords, the US-sponsored Trafficking Victims' Protection Act (TVPA) and its associated *Trafficking in Persons Reports* (TIP), and an ever-expanding series of legislative interventions that have spanned local, national, and transnational contexts.[5] As these analyses suggest, the political origins of trafficking, including the TVPA, have the US at their epicenter, but any unidirectional model of travel is not adequate to explain how this discourse has been taken up in each of our cases.[6] In this essay, we take this body of scholarship as our starting point, while also proceeding to ask a series of additional, critical questions pertaining to the geopolitics of sex and gender, and to the uneven trajectories of neoliberalism across different temporal periods and national contexts. Specifically, we suggest that the travels of trafficking and the asynchronic dissemination of the trafficking discourse can be deciphered in terms of the disparate forms that neoliberalism has taken in different regions, in combination with more "serendipitous," locally relevant factors.

As we describe in more detail below, the multiple genealogies of sex trafficking require unpacking within the different temporal and regional contexts to which they pertain. Previous commentators have observed that sex trafficking discourses have arisen and traveled in times of increasing human movement (especially of women) across domestic and national borders, alongside concerns about the expansion of markets and ensuing social "insecurity," and accompanying anxieties about the transgression of women's sexuality outside of a middle-class imagination of gendered respectability.[7]

We add our four contrasting case studies to this discussion in order to demonstrate the ways in which the discourse of sex trafficking both emerges out of and provides reinforcements for neoliberal social transformations in ways that have not received sufficient attention. As suggested by our analysis of neoliberal vulnerability in Chapter 3, these transformations include shifts from a structural discourse of social justice and liberation to visions of gender justice that are understood primarily in terms of criminal law; new configurations of the relation between national and transnational or global interests; and attempts by national governments to respond to the negative consequences of neoliberal policies in a way that does not fundamentally disrupt neoliberal economic trends. Overall, these cases show the ways in which issues related to gender and sexuality provide tensile strength for neoliberal formations, reinforcing support for stable social hierarchies even as neoliberal policies and practices have been transformative of so many peoples' lives. Importantly, the circulation of the trafficking discourse has been accomplished through a discourse of gender emancipation, one which has facilitated locally specific agendas of neoliberal economic restructuring, border control, and policing in each of the four cases that we consider.

112 Bernstein, Cheng, Plambech, and Pecheny

Across all of our cases, drastic social and economic changes effected by neo-liberal policies and practices have concocted a volatile matrix of class, racial, and gender tensions that are taken to justify an array of further state interventions. Notably, what is core to the grip of most anti-trafficking campaigns is a notion of innocent women (and their sexual victimhood) and dangerous male others.[8] Given this context, we view the emergence of "sex trafficking" in both national and regional histories as a vehicle for instantiating particular sexual and gender regulatory regimes within extensive projects of political and economic control. In this way, the deployment of "sex trafficking" discourse can contribute regulatory force not just toward men and women but also toward transgender and gender non-conforming people.[9] In order to understand the mechanisms by which this discourse proliferates, we bring into consideration not only the role of the state, but also activist networks, private sector initiatives, and the role of mass and social media in shaping "sex trafficking" as a powerful yet malleable concept.

As occurred during the global "white slavery" scare of the late nineteenth and early twentieth centuries, the more recent resurgence of anti-trafficking discourse has proved flexible enough to accomplish multiple goals in different instances, from the expulsion of migrants to the reinstation of particular forms of sexual and gendered morality, from the incarceration of racialized Others to the (paradoxical) redemption of the free market. In the sections that follow, we trace some of these agendas in more detail, exploring how and why the transnational anti-trafficking agenda has been able to circulate so widely and effectively across the globe.

Militarized humanitarianism, carceral feminism, and redemptive capitalism: tracking trafficking's travels within and beyond the US

We begin this analysis with a consideration of the role played by the US in globally disseminating the anti-trafficking framework in the late 1990s and early 2000s. Although the US has been rightly identified by many critics as the key global instigator of contemporary anti-trafficking policies, it is worthwhile to keep in mind that, up until the mid-1990s, most forms of sexual commerce were regulated at state and local, rather than at national and transnational levels. At the time, the specter of sex trafficking was of concern only to small groups of committed feminists and to sex worker activists.[10] By the year 2000, however, local frameworks for regulating sexual commerce would be powerfully challenged by a bevy of anti-trafficking laws and policies that equated all prostitution with the crime of human trafficking and that rhetorically captured both of these activities under the rubric of "modern slavery."[11]

Anti-trafficking laws were pushed forward by a broad array of social activists and policy makers – a coalition spanning from left to right and comprising secular feminists, evangelical Christians, human rights activists of diverse stripes, as

The productive incoherence of "sex trafficking" **113**

well as prominent celebrities and corporate officials. Despite renowned disagreements around the politics of sex and gender, these groups would come together to advocate on behalf of stricter control of prostitution markets domestically, and on behalf of the US's role as "global sheriff" internationally (Chuang 2006). Concretely, these demands took the form of harsher criminal and economic penalties against traffickers, prostitutes' customers, and nations deemed to be taking insufficient steps to stem the flow of trafficked women.[12]

A common explanation for the surge in attention to sex trafficking in the US, despite consistently meager case numbers, has been provided by the theory of "sex panics." Arguing in this vein, many commentators have noted the similarities between the "moral panic" around sex trafficking at the current moment and that which surrounded global campaigns against "white slavery" in the late nineteenth and early twentieth centuries.[13] The heightened presence of US evangelical Christians in disseminating particular visions of sexual freedom and human rights on a global scale, through transnational institutions like the UN, has also been aptly observed (Zimmerman 2013). It is also incontrovertible that evangelical Protestants have played a major role in US policy and politics since at least 1980, as part of a coalition which has advocated staunch conservatism in US foreign and domestic policy on issues of both gender and sexuality. The most frequently cited examples of this conservatism include the repeated US deployment of worldwide restrictions on women's reproductive freedoms, promotion of the male-headed nuclear family as the optimal model for personal life, and the dismantling of government offices and programs that had been dedicated to ending gender discrimination in economic sectors. The dissemination of anti-trafficking campaigns on a global scale can thus be considered part and parcel of this larger project (Bernstein and Jakobsen 2010).

Yet notably, US evangelical engagement with anti-trafficking politics has not diverged from the proclivity displayed by *all* significant political constituencies – including secular liberals, human rights activists, and bipartisan political officials – to remain tightly wedded to the imperatives of neoliberal globalization in forging effective policy remedies. While a focus on "sex panics" suggests a cycle of moral combustion that is destined to be endlessly repeated, present-day attention to trafficking has emerged at the juncture of cultural and political formations that are not only entrenched and self-replicating, but also quite new. Significantly, contemporary evangelical anti-trafficking activists reveal a set of political commitments that both encompasses and transcends prior depictions of conservative Christians' sexual worldviews. The alliance that they have forged with secular feminists has occurred both around a particular relational configuration of gender and sexuality and around a shared commitment to neoliberal economic and cultural agendas. With regard to gender and sexual relations, this alliance invokes a commitment to an ideal of amatively coupled heterosexuality, one that cannot imagine a place for prostitution outside the scope of women's exploitation. And, with regard to neoliberal agendas, the pursuit of "women's human rights," in this shared vision, is imagined in terms of women's (legitimate) reinsertion into market economies, and their protection by state apparatuses of criminal justice.

These approaches have been enforced both domestically and globally, through advocacy of heightened policing of both domestic and global sex markets, strategies that Bernstein (2018) has described in terms of *militarized humanitarianism* and *carceral feminism*. At home and abroad, feminists and evangelicals have teamed up and partnered with the local police to conduct brothel raids and to arrest sex workers, clients, and presumed traffickers alike. They have also engaged in advocacy for the tier-ranking of countries *via* the US Trafficking in Persons Report (based on the extent to which a nation's prostitution markets are successfully curtailed), and through the imposition of ameliorative strategies that seek to redirect sex workers to the formal sectors of service and domestic economies. Relying on digital technologies provided by firms such as Palantir and Google, they have tethered rhetorics of gender emancipation and humanitarian intervention to platforms for online surveillance and algorithmic profit.

In the succinct words of one US anti-trafficking activist who, in 2010, described her organization's successful transformation of Cambodia's Svay Pak (a district formerly known for underage prostitution) into "a nice tourist town," "Our real goal is to bring people out of slavery into the free market" (Bernstein 2018, 19). This view has also been manifest in the growing number of Christian humanitarian organizations globally that orient former prostitutes towards entry-level jobs in the service economy, teaching women to bake muffins for Starbucks and to prepare Western-style drinks and food. Evangelical as well as secular human rights groups have increasingly committed themselves to this approach – rather than framing the problem of human trafficking in terms of broader dynamics of globalization, gendered labor, and migration, it is cast as a humanitarian issue that the criminal justice system and global capitalists, working in tandem, can help combat.

In this regard, these groups followed the lead of Pulitzer prize-winning journalist, Nicholas Kristof, who, as early as 2004, was avidly endorsing the construction of what he openly termed "sweatshops" in the developing world as an antidote to sex trafficking (Kristof 2004). Whereas an earlier wave of anti-globalization activists had argued that the daily practices of capitalism created sweatshop conditions of labor that were unacceptable, "new internationalist" evangelicals, along with their secular champions, have come to identify such practices with the very definition of "freedom."

Within the US anti-trafficking movement, as in other globally directed political projects (including the deployment of microfinance and development policies), the shift to market-based visions of freedom and justice has occurred amongst secular and faith-based, and socially liberal and conservative constituencies alike (see also Karim 2011; Roy 2010). The discourse of sex trafficking is thus woven into a broad pattern in which the extension of the free enterprise system is figured as a gender-progressive quest. Capitalism itself can then be configured as the solution, rather than the source, of gender injustice. We might best

The productive incoherence of "sex trafficking" **115**

term this new configuration *redemptive capitalism*, whereby neoliberal formations are understood to be beneficial and transformative not only of gendered selves, but of gendered worlds. Redemptive capitalism – in which critiques of capitalism are not pushed aside, but rather morally and politically reconfigured – thus points us toward another key reason that the discourse of sex trafficking has been able to travel so widely and well in the neoliberal era.

South Korea: neoliberalizing and democratizing women's human rights

Contrary to the trend of de-democratization that has been consistent with neo-liberalism in the US, neoliberal and democratization reforms took place con-temporaneously in South Korea.[14] Notably, anti-trafficking initiatives provided a site for articulating both nationalist and internationalist discourses within the South Korean context. South Korea faced a conundrum in that the emergence of expanding democratic reforms coincided with both a political appeal to South Korea's international position among other democracies and the economic necessity of accepting a loan from the International Monetary Fund (IMF) with its attendant (transnationally imposed) package of policy constraint. As we will show below, anti-trafficking discourses addressed this conundrum, providing a discursive path by which South Korea might position itself as an emergent liberal democracy and a free market economy, while being morally and cultur-ally distinct as a nation. These tensions allowed for the positioning of the coun-try's 2004 anti-prostitution laws *as* anti-trafficking laws, and the equivalence of women's human rights with the protection of women from prostitution in South Korea (Cheng 2011).

In South Korea, democratization reached a new height with the election of former dissident Kim Dae-Jung as President in 1997, but, in the same year, the country received the largest-ever loan package of $55 billion in the history of the IMF. The new President established the first National Human Rights Commission and the Ministry of Gender Equality, and supported an emerging wave of civic organizations, but the neoliberal reforms and concomitant austerity agenda required by the loan package economically disenfranchised many people and expanded the informal labor economy in the following decade.

One way in which these potentially opposing currents between a new focus on human rights and gender equality and a stratified economic policy could be channeled together was through the adoption of anti-trafficking discourse as the central issue for women's rights. Disparate women's groups found cohesion around the cause of combating prostitution in 2000 – the same year as the adop-tion of the TVPA and the UN Protocol, as well as the deaths of five women in a tragic brothel fire (Choi 2004). As was the case in the US, women in prostitu-tion had not been a key focus of the South Korean women's movement before 2000. Rather, their primary areas of concern were domestic violence, sexual vio-lence, and the family headship system. The merging of international and national concerns around prostitution *as trafficking* catapulted the women's movement into a prominent voice for social reform.

The anti-prostitution/anti-trafficking movement also marked the launch of a collaborative partnership between the women's movement and the South Korean state – a significant departure from the antagonistic relations between civil society and the military dictatorship before the 1990s. The National Solidarity against Prostitution was formed in 2001, and actively deployed transnational activist networks and worked with US abolitionist organizations, such as the Coalition Against Traffic in Women (CATW). The abolitionist approach identified prostitution as inherently a form of violence against women and promoted "women's human rights" within this framework.

After being categorized as a "Tier 3" country in the first U.S. *Trafficking in Persons Report* in 2001, the South Korean state and women activists worked feverishly to introduce the first anti-trafficking laws in 2004 – the Act to Punish Prostitution and Related Acts and the *Act to Protect Victims of Prostitution*. Previously, the laws identified women in prostitution as "fallen women." The new laws introduced labels to recognize women's victimhood in prostitution – now as "prostituted persons" (*seongmaemae-dwean-ja*) or "victims of prostitution" (*seongmaemae-pihae-ja*). Although prostitution has been criminalized in South Korea since the end of Japanese colonialism in 1945, it was only after 2000, with the passing of the UN Protocol and the US Trafficking Victims Protection Act (TVPA), that South Korean women activists adopted the abolitionist language of "sex trafficking" and "prostituted women" to refer to all forms of prostitution (in Korean, "*seongmaemae* [the buying and selling of sex]") and their (presumably female) victims.

The UN Protocol – which clearly specifies that trafficking can also occur in labor sectors other than sex – failed to interrupt the customary and legal conflation of prostitution with trafficking, allowing sex to mark the limits of human trafficking in South Korea. The newly discovered sexual victimhood of sex workers reinscribed the nationalist historiography that highlighted South Korean women as targets of foreign aggression – as in the examples of the "comfort women," and women who served the US military in Korea. Under the auspices of the new laws that claimed to protect women's human rights, the intensive police crackdowns and increased penalties for sex workers, their employers, and their clients have been celebrated by South Korean activists, the South Korean state, and the US State Department as "best practices" in combating trafficking. With abundant government support available, existing women's organizations reconfigured themselves and new ones were founded in a flurry, all with the goal of eliminating "sex trafficking" and protecting innocent victims.

The new laws generated a two-tiered system of women in prostitution – comprised of "authentic victims," who deserve protection, and of "real prostitutes," who deserve punishment. Undergirding this legal distinction of victims and criminals is the construction of Korean womanhood and Korean culture as antithetical to prostitution. Activists and state discourses have been constructing

The productive incoherence of "sex trafficking"   **117**

prostitution as an evil of colonialism and postcolonialism – brought in by the Japanese and the Americans and expanded by globalization. By capitalizing on women's sexual victimhood and its echoes in Korean nationalist historiography, South Korean women activists found a way to render women's human rights compatible with the national interest, compelling state actions to introduce anti-trafficking laws. In the Ministry of Gender Equality promotion of the 2004 laws, it uses the image of the "good daughters of the [South Korean] nation" to call on the prodigal daughters [prostitutes] to help build a country without prostitution. Eradicating prostitution is therefore a project of both restoring "tradition" and enforcing the "modern" – both the female virtues of precolonial Korea and the gender equality of the democratic nation-state.

This method of embodying gender equality by passing laws against sex trafficking did nothing, however, to shift gender-stratification in the economy or to end women's economic precarity. In 2002, 66.9% of women were either day laborers or temporary workers, while the figure for men was between 35 and 41% (Kim and Park 2006, 447), with 70% of women workers being irregular workers in 2004 (Kim and Park 2006, 492). South Korea continued to have the highest gender wage gap, of almost 40%, in OECD countries up to 2016 (OECD 2017). As South Korea's economic growth slowed down over the past decade, the youth unemployment rate has steadily increased, tripling the overall unemployment rate, with the NEET rate (Not in Education, Employment or Training) for ages 20–25 being particularly high at 37.7% amongst low-income youth, compared with 9.5% in high-income groups in 2014 (Noh and Lee 2017). None of these broader questions of gendered socio-economic inequalities appeared in the anti-trafficking campaigns, which nonetheless offered to redeem the nation through women's human rights, freedom, and global stature, and are therefore celebrated as a sign of progress by the state and women's groups.

The new laws did lead to women in prostitution protesting in mass rallies and demanding recognition of their right to live and to work for the first time in South Korea's history. The first sex workers' organization was formed in 2005, and different reiterations of their demands took place in the next decade. These protests, however, have had little effect on the continual expansion of the number of anti-trafficking non-governmental organizations (NGOs) and their partnership with the state to eliminate prostitution as violence against women *par excellence*. The translation of global initiatives to combat human trafficking into South Korea was thus a highly political act rife with feminist pretensions but also highly incoherent: not only was human trafficking conflated with prostitution, in which the figure of the prostitute had come to be a symbol of national suffering, but the refraction of these initiatives through contested "national values" of womanhood, victimhood, and modernity had further silenced claims by sex workers for rights and protection in South Korea.

Through the travels of trafficking and the political reforms that have accompanied this discourse, sex workers have ended up with fewer legal protections and less access to economic power.[15] Yet the incoherence of this policy has been highly productive, creating a distinctly South Korean national identity even as South Korea has been economically subjected to neoliberal austerity policies dictated by transnational institutions like the IMF. *Via* governmental claims to advancing gender justice, this distinctive national identity draws upon specific points in Korea's history and traditions and imagines the South Korean nation as a subject of – not just subjected to – the norms and practices of contemporary global governance.

Sex trafficking, statecraft, and sovereignty in postcolonial Nigeria

The US and South Korean cases illustrate how trafficking discourses form part of broader neoliberal shifts, as well as the extent to which these shifts have been productively incoherent. Thus far, we have followed moves towards heightened policing and toward market-based visions of freedom and justice, along with greater transnational control over emerging markets and the recurrence to long-standing traditions of women needing masculine and governmental protections (even as they face increasingly scarce access to economic resources). The South Korean case further illustrates how human trafficking, when conflated with prostitution, came to stand in for the forms of gendered suffering brought about by colonial and postcolonial political incursions.

In Nigeria, as in the US, faith-based organizations have comprised a significant part of the contemporary anti-trafficking movement. Certainly, the Christian presence in Nigeria and the extent of Christian work on this issue indicate continuities with a longer history of colonial relations. But the Christian influence on trafficking discourse is also indicative of the ways in which neoliberal formations bring new layers of inequality to these long-standing global hierarchies. Likewise, anti-trafficking discourses are, as in South Korea, embedded in broader debates about emerging paradigms of gender and nationhood, particularly, in the Nigerian case, as they pertain to Nigerian women's increasing migration into Europe.

Transnational Christian organizing has contributed to a striking proliferation of faith-based NGOs in Nigeria, working on behalf of a range of issues (Smith 2006). The general proliferation of NGOs in Nigeria is one marker of how neoliberal relations are formed in Nigeria, as potentially public functions move not just into the private sphere of market relations but also into private non-profit organizations that are nonetheless tied to redemptive capitalism. Trafficking's travels to and through Nigeria are enabled by the mushrooming of anti-trafficking NGOs in the southern part of the country, which have become emblematic of how, in a neoliberal era of outsourcing, the Nigerian state privileges NGOs for service provision and as solutions to broader structural challenges of inequality, unemployment, and migration.

What is significant for and unique to Nigeria, when comparing it with the US and South Korean cases, is the pervasiveness of unemployment and poverty.

The productive incoherence of "sex trafficking" **119**

In 2017, the unemployment rate in Nigeria was 25.8% in rural areas (and even higher for women than for men), while 68% of the population lived below the poverty line. The average life expectancy at birth is only 54 years (World Bank 2018). Thus, trafficking discourses in Nigeria cannot be explored outside of conditions of rampant poverty and the reality that Nigerians, and, in recent years, Nigerian women in particular, have migrated to Europe in search of better livelihoods. Nigeria's postcolonial context also means that anti-trafficking interventions and discourses are deeply ingrained in the fabric of nation-building strategies that have arisen since independence.

These developments form the contemporary context for the travels of trafficking to and within Nigeria. Notably, prior to the early 2000s, the Nigerian government did not intervene much in the lives of sex workers or migrant women (Ekpootu 2013). But, in 2003, following a series of deportations of Nigerian female sex workers from Italy, Nigeria's National Agency for the Prohibition of Traffic in Persons and Other Related Matters (NAPTIP) was established.[16] Beginning in the early 2000s, the increase in Nigerian women traveling undocumented to Europe to work in the sex industry spurred anti-migrant sentiment and a range of anti-trafficking initiatives among EU member states and NGOs. In Nigeria, although women's migration into the sex industry is also a matter of domestic concern, contemporary anti-trafficking interventions are primarily a product of concerns among EU and US donors, both governmental and nongovernmental. In particular, Nigeria was (and still is) under intense pressure to combat trafficking as part of pervasive European anxieties about the undocumented migration of Nigerians to Europe. Meanwhile, concerns in Nigeria pertain not only to human rights and to the protection of women migrants; Nigeria has also started to emphasize how the migration of women into the sex industry in Europe is harmful for Nigeria's image abroad (de Haas 2007).

Nigerian state interventions targeting female migrants have included interceptions at the international airports in Lagos and Abuja and along territorial borders of women on their way to Europe, to pre emptively prevent human trafficking. Thus, most of the women sitting at NAPTIP's anti-trafficking shelters have been intercepted at the airport and not deported from Europe, as was the initial purpose of the shelters (Vanderhurst 2013). Up until the 1940s, Nigerian women required the permission of their fathers or husbands to receive passports or travel documents (Aderinto 2012). In twenty-first-century Nigeria, however, women increasingly need the acceptance of the Nigerian state to migrate by air. Although enacted to prevent trafficking in women and girls, the interceptions not only affect women's freedom to travel, but also push them into high-risk migration journeys through the Sahara Desert and across the Mediterranean.

Nigerian women's migration to the sex industry in Europe was initially spurred by the dual dynamics of demand for labor in southern Europe and the adoption of the Structural Adjustment Programme (SAP) in June 1986 in Nigeria.[17] The SAP dictated a shift to reduced government spending on critical services, such as healthcare, education, and housing, which created substantial unemployment within the governmental sector and a greater tendency to migrate. This was particularly true for women, who found few jobs within other sectors, such as the oil industry, and who often chose to migrate after the male family breadwinner lost his job (Plambech 2017). More recently, SAP must also be included within a range of other developments in Nigeria spurring emigration, including falling oil prices and an expanding migration industry facilitating transport to Europe across the Sahara Desert. Nigeria remains the biggest oil exporter in Africa and close to 90% of the country's exports emanate from the oil industry, yet poverty and unemployment continue to be significant (World Bank 2013).

Although the SAP and the general situation in Nigeria of poverty and unemployment have contributed in important ways to the migration flow, women migrants often note that they migrate for a variety of reasons, including their desire for greater autonomy and adventure, divorce, love, and familial expectations (Plambech 2017). These desires mirror broader and widely debated transformations of sexuality and gender roles in postcolonial Nigeria. In this context, the migrant sex worker has emerged as the emblem of a lost, morally worthy past and the imagined disintegration of traditional and conservative family values and gender roles in the present. From this perspective, rescuing Nigerian women migrants from sex work is both about rescuing Nigeria from corruption and collapse and establishing a modern nation-state for the future.

In contemporary anti-trafficking work in Nigeria, myths, past events, and ideas about what womanhood was in precolonial Nigeria, what it is now, and what it should be in the future are directly and indirectly drawn into the debate. Ideas of a more coherent and purer past, where women's morality was not depraved, spur pleas for morally decent female behavior. For instance, one of the anti-trafficking NGOs in Benin City in southern Nigeria, funded by European donors, carries the name Idia Renaissance after Queen Idia, a sixteenth-century Benin Kingdom Queen Mother, who is taken to serve as a model for all that was "dignifying to womanhood" (Adesina 2005, 2). Idia Renaissance describes how their anti-trafficking work is meant to bring about a renaissance in "true womanhood." Thus, the invocation of the Queen Mother's name and an idealized past lend rhetorical power to complaints about contemporary women's behavior, migration, and sex work.

Normative prescriptions for women's lives and livelihoods are, thus, embedded in nationalist discourse as they circulate within the Nigerian context. As the Nigerian historian Uyilawa Usuanlele argues: "The social crusade against international export of teenage girls into prostitution and sex slavery ... is [deemed] a worthy and noble cause that should be supported and fought with all our might ... it is a battle for survival and national rebirth" (Usuanlele 1999, 5).

The focus on history, purity, and morality – what the anthropologist Daniel Jordan Smith terms the *domestication of religious morality* in Nigeria – diverts attention from the Nigerian state and the structures that produce poverty and inequality (Smith 2006, 217). Yet Nigerian anti-trafficking NGOs are not merely propounding ideals of women's purity because they are moralistic as such; rather, the organizations most often do not trust the Nigerian state apparatus. Nor

The productive incoherence of "sex trafficking"   **121**

are they uncritically nationalistic; rather, they also invoke a language of faith, morality, and modesty because they have very few resources to offer migrant sex workers in terms of employment. By framing sex work migration as predominantly a moral problem, they hope that this might steer the women away from sex work and migration, even in the absence of promising labor market alternatives.

This background is important if we want to understand why current anti-trafficking policies have traveled so well in Nigeria, as well as the multiple purposes they serve. Beginning in the 1990s, NGOs, and anti-trafficking NGOs in particular, would become among the fastest-growing industries in Nigeria (Adunbi 2016). The mushrooming of anti-trafficking NGOs serves as a prism to illustrate the ambiguous and complex role of neoliberalism in postcolonial Nigeria, where some state functions and social programs were built, some were never formed, and others have been decimated or outsourced. At the same time as state structures have been depleted, rich international funding streams have made it possible to establish an abundance of NGOs. Thus, the culture and practices of anti-trafficking NGOs are illustrative of how neoliberalism has decimated the Nigerian state in ways that outsource public functions to the burgeoning NGO sector, funded by transnational organizations such as the Ford Foundation, The Global Fund, and the EU (Ibid).

The travels of trafficking to Nigeria demonstrate the intertwining of moral discourses that are grounded in both nationalist sentiment and historical traditions: the effects of transnational political–economic trends (including both the fall in oil prices and the actions of institutions like the IMF), transnational funding streams that circuit through private foundations, and state institutions that have been repeatedly undercut by neoliberal privatization. Anti-trafficking discourse has served to support these trends in myriad ways, for example, by providing political legitimacy to the outsourcing of state responsibilities and thus contributing to the neoliberal NGO-ification of state functions. Anti-trafficking discourses also recast the inability of many Nigerians to make a living as a question of individual responsibility and moral behavior rather than one of political economy and social policy. Anti-trafficking discourses provide a gendered language through which to call upon Nigerians to support nationalism through their intimate behavior and moral commitments rather than through, for example, political participation. In this way, when anti-trafficking organizations import and then disseminate the increasingly hegemonic human rights-based language of anti-trafficking, they in fact contribute to making the state less responsive to the needs of Nigerians – and the needs of female Nigerians, in particular.

Sex trafficking discourse in "post-neoliberal" (and post-transitional) Argentina

If the US, South Korean, and Nigerian cases together illustrate the disparate ways in which trafficking discourses contribute to neoliberal political formations, the Argentinian case at first glance appears to represent the opposite. In Argentina, anti-trafficking policies emerged in the early 2000s as part of a broader agenda of transitional justice and "reparations" for previous decades' human rights violations, and as an apparent corrective to neoliberal structural adjustment paradigms. The 1990s represented a period of state retrenchment and a decline in formal sector employment, with the consequent growth of social and economic precarity and the proliferation of informal subsistence practices, some of which bordered on illegality (such as sex work and the drug trade). The conjunction of economic crisis, brutal and sudden unemployment, and the devaluation of currency resulted in state and activist commitments to respond to the effects of structural adjustment through various kinds of social interventions. The years that followed the neoliberal period were characterized by the ascent of center-left, populist administrations which propounded a new social justice discourse, including a discourse of gender justice and sexual rights. Thus, it is within the context of purportedly progressive politics that the issue of sex trafficking in Argentina was first articulated and disseminated. However, as we shall describe in more detail below, the emergence of these policies as a "corrective" to neoliberalism was more complicated and contradictory than it at first appeared, as other policies supporting neoliberal economic agendas, globalization, and capital accumulation were allowed to remain unchanged.

This combination – new commitments to social justice discourse and the continuation of neoliberal economic policies – produced an incoherence that anti-trafficking discourses could make productive. Understandings of human rights and social justice as allied, similar, or even synonymous projects can make human rights-based anti-trafficking campaigns amenable to claims for social justice, even as anti-trafficking discourses facilitate neoliberal responses to injustice. As a result, anti-trafficking discourses can also suture efforts to address injustice into existing neoliberal frameworks. If human rights are sufficient for social justice, and anti-trafficking is part of human rights, then these discourses can hold together to provide the links needed to pin back other claims to justice that might be made in response to the deleterious effects of neoliberalism.

During the first decades of the twentieth century, the "white slave traffic" had also been an issue in Buenos Aires, in the context of massive male migration, anti-anarchist and anti-unionist policies, and hygienist (anti-homosexual) prevailing discourses. Since that time, prostitution has not been criminalized as such, even though local regulations have allowed for police harassment and persecution. AMMAR, the main organization of female sex workers in Argentina, was created in 1994, claiming labor rights for sex workers; in 1995, AMMAR joined the Argentine Workers Central Union (CTA). Anti-prostitution discourses have only appeared more recently, in the context of contemporary anti-trafficking campaigns, beginning in the early 2000s.

It is also significant that anti-trafficking policies arose in Argentina in 2001 within the context of a political and economic crisis. At the time, a widespread and devastating economic crisis resulted in increasing rates of unemployment, gender-based violence, and burgeoning informal economic sectors,

The productive incoherence of "sex trafficking" **123**

including sex work. As a result of the crisis, President de la Rúa was forced to resign, a provisional president was designated, and elections were held in 2003, when Néstor Kirchner, a center-left populist leader, was elected President. It was under Kirchner's presidency, during a "recovery period" after the financial crisis, when the anti-trafficking discourse first entered the country, becoming part of a broader human rights and "post-neoliberal gender justice" agenda, both as a counter to neoliberalism and, paradoxically, also to reinforce it.

Beginning in the 1980s, the installation of political democracy, a progressive agenda on reproductive, gender, and sexual rights, and the language of human rights and democratization all expanded in Argentina. Since the 1990s, neoliberal reforms have led to unemployment, precarity, and social fragmentation; in this context, women's labor market access has been more and more limited to the informal sector, including domestic labor and extra-legal survival economies, such as petty drug dealing and in particular sex work. In the 2000s, following the political and economic crisis, a decade of "post-neoliberal" governments implemented policies to alleviate the social consequences of the previous decades' neoliberal reforms. In terms of gender, this period included advances in liberal reforms related to sex and gender (e.g., gay marriage and transgender rights), but also a construction of female sexual subjects mostly as victims. This approach crystallized in two of the most important current issues within the gender and democratization agenda: violence against women and anti-trafficking policies. Both were framed as cornerstone issues of progressive policies and as being integrally related to structural gender inequalities.

These issues aimed at repairing historical and structural aspects of gender injustice without questioning a discourse that placed women (and other feminine subjects) as victims, and without questioning the ways that capitalism and the labor market determined the boundaries of social and gender relations. As a post-neoliberal project, anti-trafficking campaigns in Argentina tried to respond to the gender-negative consequences of patriarchal neoliberalism, but without initiating transformations in capitalism that would modify the very conditions of the emergence and reproduction of unequal gendered relations. The precarity created by neoliberalism slipped into a discourse of victimization and was articulated with the expansion of survival economies. Extra-legal economic endeavors that helped people survive the vagaries of neoliberalism could now be configured as the problem of neoliberalism, so that opposing sex work as victimization – i.e., taking up anti-trafficking campaigns – came to be seen as a way of opposing neoliberalism, even as these campaigns were aligned with market solutions to neoliberal problems.

This ambivalence might help to explain why radical feminists and social justice advocates, as well as conservative and neoliberal leaders, embraced campaigns against gender-based violence and the fight against sex trafficking and prostitution. By the same token, within a democratic culture that no longer accepted misogynist discourses and authoritarian regulations of sexuality, these victim-based discourses about gender democratization reinstated particular

124 Bernstein, Cheng, Plambech, and Pecheny

forms of sexual and gendered morality: in a context of (neo- and post-neo-) liberal values and discourses about autonomy, only "feminist-framed protections" could be accepted as legitimate. Notably, in 2015, a new neoliberal right-wing government did not have any trouble incorporating the anti-trafficking policies of the previous post-neoliberal administrations into its own governing regime.

As in the South Korean and Nigerian cases, US and global pressures are part of explaining the adoption of anti-trafficking policies in Argentina, but local dynamics and framing processes explain the shape and content that they have assumed. Local actors and discourses framed the issue of trafficking as a women's rights issue, in which any woman involved in sex work was considered *a priori* a victim of trafficking. Thus, "sex trafficking" in Argentina, in contrast to places such as Nigeria, has not meant crossing national borders, but rather all forms of sex work that might or might not include displacement. Displacement, when it occurs in Argentina, is mainly imagined as the movement from one province to another and is not seen as a transnational issue.[18]

Anti-trafficking laws were initially discussed and voted upon following a trial with high impact (the disappearance and probable murder of a young woman, Marita Verón, at the hands of traffickers), as well as the struggle of her mother, Susana Trimarco. This trial made the issue of trafficking publicly visible for the first time. A popular soap opera even told the story on TV.[19] But this case is clearly not a sufficient explanation for the "success" of the anti-trafficking discourse. Thus, in addition to the crucial context of "post-neoliberal" reforms mentioned above, two additional factors explain why this case did not remain at the social or cultural level, and why it came to trigger significant political responses: first, an active governmental policy of reparation, in the context of post-transitional justice; second, the US and global exportation of the anti-trafficking discourse and the constitution of an anti-trafficking or anti-sex work social movement (Varela 2013; 2014).

In 2003, the Ministry of Justice launched a program to examine some key "unsolved" criminal cases, meeting with relatives and families of the victims. In this context, Susana Trimarco met with state authorities, including the President, and got resources to investigate the disappearance of her daughter in the context of a wider investigation of prostitution networks. The unsolved case of Marita Verón became a "leading case" (*caso testigo*) and an example of impunity, reminding the public of the disappearances during state terrorism in the 1970s.

Before 2005, sex work (which was not illegal in Argentina) and sex trafficking were still considered separate issues. This situation changed when a global anti-sex trafficking discourse entered the country. Since 2004, the International Organization for Migration (IOM), supported by the US government, installed the theme of trafficking in the political agenda, organized workshops to sensitize and train officials and NGOs, and launched programs to assist "victims of trafficking." Between 2004 and 2007, through US pressure and the dissemination of *Trafficking in Persons Reports* increasingly critical of the Argentine government (urging Argentina to adopt penal measures), the country progressively adjusted

The productive incoherence of "sex trafficking" **125**

its approach to those anti-trafficking policies promoted by the US, for example, through a public campaign against "modern slavery" and the discussion of a criminal law. As in other global regions, an active field of anti-trafficking NGOs emerged, in part supported by transnational funds. Most of those "abolitionist" NGOs had not focused on sex work or trafficking before but converted their goals to adopt a radical anti-sex work/anti-trafficking perspective.

In fact, local dynamics and global (or US) actions served to reinforce one another. To consider just one example: On 8 March 2007, the US Department of State honored Susana Trimarco, Marita's mother, with the International Women of Courage Award, conferred by then-Secretary of State Condoleezza Rice. In April 2007, on the fifth anniversary of Marita Verón's disappearance, Casa del Encuentro, a feminist NGO with no previous experience working on trafficking issues, organized a demonstration at the national Congress, with the following claim: "Disappeared women: we want them back alive! Punish the responsible!" ("*aparición con vida de las mujeres desaparecidas en democracia y castigo a los responsables*"). With this event, the anti-trafficking discourse was successfully inscribed in the national commitment to historical memory and justice. In summary, both external and internal political pressures contributed to an emerging and powerful social movement against sex trafficking, one that has been unmatched in scale or intensity in other Latin American countries. The local movement of sex worker activists was not strong enough to nuance this framing.

Beginning in 2007, multiple anti-trafficking organizations were formed, and several prominent campaigns were launched against "prostitution networks" and sex trafficking. Some have been critical of the UN Protocol, which differentiates between forced and free forms of sex work, and of the very notion of "consent" within sexual labor. Since that time, the crime of trafficking has been defined as "the offer, recruitment, transport, receipt, or hosting of persons for the purpose of exploitation, within the national territory, and from or to other countries," with the distinction between adults and minors being suppressed.[20] All those who came to the country as migrants, or who become involved in the sex market through an arrangement with a third party – regardless of the existence of violence, threats, or coercion – are considered victims of trafficking or sexual exploitation, and become both the object of policies of "rescue" and of "social reintegration." Helpers within the migration processes, who often come from close networks of acquaintances and relatives, can be considered "traffickers" regardless of the positive self-assessment that people make of their migration project and participation in the sex market. Anyone who facilitates the practice of prostitution of another person can be considered a perpetrator who is guilty of the "promotion" of prostitution. The only instance of sexual services that remain outside the trafficking frame are cases of prostitution in which no third party obtains any economic benefit. In addition, a set of legal regulations and bureaucracies was established in order to monitor and prosecute commercial sex under the categories of "human trafficking" and "rescuing" its victims (including the closing of whiskey bars and cabarets, the prohibition of ads, police entry

126 Bernstein, Cheng, Plambech, and Pecheny

into private homes, etc.). The campaign has thus changed dramatically from its original purpose – fighting trafficking and sexual exploitation – and has become increasingly oriented towards the elimination of commercial sex in all its forms.

The vernacularization of a discourse

Our discussion of trafficking and its travels is a way to examine not only how the language of trafficking and its attendant ideas of protection and punishment, human rights, and gender justice become vernacularized in different national contexts, but also when such translation and integration processes become possible and desirable. We have demonstrated in this chapter that global anti-trafficking initiatives, initially spurred by the US and Europe, are translated into locally resonant discourses of gender and "modern" nationhood in unique ways in post-colonial South Korea and Nigeria, and in the post-transitional Argentinian context. At the same time, the common focus on prostitution in anti-trafficking efforts has led to a revival of ideal images of womanhood as a symbol of authentic national values, asserted in defense of nationalist cultures and traditions, including through the new *lingua franca* of human rights. Meanwhile, the universal values and paradigms proclaimed in anti-trafficking discourses – for example *via* the UN Protocol and the US TVPA, which mandates the publication of the *Trafficking in Persons Report* – serve to motivate local efforts by states and activists alike to gain and retain membership in a new world order that is characterized by neoliberal imperatives.

We have also shown how the discourse of trafficking is materially supported by the international power of the US, by transnational institutions that enforce neoliberalism, and by culturally and historically specific articulations in different sites through the evocation of local memories, common values, and national identities. As we have seen, even a "local" emphasis on common values, history, and language, as well as the discourses' integration into common public institutions, may create barriers, burdens, or disadvantages to those who are already politically and economically disempowered.[21]

While women working in prostitution and sex trafficking victims serve as proof of the moral downfall of the nation and of the failure of the state, different images of gender justice are offered up as promises of the nation-state's future. This is particularly the case in countries which have a long history of struggles with colonial and imperial forces, and/or authoritarian regimes: Queen Idia in Nigeria and the good South Korean daughters play the common role of evoking a morally pure, socially just, and nationally authentic past. In Argentina and in the US, gender justice is instead imagined through the present and future redemption of the disappeared women of the dictatorship, or, in the US case, *via* the proliferation of "access to" or "entry into" the freedom of the market, even when global sweatshops provide the portal of entry.

The language of "women's human rights" has become part and parcel of anti-trafficking discourses that focus on prostitution. The globalization of universal

The productive incoherence of "sex trafficking"   **127**

rights and international laws interface with local ideas and national values to provide not only competing claims about norms and ethical practices, but also gendered ideas of personhood and nationhood. Within the transnational and national debates about what kind of interventions and policies are compatible with women's human rights, we note particularly that the state, middle-class activists, and the subjects of these rights' interventions may disagree as to what constitutes the violation as well as the protection of these rights, whether or not patriarchy is the main culprit, and what to do about it (Cheng 2011, 479). Nevertheless, sex workers continue to be criminalized, exposing the restrictive scope of "women's human rights" as it has been translated through anti-trafficking campaigns. In each of the cases under consideration, "women's human rights" on the one hand challenges the state and propels forward reforms, but on the other hand also bolsters state projects of nation building, constituting what Cheng has called the "paradox of vernacularization" (Cheng 2011). We therefore observe a gendered geopolitical paradox in these new anti-trafficking measures: while they reinscribe women's mobility and sexuality outside of the domestic sphere as inherently out of bounds and therefore dangerous, they also celebrate efforts to combat trafficking as liberatory, modern, and enlightened.

In turn, the coupling of sexual victimhood with "women's human rights" creates a narrowly circumscribed vision of women as sexual subjects. The US's TVPA and the Swedish *Sex Purchase Act*, as well as the activist groups that helped to implement them, have been crucial in blurring the distinction between prostitution and sex trafficking, to such an extent that in much of popular discourse they have now become indistinguishable. Thus, the new trafficking law in Argentina that considered any mediated acts of prostitution to be trafficking eliminated prior distinctions between adults and minors and rendered irrelevant issues of consent. Similarly, the Nigerian and South Korean anti-trafficking laws targeted prostitution and categorized women as either "victims of trafficking" or, in the case of those who work and migrate independently, as criminals who deserve to be punished. These have not prevented the states from proclaiming that such legal reforms are effective means to combat trafficking, to protect women, and to assert national sovereignty. In each of these cases, women's mobility, sexuality, and the situations labeled as trafficking continue to be perceived as threats to national ideals of reproduction, respectability, and morality (Aderinto 2012a), and thus antithetical to the goals of gendered progress, rights, and freedom.

We have also considered the temporality of how trafficking and its discourses become possible and desirable in different contexts. Most crucially, these anti-trafficking reforms should be seen as both a response to and an expression of neoliberalism. The UN Protocol adopted in 2000 was the culmination of a range of concerns about migrants' rights, prostitution, and border control that took shape in relation to the increase in mobile populations – particularly with the "feminization of migration" in the late 1990s, when statistics showed that women had become the majority of migrants. At the same time, neoliberal reforms in different sites have exacerbated social and economic inequalities, displacing and disenfranchising significant populations. This was accompanied by an expansion of humanitarian initiatives and funding to "save the poor" – clearly evident in the growth of both local and transnational anti-trafficking NGOs in South Korea, Nigeria, and Argentina. In times of economic and cultural flux such as ours, sex work has become an easy and frequent target of campaigns for state regulation and contemporary conflicts around intimate relations (Aderinto 2012b).

The late twentieth and early twenty-first centuries' "traffic in women" has been accompanied by a global traffic in feminism, and by a circulation of both old and new forms of sexual politics. Situated at the nexus of sex, morality, humanitarianism, and political economy, contemporary anti-trafficking campaigns provide a useful lens on the ongoing social transformations that are reshaping each of these domains. Although the contemporary rubric of "fighting trafficking" has done little to protect most sex workers or others laboring under exploitative conditions,[22] it has been highly effective as an ideological constellation that can travel widely and well, brokering alliances amongst otherwise disparate social groups – not despite but rather *because* of its ultimate incoherence as a discourse of social suffering.

Given the efficacy and breadth of the travels of "trafficking," the more salient question may not be why and how such discursive regimes succeed but if and when they ever falter. Because history suggests that existing discursive formations of power can quickly unravel and reconfigure, we end by considering the potential for a different vision of gender justice to emerge in the context of the broad and sweeping political transformations that have arisen in the second decade of the twenty-first century – with the rise of new populisms, authoritarian regimes, the 2020 coronavirus pandemic, and what some have described as a new crisis of neoliberal authority, particularly in the US and Europe. It can certainly be argued that, with migration stalled and sex markets curtailed under current pandemic conditions, the issue has diminished in prominence (while fears of viral contagion have closed borders entirely, and other biopolitical concerns have surged to the fore).[23] At the same time, we can observe that the discourse of sex trafficking has continued to reinvent itself and to shapeshift in accordance with new political interests, including those associated with ethno-nationalist variants of neoliberalism and virtually circulating far-right conspiracies.[24] We would argue that it is precisely this waxing, waning, and redirecting of attention that points to the broader cultural and political work that the discourse of "trafficking" has accomplished since its inception – securing geographic borders, sexual boundaries, and particular visions of gendered progress and freedom – rather than the lives of sex workers themselves.

Notes

1 Sex worker rights activists have objected to the prevailing rubric of "sex trafficking" because it enforces a politically contested distinction between sexual and non-sexual forms of labor.

The productive incoherence of "sex trafficking" **129**

2 On the "productive incoherence" of contemporary cultural formations around gender and sexuality, see Sedgwick (1993, xii) and Duggan (2003,14).
3 For Grabel, evidence for productive incoherence can be found by carefully tracing responses to major global events, such as the Asian financial crisis of the late 1990s and the global financial crisis of 2008. Grabel sees in the uneven responses to the global financial crisis the possibility for productive change toward "democratic, ethically viable development institutions" (2015, 388). Thus, for Grabel, the sense of a "productive" incoherence has a positive ethical valence. Our use of the term understands that what is "produced" by the type of incoherent initiatives that Grabel describes may well not carry the positive ethical valence she asserts. In other words, incoherence may be as likely to produce unequal hegemony as it is to lead to democratic development. For example, the idea of "development" may itself be part of the infrastructure for hegemonic inequality (Grabel 2015, 392).
4 See also Moyn (2012).
5 See, e.g., Kempadoo (2005); Doezema (2010); Hua (2011); and Chuang (2006).
6 With the Swedish Sex Purchase Act introduced in 1999, a legal decision to criminalize only the act of the sex buyer, not the selling of sex, the epicenter expanded to include Sweden, as well as other Scandinavian countries who shortly therafter adopted the "Swedish Plan." The Swedish government, in tandem with international abolitionist organizations, has made great efforts to export the law and to influence debates about prostitution and sex trafficking internationally (despite its initial focus on prostitution, The Swedish Sex Purchase Act is commonly framed as a measure to combat trafficking). See Bernstein (2007) and Skilbrei and Homström (2016). After the US election of President Trump in 2016 and his retreat from international human rights agendas, the US relinquished some of its role as the global enforcer of anti-trafficking interventions.
7 See, e.g., Kempadoo (2005); Sharma (2005); Davidson (2015); Zimmerman (2013); and Cheng (2011).
8 For critiques of the heterosexual imagery in contemporary anti-trafficking campaigns, see Kaye (2018) and Mai (2012).
9 Notably, the types of claims made in "sex trafficking" discourse about dangerous men and female victims have reappeared in trans-exclusionary discourses in which transwomen are depicted as "men" who are a danger to "women," particularly in public spaces like restrooms and changing rooms. It is also significant that some of the same political formations, such as an alliance between certain feminist activists and Christian evangelicals, provide the infrastructure for both "sex trafficking" discourses and anti-trans claims. See, e.g. LaFleur and Bassi (2022).
10 See e.g., Barry (1995).
11 See, for example, the US 2013 *Trafficking in Persons Report*, in which then-President Obama declared that "the injustice, the outrage, of human trafficking … must be called by its true name – modern slavery" (US Department of State 2013, 7).
12 At the federal level, see the Trafficking Victims Protection Act (United States Department of State 2000) and its successive reauthorizations. At the transnational level, see the UN Protocol to Prevent, Suppress and Punish Trafficking in Persons, Especially Women and Children, Supplementing the United Nations Convention against Transnational Organized Crime (United Nations General Assembly 2000).
13 See, e.g., Doezema (2010); Vance (2012); and Rubin (2011).
14 See also Brown (2006).
15 See also Cheng (2011).
16 NAPTIP (2003), Nwogu (2005). NAPTIP's terms of reference can be classified into two types of intervention: those that aim to prevent trafficking from occurring (public education and awareness) and those that protect and assist people who have already been trafficked (provision of shelter, rehabilitation, skills acquisition, family tracing, provision of scholarships and health care, legal aid, reintegration, counseling, and financial assistance).
17 Afolayan, Ikwuyatum, and Abedjide (2008); Attoh (2009).

18 In relation to migration and sex migration, Argentina is thus different from the Nigerian or the South Korean cases. In terms of national policy, migration is framed as a human rights issue. A progressive law on migration, voted on in 2010, included a right to migration defined as an "essential and inalienable" human right, based on "the principles of equality and universality." Between 2015 and 2019, anti-migrant rhetoric was deployed by the right-wing government, but the legislation on migration remained unchanged. In 2019, a new center-left administration came to power, with a more moderate discourse on migration and an explicit legitimation of migration through human rights discourse. It is within this context that policies against trafficking, including sex trafficking, have been implemented.

19 Varela (2013); Varela and Daich (2014).

20 In 2008, the Argentinian Congress passed a law on "Prevention and sanction of trafficking in persons and assistance to victims." (*"Prevención y sanción de la trata de personas y asistencia a sus víctimas."*) The law nonetheless distinguished between "forced" and "free" prostitution, accepted the possibility that an adult could voluntarily migrate in order to work in the sex trade, and did not criminalize those who promote or facilitate migration in those cases. In line with discussions taking place at the transnational and supranational levels, the distinction between "free" and "forced" prostitution, and the issue of the "impossible consent to slavery," have become controversial subjects for local anti-trafficking organizations. In 2012, the law was reformed to align more directly with the argument offered by these activists.

21 In his discussion of the nation as an imagined community, Benedict Anderson (1991) first raised the importance of vernacular language and nationalism in refracting "world events" into a specific imagined world of vernacular readers. Our cases demonstrate some uncanny parallels in the conservative gender projects that anti-trafficking discourses have facilitated, as well as the specific, political–economic dynamics in which they have taken shape.

22 For example, in the US alone, to date only a scant number of T-visas have been issued relative to the government's estimated prevalence of sex trafficking, despite the fact that this was supposed to be one of the major resources offered to help victims. For empirical accounts of the failure of contemporary anti-trafficking policies to assist sex workers, including those laboring under exploitative conditions, see also Bernstein (2018); Cheng (2011); and Plambech (2017).

23 See, e.g. Slater, Fahim, and McQue (2020); Favell and Recchi (2020).

24 See Bernstein (2018); Chávez (2020).

References

Aderinto, Saheed. 2012. "Sex Across the Border: Researching Transnational Prostitution in Colonial Nigeria." In *The Third Wave of Historical Scholarship on Nigeria: Essays in Honor of Ayodeji Olukoju*, edited by Ayodeji Olukoju, Saheed Aderinto, and Paul Osifodunrin, 76–94. Newcastle: Cambridge Scholars Publishing.

Adesina, O. A. 2005. "Between Culture and Poverty: The Queen Mother Phenomenon and the Edo International Sex Trade," *Humanities Review Journal* 5, no. 1 (1 January): 28–46. https://doi.org/10.4314/hrj.v5i1.5959.

Adunbi, Omolade. 2016. "Embodying the Modern: Neoliberalism, NGOs, and the Culture of Human Rights Practices in Nigeria," *Anthropological Quarterly* 89, no. 2 (21 July): 431–64. https://doi.org/10.1353/anq.2016.0031.

Afolayan, Adejumoke, Godwin Ikwuyatum, and Olumuyiwa Abedjide. 2008. "Country Paper: Dynamics of International Migration in Nigeria," Ibadan, Nigeria: University of Ibadan, Department of Geography. https://www.imi.ox.ac.uk/files/completed-projects/nigeria-country-paper.pdf.

Anderson, Benedict. 1991. *Imagined Communities: Reflections on the Origin and Spread of Nationalism*. Revised edition. London, New York: Verso Books.

Attoh, Franca. 2009. "Trafficking in Women in Nigeria: Poverty of Values or Inequality?" *Journal of Social Sciences* 19, no. 3 (1 June): 167–71. https://doi.org/10.1080/09718923.2009.11892705.

Barry, Kathleen L. 1995. *The Prostitution of Sexuality*. New York: NYU Press.

Bernstein, Elizabeth. 2007. *Temporarily Yours: Intimacy, Authenticity, and the Commerce of Sex*. 1st edition. Chicago, IL: University of Chicago Press.

Bernstein, Elizabeth. 2018. *Brokered Subjects: Sex, Trafficking, and the Politics of Freedom*. Chicago, IL: University of Chicago Press.

Bernstein, Elizabeth, and Janet Jakobsen. 2010. "Sex, Secularism and Religious Influence in US Politics," *Third World Quarterly* 31, no. 6: 1023–39. http://www.jstor.org/stable/27896595.

Brown, Wendy. 2006. "American Nightmare: Neoliberalism, Neoconservatism, and De-Democratization," *Political Theory* 34, no. 6: 690–714. http://www.jstor.org/stable/20452506.

Chávez, Aída. 2020. "How QAnon Conspiracy Theories Spread in My Colorado Hometown," The Intercept. https://theintercept.com/2020/09/23/qanon-conspiracy-theory-colorado/.

Cheng, Sealing. 2011. "The Paradox of Vernacularization: Women's Human Rights and the Gendering of Nationhood," *Anthropological Quarterly* 84, no. 2: 475–505. http://www.jstor.org/stable/41237502.

Choi, Jae-hyuk. 2004. "Gov't Responsible for Victims of 2000 Gunsan Brothel Fire," *The Choson Isbo*, 23 September. http://english.chosun.com/site/data/html_dir/2004/09/23/2004092361028.html.

Chuang, Janie. 2006. "The United States as Global Sheriff: Using Unilateral Sanctions to Combat Human Trafficking," *Michigan Journal of International Law; Ann Arbor* 27, no. 2 (437–94) http://search.proquest.com/docview/208562020/abstract/D67CB48C323B48CBPQ/1.

Davidson, Julia O'Connell. 2015. *Modern Slavery: The Margins of Freedom*. First edition, 2015 edition. London: Palgrave Macmillan.

de Haas, Hein. 2007. "International Migration, National Development and the Role of Governments: The Case of Nigeria," in *International Migration and National Development in Subsaharan Africa: Viewpoints and Policy Initiatives in the Country of Origin*. Leiden: Brill Publishers.

Doezema, Jo. 20120. *Sex Slaves and Discourse Masters: The Construction of Trafficking*. London: Zed Books, 2010.

Duggan, Lisa. 2003. *The Twilight of Equality?: Neoliberalism, Cultural Politics, and the Attack on Democracy*. Boston, MA: Beacon Press.

Ekpootu, Mfon Umoren. 2013. "Interrogating Policies on Human Trafficking in Nigeria," in *The Power of Gender, the Gender of Power: Women's Labor, Rights and Responsibilities in Africa*, edited by Toyin Falola and Bridget Teboh, 543–558. Trenton: Africa World Press.

Favell, Adrian and Ettore Recchi. 2020. "Mobilities, Neo-nationalism and the Lockdown of Europe: Will the European Union Survive?" *COMPAS Coronavirus and Mobility Forum*. https://www.compas.ox.ac.uk/2020/mobilities-and-the-lockdown-of-europe-will-the-european-union-survive/.

Grabel, Ilene. 2015. "Post-Crisis Experiments in Development Finance Architectures: A Hirschmanian Perspective on 'Productive Incoherence'," *Review of Social Economy* 73, no.4: 388–414. https://doi.org/10.1080/00346764.2015.1089111.

Hua, Julietta. 2011. *Trafficking Women's Human Rights*. First edition. Minneapolis, MN: University of Minnesota Press.

Karim, Lamia. 2011. *Microfinance and Its Discontents: Women in Debt in Bangladesh*. Minneapolis, MN: University of Minnesota Press.

Kaye, Kerwin. 2018. "The Gender of Trafficking, Or, Why Can't Men Be Sex Slaves?" In *Understanding Sex for Sale*, edited by May-Len Skilbrei and Marlene Spanger, 180–198. London: Routledge. https://doi.org/10.4324/9781315107172.

Kempadoo, Kamala. 2005. "From Moral Panic to Global Justice: Changing Perspectives on Trafficking," in *Trafficking and Prostitution Reconsidered: New Perspectives on Migration, Sex Work, and Human Rights*, edited by Kamala Kempadoo, Jyoti Sanghera, and Bandana Pattanaik, Second edition, 249–261. Boulder, CO: Paradigm.

Kim, Andrew Eungi, and Innwon Park. 2006. "Changing Trends of Work in South Korea: The Rapid Growth of Underemployment and Job Insecurity," *Asian Survey* 46, no.3: 437–456. https://doi.org/10.1525/as.2006.46.3.437.

Kristof, Nicholas D. 2004. "Inviting All Democrats," *The New York Times*, January 14, sec. Opinion. https://www.nytimes.com/2004/01/14/opinion/inviting-all-democrats.html.

LaFleur, Greta and Serena Bassi. 2022. "Trans-exclusionary Feminisms and the New Right," *TSQ: Transgender Studies Quarterly*. 9: 3.

Mai, Nick. 2012. "The Fractal Queerness of Non-Heteronormative Migrants Working in the UK Sex Industry," *Sexualities* 15, no.5–6 (1 September): 570–585. https://doi.org/10.1177/1363460712445981.

Moyn, Samuel. 2012. *The Last Utopia: Human Rights in History*. Cambridge: Belknap Press of Harvard University Press.

Nigeria: Act No. 24 of 2003, Trafficking in Persons (Prohibitions) Law Enforcement and Administration Act [Nigeria], Cap T23 LFN 2004, 14 July 2003, available at: https://www.refworld.org/docid/54f989d24.html.

Noh, Hyejin and Bong Joo Lee. 2017. "Risk factors of NEET (Not in Employment, Education or Training) in South Korea: an empirical study using panel data," *Asia Pacific Journal of Social Work and Development* 27, no.1: 28–38. https://doi.org/10.1080/02185385.2017.1289860.

Nwogu, Victoria Ijeoma. 2005. "Trafficking of Persons to Europe: The Perspective of Nigeria as a Sending Country." Presented at an International Conference on the theme: Trafficking and Migration; A Human Rights Approach organized by Anti-slavery International and OIKOS Portugal, on 4 and 5 March, in Lisbon, Portugal.

Organization for Economic Co-operation and Development (OECD). 2017. "Gender Wage Gap," https://data.oecd.org/earnwage/gender-wage-gap.htm.

Plambech, Sine. 2017. "Sex, Deportation and Rescue: Economies of Migration among Nigerian Sex Workers" *Feminist Economics* 23, no.3 (3 July): 134–59. https://doi.org/10.1080/13545701.2016.1181272.

Roy, Ananya. 2010. *Poverty Capital: Microfinance and the Making of Development*. 1st edition. London: Routledge.

Rubin, Gayle. 2011. "The Trouble with Trafficking," in *Deviations: A Gayle Rubin Reader*. Durham, NC: Duke University Press.

Sedgwick, Eve Kosofsky. 1993. *Tendencies*. Durham, NC: Duke University Press.

Sharma, Nandita. 2005. "Anti-trafficking Rhetoric and the Making of a Global Apartheid," *NWSA Journal* 17, no.3: 88–111. muse.jhu.edu/article/189422.

Skilbrei, May-Len, and Charlotta Holmström. 2016. *Prostitution Policy in the Nordic Region: Ambiguous Sympathies*. First edition. London: Routledge.

Slater, Johanna, Kareem Fahim, and Katie McQue. 2020. "Migration, in Reverse," *Washington Post*. https://www.washingtonpost.com/graphics/2020/world/coronavirus-migration-trends-gulf-states-india/.

Smith, Daniel Jordan. 2006. *A Culture of Corruption: Everyday Deception and Popular Discontent in Nigeria*. Princeton, NJ: Princeton University Press.

The World Bank. 2013. *Migration and Development Brief*. http://pubdocs.worldbank.org/en/471191444756853938/MigrationandDevelopmentBrief21.pdf.

United Nations General Assembly. 2000. *Protocol to Prevent, Suppress and Punish Trafficking in Persons, Especially Women and Children, Supplementing the United Nations Convention against Transnational Organized Crime*. https://www.ohchr.org/en/professionalinterest/pages/protocoltraffickinginpersons.aspx.

United States Department of State. 2000. "Victims of Trafficking and Violence Protection Act of 2000," Washington, DC: US Department of State (October 28). https://www.govinfo.gov/content/pkg/PLAW-106publ386/pdf/PLAW-106publ386.pdf#:~:text=To%20combat%20trafficking%20in%20persons,women%2C%20and%20for%20other%20purposes.

United States Department of State. 2001. "Trafficking in Persons Report 2001," Washington, DC: US Department of State. https://2009-2017.state.gov/documents/organization/4107.pdf.

United States Department of State. 2013. "Trafficking in Persons Report 2013," Washington, DC: US Department of State. https://www.state.gov/j/tip/rls/tiprpt/2013/.

Usuanlele, Uyilawa. 1999. "Colonialism and the Origin of Female Prostitution Among the Benins of Edo State," *Benin Studies Newsletter* 4, no.3: 1–7.

Vance, Carole. 2012. "Innocence and Experience: Melodramatic Narratives of Sex Trafficking and Their Consequences for Law and Policy," *History of the Present* 2, no.2: 200–218. https://doi.org/10.5406/historypresent.2.2.0200.

Vanderhurst, Stacey. 2013. *God Rescued You: Religious Subjectivity and Citizenship in a Nigerian Counter-Trafficking Shelter*. Providence: Brown University Press.

Varela, Cecilia and Deborah, Daich. 2014. "Entre el combate a la trata y la criminalización del trabajo Sexual: las formas de gobierno de la prostitución," *Delito y Sociedad* 38: 63–86. https://doi.org/10.14409/dys.v2i38.5554.

Varela, Cecilia Ines. 2013. "Del tráfico de las mujeres al tráfico de las políticas. Apuntes para una historia del movimiento anti-trata en la Argentina (1998–2008)," *Revista Publicar*, 12 (25 August). http://ppct.caicyt.gov.ar/index.php/publicar/article/view/1565.

World Bank. 2018. https://data.worldbank.org/indicator/SP.DYN.LE00.IN?end=2018&locations=NG&most_recent_year_desc=false&start=1960&view=chart.

Zimmerman, Yvonne. 2013. *Other Dreams of Freedom: Religion, Sex, and Human Trafficking*. Oxford: Oxford University Press.

5

BORDERS AND BOUNDARIES

Thinking migration, sexuality and precarity in a neoliberal age

Sine Plambech, Mark Padilla, Sealing Cheng, and Svati Shah

During the neoliberal period, migration has increased and migratory restrictions around the globe have also intensified, producing correlative restrictions for migrants' access to livelihoods and opportunities (De Genova 2003; Nyers 2019). The regimes that produce these effects, making life hard enough in some places to induce migration, while also making life harder for migrants, create any number of paradoxes in both policy and practice. There is much debate over the likely effects of the COVID-19 pandemic on migration globally, but whether or not the number of migrants remains high, it seems safe to posit that the movement of peoples within and across borders will remain stratified, perhaps increasingly so, whereas the paradoxical social and political conditions that migrants have faced will continue to accumulate.[1]

This chapter shows in detail how the paradoxes of neoliberalism work out in practice. We argue that the incoherence of neoliberal migratory regimes is often productive of both governmental power and of economic value. Most importantly, we show how these regimes and their attendant paradoxes create double binds and resulting ambivalences for people who are the objects of these policies and practices, who must in turn respond with highly creative strategies and tactics for survival. We further demonstrate how these strategies and tactics cannot be understood without an understanding of how gender and sexuality are creatively deployed in many migratory trajectories.

We concisely explore four ethnographic case studies conducted among distinct migrant groups: asylum seekers in Hong Kong, deportees in the Dominican Republic, Nigerian migrant sex workers in Italy and Denmark, and rural-to-urban labor migrants in Mumbai, India. Our studies address the question of migrant labor and precarity in informal economies amongst both international and domestic ("internal") migrants. For example, Svati Shah's (2014) research on sex work and migration shows that people have migrated from all over India to

DOI: 10.4324/9781003252702-5

Mumbai in search of paid work. These migrants face administrative challenges, which we describe below, that are not dissimilar to those faced by cross-border migrants. The significant regional differences within India make migration within the country's borders sometimes even more fraught than migrating for work abroad, e.g., to the Gulf states.

This juxtaposition between domestic and cross-border migration indicates both the cross-site constancy and the local variations that simultaneously operate across all of our settings; whereas the policing of mobility and the stigmatization of migrants universally generates conditions of precarity, the categories and stereotypes that shape this precarity are specific to each case. For example, although the economic impacts of COVID-19 were felt universally, these impacts were especially severe in places that had embraced the neoliberal economic ethos of austerity and the roll-back entitlements for people living in poverty. As a result, hunger rates amongst migrant workers in India, for example, went off the charts during the pandemic (Mishra and Rampal 2020). In the Dominican Republic, food insecurity is also an issue that, along with precarious access to health care, has intensified during the pandemic, particularly because public health facilities were already overstrained, with private health care being inaccessible to many people. According to a 2020 household survey in the Dominican Republic (United Nations 2020), those households dependent on employment in the informal sectors were also likely to experience intensified precarity as informal jobs were the ones that immediately disappeared, particularly in the tourism-dependent sector of the economy. These workers may be pushed toward other informal employment (security, maintenance, cleaning, food delivery, taxi services, or the local sex or drug economies) even as such jobs also became scarcer. Overall, barriers to trans-border migration are likely to become even more significant, while internal migration may become more fraught in countries like India, China, and Brazil, where administrative legibility and access to services may lag behind the where and how of migrants actually moving, settling, and navigating administrative illegibility and violence.

In the discussion that follows, we aim to complicate the conventional understanding of borders as being primarily geopolitical by attending to the interplay of race, gender, and sexuality, as well as region and nation. Rural migrants who cross vast distances within their own country, as in India and China, for example, may be racialized as a foil to unmarked, non-migrant citizen subjects (Zhang 2002; Yang 2012). In the Indian case (Shah 2014), hierarchical social categories are maintained through the reification of differences in religion, caste, and region, in which migrant laborers represent the lowest rungs of these hierarchies. The interplay between migration and border control policies is not a linear process of transgression and control, but is rather often unpredictable and messy, producing iterative effects that are locally inflected and continually evolving.

These different cases also highlight how sexuality as a form of social capital is both embodied and enacted. Emotional and erotic labor constitute sites for negotiating both interpersonal and institutional inequalities, and sex, desires, dating, and love can function as a form of proof that one is alive, able, and capable of pleasure (Scheper-Hughes 2003). Our examination of "sexuality" here focuses on two major social domains – marriage and sexual commerce – both of which are powerfully shaped by global regimes of migration and citizenship. In our analysis, we read across our varied ethnographic contexts to identify patterns and points of divergence, rather than trying to offer a complete picture of each local setting.

For instance, Padilla introduced us to Samuel briefly in Chapter 2, and his experiences serve to further illuminate our analysis in this chapter. Samuel was a 57-year-old informal tourism employee in the Dominican Republic, who was interviewed by Padilla in 2017 for a broader ethnographic study on migration and tourism (Padilla et al. 2018). Having been deported multiple times from the United States (US) and Puerto Rico (a US territory and a primary destination for undocumented Dominican migration), and having experienced problems related to drug addiction and small-scale drug dealing in all of the countries in which he has lived, Samuel was contemplative when reflecting on a life in which he had faced blocks at crucial moments, including the particularly scarring block to seeing relatives in the US created by his deportation. And yet he had also put together meaningful life projects and relations. He was an active participant in "*buscándose la vida*" (looking for life) – a phrase that is used in the Dominican Republic to describe the multiple informal strategies that people use to make ends meet in the context of labor exclusion and a precarious informal economy.

Unable to obtain formal employment due to a Dominican policy that functions to deny employment to deportees despite having never committed a crime within the Dominican Republic, he resorted to working in the sale of drugs and sex in the tourism economy of Santo Domingo. His linguistic skills in English allowed him to negotiate sexual services in an economy that relied fundamentally on his ability to connect intimately with foreign tourists.

In this way, Samuel was able to insert himself into a particularly Dominican expression of neoliberalism – the erotic markets and intimate spaces created by global corporate tourism in the Caribbean – but crucially, his sexuality and gender identity were essential resources for him in navigating the constraints he encountered within it. These are ripple effects of policies that were not initially conceived in the promises of neoliberalism in resource-poor nations such as the Dominican Republic, but which nevertheless have become an essential part of contemporary Dominican reality. As the US deportation regime forcibly moves an increasing number of Dominican men back to their "homes," pleasure-related markets emanating from the Global North simultaneously drive deported men's labor to the service economies of tourism.

In Hong Kong, asylum seekers, who are predominantly men from Africa and South Asia, face even more extensive legal prohibitions from work, study, and volunteering, with no legal access to cash. Asylum seekers are dependent on the meager assistance that the Hong Kong government and local NGOs provide, while they wait – sometimes for over a decade – for a decision on their asylum applications. In the 2010s, an increasing number of African asylum-seeking men began marrying Hong Kong residents, as the asylum approval rate of 0.6% made many turn to means of seeking a better life outside of the asylum process.[2] For African asylum seekers and refugees in Hong Kong, marrying Hong Kong residents became virtually the only way to stay in Hong Kong as legal residents (Cheng 2021). Entering an intimate relationship is thus a medium by which to create a different set of possibilities for the future. Simultaneously, many asylum seekers risk arrest and imprisonment to work in criminalized economic sectors. Although the government creates the conditions for work in illegitimate survival economies by denying asylum seekers either a regularized status or the necessary benefits to live while waiting, within the popular media they have been dubbed "fake refugees," who purportedly perpetrate crime and violence in Hong Kong while posing an undue burden on government resources. These political and popular discourses create a double bind for migrants that leave them with no legitimate avenue for survival (we revisit the double binds of neoliberalism in Chapter 6).

The undocumented migrant Nigerian women in Plambech's study were not legally barred from employment as Samuel was or as the asylum seekers in Hong Kong are, but they have faced similar problems in finding jobs upon their arrival to Europe.[3] They often described how it was difficult for them to find work in restaurants, hotels, or on farms in Europe because the employers "don't trust African people." As one of the women explained, "When I come in as Black, they don't see me," while another reported, "I don't have a white person who can say that I am OK." By contrast, in the sex market, African women find that they are desired by local men and that there is money to be earned. One of the more experienced women shared that her solution to the dilemma was "women's built-in ATM machine," a gendered rendering which both naturalizes heterosexual power relations and argues for a subversive space to maneuver within them. Others made reference to the multiple dating websites that many Nigerian women turn to for connections and clients, such as *Afro-Introductions .com*. Here, the women strategically create profiles that play upon exotic imaginations of lustful African women, displaying their long, braided hair, mentioning their "African bumps," or dancing in provocative ways on live video feeds. Some of the women said that they were actively looking for men to marry them or for more steady kinds of relationships, but regardless of the kind of arrangement that they were seeking, what they were most hoping for was a source of income that was more reliable and lucrative than the precarious formal job market available to them in Europe.

In Mumbai, we turn our focus to domestic or internal migrants. As with cross-border migrants, domestic migrants often share challenges in accessing government entitlements. Labor migrants in Mumbai, and throughout India, lose access to food subsidies through India's Public Distribution System (PDS) when they leave their places of origin, as the ration cards that allow access to the PDS are non-transferable (Sriraman 2018). Although the Indian government is

138 Plambech, Padilla, Cheng, and Shah

aiming to digitize this system with the promise of making benefits more mobile, critics have decried the new regime of a digitized, unique-ID system as yet another means of stripping the poor of entitlements (Nigam 2017).

To be sure, when cross-border labor migrants leave their countries of origin, legally or extra-legally, they too knowingly lose access to basic entitlements they would have received in their home countries. Whereas domestic migrants are not technically "stateless" or undocumented, their participation in urban informal economies is highly regulated. Domestic migrants can, for example, be driven away from certain sectors and spaces by being given reduced access to labor markets or by being driven out of slum and squatter settlements (also sometimes known as "encroachments") without being given compensatory accommodation. In this situation, wherein everyday life can be so uncertain, sexual and affective exchanges again become a means for some of securing basic necessities, even if they are only secured precariously and transiently by the domestic migrants who seek them.

As these four cases illustrate, the paired effects of imbricated social hierarchies and neoliberal practices, including migratory surveillance and expanded economic informalization, have created a perfect storm for migrants who are "looking for life."[4] In Hong Kong, ongoing coloniality and racialization have resulted in direct and intensifying regulation of asylum seekers, turning the humanitarian category of asylum into a site for social containment. As we noted in Chapter 2, the racialized sexualization of the Caribbean has helped to fuel the expansion of tourist economies, including both formal and informal sectors, throughout the region and particularly in the Dominican Republic. In the current chapter, we explore in more detail how migratory regimes help to ensure that workers like Samuel are available for sexual provisions within the informal economy. For Nigerian migrants to Europe, the economic effects of a racialized and sexualized economy are not enforced by the government, but they are nonetheless shaped by the lived contours of political blockages and openings. And for migrants in Mumbai, the boundaries of region, language, and caste create access that is precarious at best in terms of both work and government benefits.

Gender and sexuality as they are embedded in racial capitalism are, in this way, sites of paradox; mobilizing gender and sex can provide both more pronounced agentive action for migrants and can also be sites of state regulatory and carceral responses. In this chapter, we aim to capture the diverse ways in which migrants engage in various deployments of sexuality in order to negotiate policies meant to restrict their movements – either across political borders or within nation-states. Our recognition of international and regional borders as not only territorial, but also as social and intimate, has allowed us to see immigration control, criminalization, and discrimination on a continuum of exclusionary practices that are embedded in structures of inequality, with gender, sexuality, race, class, and caste most pertinent to our discussion here. As in prior chapters, we focus our attention on some of the groups who are most negatively impacted by neoliberal policies – in particular, those who are precariously sustained through informal survival economies. In the pages that follow, we analyze how migrants deploy gender and sexuality for access to money, immigration documents, and the social and geographical mobility that border regimes deny them. For migrants who have limited access to social and financial capital, the ability to deploy sexual capital serves as a means to mitigate the effects of migratory restrictions, while facilitating alternative, informal strategies for generating both economic and social resources.[5]

Informal economies and neoliberalism

We wish to highlight three key aspects of neoliberalism in relation to the ways in which migrants survive economically. First, although neoliberal economic policies are far from uniform in their application or effects across national contexts, the general confluence of reduced tariffs, weakened labor protections, and an impulse toward privatization has, among other things, resulted in far fewer entitlements that people living below the poverty line may demand from their own governments. Reduction or elimination of economic safety nets necessarily stimulates more labor migration, as people seek better opportunities by crossing borders (Cheng and Kim 2014). Second, the move toward privatization has expanded the numbers of people surviving in the informal economies, the untaxed and largely cash-based segment of the economy in which people generally live hand to mouth, earning wages as either a piece rate or a daily wage. The majority of poor migrants work informally, and even more people will do so as economic informalization expands (De Genova 2013). Third, global labor regimes and seasonal changes in neoliberal markets can produce ebbs and flows of informal labor demands, resulting in the patterns of internal or cross-national migration that we have witnessed in our research sites (Brotherton and Barrios 2011). These flows of laborers – many of whom are engaged in sexual and affective exchanges – are part and parcel of the ways that neoliberalism operates to shape precarity as well as the rhythms of mobility.

The precarity that we reference among the migrants in our studies derives from the categories, labels, and migrant statuses they must inhabit when they leave their places of origin. Categories such as "overstayer," "immigration offender," "deportee," "encroacher," and even "asylum seeker," contribute to already economically impoverished migrants being marked as "criminals," "failures," "outsiders," or "victims." These terms become means of rendering people as appropriate targets for subsequent interventions that include the need to be "arrested," "screened," "rescued," "removed," or "deported."[6] Even when the categories invoke humanitarian values (such as "asylum"), we have found that the ways in which border security concerns intersect with humanitarian demands produce effects that are paradoxical at best.

Migration regimes – the institutional, political, and symbolic mechanisms through which the mobility of populations is controlled – are created for the purpose of maintaining a collective "community of value" within certain social

140 Plambech, Padilla, Cheng, and Shah

and geopolitical boundaries, a project that requires both including and excluding others (Anderson 2013). Shared convictions about the value of borders are built upon the faith that the stability and security of the imagined national, urban, or regional community hinge on how well such borders are maintained. Migrants threaten the "community of value" in both conceptual and embodied ways, thereby exposing the fragility of borders and compelling new strategies of reinforcement and defense. At the same time, migrants may well contribute to – and be necessary for – the sustenance and even expansion of neoliberal economies.

Cheng has observed these paradoxical dynamics in her study of the survival strategies of African migrants in Hong Kong. In 2012, online Chinese forums, dominated by young Hong Kong male users, began denouncing intimate relationships between BLACK African men and Hong Kong Chinese women – claiming that African asylum seekers were unscrupulous men marrying local women solely for ID cards, and that women were "stupid" and "sex crazed" to be attracted to African men (an attraction that was attributed on these forums to a racist narrative about penis size) (HK Golden Forum 2009). The social boundaries articulated through racist message boards and the state's political control of migrants mutually reinforced each other in the constitution of a community of moral value. In 2016, the Hong Kong government started rejecting dependent visas to any asylum seeker with a "suspected offence" (not conviction), reiterating migrants' illegality and deportability. These "suspected offences" were often related to immigration infractions, so that the state's punishment of the migrants through the denial of marriage visas effectively created a "state of exception", (Agamben 1998) in which the construct of asylum seekers as always already illegal closed off even legal paths to citizenship. Excluded from the protections of even the most basic rights, many African migrants in Hong Kong were instead pushed into informal economies, doing forms of labor in construction, goods moving, recycling, and trading to sustain the city's economic growth (Vecchio 2014).

The legitimation provided by communities of value sustained through the idea of secure borders, thus, also draws boundaries that protect capital. Although much has been made of the movement of capital in the neoliberal period, it has also been a time in which capital has become increasingly bounded, as the concentration of wealth means that fewer and fewer people have access to more and more capital.[7] Jodi A. Byrd et al. (2018) argued that primary accumulation is not a stage in capitalism that has long been superseded, but is instead, like coloniality, an ongoing and dynamic process that continues to sustain capitalism. As such, the enclosures that provided for the development of private property as the material base of capitalist relations continue in some form. This movement of goods and services is accompanied by the expansion of security apparatuses (whether private security companies or campus police) that enforce the boundaries of increasingly exclusive spaces occupied by social elites, just as the expansion of border security has enforced national boundaries. And these border regimes are part of a larger suite of neoliberal policies and practices. Saskia Sassen's (2014) analysis of the continuing "expulsion" of people from land (what David Harvey (2004) terms "accumulation by dispossession") provides a way to understand border regimes as being intertwined with several inter-related aspects of neoliberalism, including privatization and financialization.[8]

One way to understand neoliberal "privatization," then, is to see it as a form of enclosure in which public goods, services, and the institutions that provide them are enclosed within private markets. The effect, as with earlier enclosures, is to place goods within the control of capitalists (e.g., private equity firms, venture capitalists, large banks, and transnational corporations) while controlling the access available to people who used to depend on those goods or who used to work in privatized sectors. In turn, much of the economic expansion in privatized sectors is controlled by transnational corporations, like Amazon (as discussed in Chapter 2). Overall, the effect of neoliberal policies and practices, like the enclosure of privatization or the expulsion and accumulation by dispossession discussed by Sassen (2014) and Harvey (2004), is to expand the precarity of both formal employment and of the informal economies that are the focus of this chapter.

We understand the expansion of informal economies in the past several decades to be part of what Lisa Duggan (2003) has identified as the redistribution upwards that is characteristic of neoliberal economies. Organizing labor through informal exchanges keeps wages lower than in sectors organized through contracted labor while also making many forms of labor organizing difficult because there are no collective points of contract negotiation. The expansion of "gig economies" and piece work has also helped corporations to reduce or deny benefits associated with formal employment. In other words, the expansion of informal labor sectors is not something that is incidental to neoliberal economies but is rather a central means by which capital is accumulated in the neoliberal period. Migrant labor in these informal sectors thus emerges as paradoxically central to contemporary relations of production.

The combination of increasingly restricted access to economic sectors with secure, formal employment and the correlative expansion of informal economies creates a dynamic of intertwining inclusion and exclusion in migratory regimes. In Europe, for example, while Nigerians constitute one of the largest groups of undocumented migrants working in informal economies, they are also among the most frequently deported.[9]

Meanwhile, in the Dominican Republic, deportees from the US experience intense and institutionalized stigma and discrimination as a consequence of their legal and social status as "deportados" (deportees). Undocumented Dominican immigrants in the US often begin their journey *via* Puerto Rico, which has historically received large numbers of Dominicans who cross the treacherous 80-mile Mona Passage in rickety fishing boats. Since the 1980s, many migrant Dominicans, particularly young men, have been unable to find formal wage labor in the US and ultimately turned to informal work in urban drug economies (Brotherton and Barrios 2011). These same informal

142 Plambech, Padilla, Cheng, and Shah

illicit activities have heightened the possibility of their eventual deportation for drug-related crimes, the primary rationale for Dominican deportation from the US. This situation has led to the current deportation crisis in the Dominican Republic, which now receives approximately two thousand deportees from the US annually.

Once they are returned 'back home' to the Dominican Republic – a home that many of them have not seen since their youth – these men face almost insurmountable barriers to formal work imposed by "*la ficha*" (the registry), a phrase used by deportees to refer to their forced registration with the Dominican state as deportees. The *ficha* essentially criminalizes them despite the fact that most have committed no crimes in the Dominican Republic (Padilla et al. 2018) and imposes intense barriers to formal employment. Thus, Dominican deportees face extreme constraints on access to formal work on both sides of the "border": in the Global North, they are "illegals," and in the Global South they are *deportados*. As a result, many Dominican men deported back to the Dominican Republic find themselves in a series of double binds, articulating the perception of being trapped or unable to escape informal sex tourism and small-scale drug sales.

The sense of being trapped in motion can also be part of the experience of movement within national boundaries. The following vignette, drawn from Shah's ethnography of sex work and migration in Mumbai, is illustrative.

> Radhabai said she was off to her village. When [Shah] asked whether she'd be coming back, she waggled her hand in both directions and turned down the corners of her mouth, indicating her ambiguity. "We came here to fill our stomachs," she said, "and instead what do we do here? Just walk up and down this street and eat slaps." Shaini said that Radha hadn't had any work for two days, and that her whole family was living back in the village. She said that Radha was off to her village and may or may not come back. Almost everyone else in this community of street-based sex workers was back in their villages as well. I was told that this was "the time" for people to go back, for a short while, at least. They would return soon, by and large, and later in the year they would go back again to help with the harvest so that they could increase the family's income for the season.
>
> (Shah 2014, 117)

Perspectives like this illustrate the ways in which both economic arrangements and state policies often result in an experience of incoherence for migrant workers, rarely addressing the paradoxes that they confront adequately.

In the other sites we discuss here, the combination of inducement and regulation, enforcement of both migration and border control, and internal and transborder movement creates any number of paradoxical situations for migrants. The incoherence that they must navigate may well be productive for capital overall, but not in any simple or direct way. Rather, our research finds repeated battles and skirmishes over both communities and value.

The incoherence of migration regimes can mean not just the simultaneous inducement and regulation of movement but the simultaneity of inducements to migrate coupled with a virtual shutdown of migration, as in the situation faced by asylum seekers in Hong Kong. In fact, our cases show that migrants often find themselves "stuck" at some point in the processes of migration – deported back from the US to the Dominican Republic but unable to make a living because of local regulations; migrating again and being deported again in a loop of mobility-for-stasis; or moving to urban areas of India for the sake of employment and then waiting and waiting for work to materialize.

In our research, we often observed that migrants find the realms of sexuality and intimacy as effective sites, not only for enterprising negotiations pertaining to survival, but also as generative of spaces that allow people to continue to strive for what their immigration and social status have proscribed. Sex, sexual commerce, romantic love, and marriage became channels, not only for reaffirming one's existence and value, but also for attaining legitimacy, wellbeing, and, possibly, upward social and economic mobility (Cheng 2012 and 2021; Freeman 2017). In this sense, we recognize the emotional and erotic labor in friendship, romance, and marriage *as part of the informal economy*, as it is, indeed, linked to material conditions and the agentive means by which individuals make ends meet in the context of scarcity or politico-legal constraints (Hart 2009).

If neoliberalism encompasses a set of policies that have contributed to the expansion of economic informalization throughout the world, the informal economy is where the migrants in each of the four studies we synthesize here negotiate economic survival (Shah 2014) and social thriving (Agarwala 2009; Hart 2009). The growth of informal economies may be bad for workers overall, but it can be good for some workers because informal sector service jobs may be better in many ways than service jobs that are available in the formal labor sectors. Sometimes workers are actively excluded from formal jobs and sometimes they choose informal jobs as offering higher wages and less demeaning working conditions. It may also be that racist social relations are more manageable in informal economies or that the work is preferable for any number of possible reasons. A foundational point of analytic imbrication between critiques of "neoliberalism" and "migration" is in the growth of informal economies, the migrant laborers on which they rely, and the ways in which surviving in the informal sector necessitates managing intense competition for limited resources.[10]

The potency of sex

Stripped of their rights and entitlements, living with the constant anxieties of removal and criminalization, migrants are necessarily aware of how they may deploy sexual capital for material and social security. Their precarious legal status also means that having sex with tourists, clients, and local partners is laden with implications for their own well-being and their aspirations to overcome the restrictions placed on them as outsiders. We find it useful to conceptualize these agentive practices as forms of sexual capital that can be deployed by migrants within the interstitial spaces of the political, economic, and social constraints of their specific setting. Furthermore, we do not intend to argue that sexual and relational intimacy are reducible only to instrumental or strategic decision-making. It is our view that social relationships – including those involving sexual intimacy – are always filtered through different social and economic incentives, and migrants' concerns for economic and migratory stability are a part, but not the only part, of their relational needs (Zelizer 2002; Cheng 2021; Constable 2014).

The social dimension of sexual capital comes from attributes such as migrants' racial and ethnic identity, their country or region of origin, their language skills and comportment, as well as their performance of gender and sexual identities. Sexuality, in the context of migration for precarious populations, can, therefore, be a way to open a space in a system that restricts migrants socially and legally. As Nicole Constable (2014) shows, migrant female domestic workers who have intimate relationships and give birth in Hong Kong (even though their children may become stateless) are contesting the immigration regulation that sees them as only workers and not as "people." Having intimate relationships, engaging in sex, and having children – with their attendant burdens and pleasures – can become embodied ways to experience one's personhood in defiance of a regime that excludes and dehumanizes migrant bodies.

Even as we deploy concepts of resistance, agency, or defiance, we do not aim to romanticize migrants' sexuality in a context where they are already exposed to harsh regulatory regimes; although the possibilities for resistance and for creatively negotiating the challenges to survival cannot be denied, we also acknowledge that, for example, migrants in Mumbai are negotiating survival and heavy policing day to day. And as Karma Chávez and Eithne Lubhéid note in the Introduction to their important volume on *Queer and Trans Migrations,* "[T]hose who are already subalternized due to country of origin, race, class, ability, religion, gender, and sexuality often find themselves facing the most difficult conditions before, during, and after migration. For example, in the process of migration, LGBTQI people, especially those who are trans and gender-nonconforming, face exacerbated risks of violence, policing, and containment at the hands of state and non-state entities" (Chavez and Lubhéid 2020: 3). If the trope of "defiance" could be brought to bear, one could consider the demands of carving out a living against a set of conditions that make survival virtually impossible. Moreover, reliance on one's sexuality for security and material gain can further put migrants at risk. For example, Nigerian sex workers working on the streets of Europe in a *de facto* criminalized sector are often exposed to many forms of violence, harassment, detention, and unintended pregnancies, which, for migrant women, includes the possibility of having "stateless" children, as well as the consequences that arise from lacking requisite medical facilities, food, and shelter (Plambech 2016). Similarly, Samuel, with whom we began this chapter, exemplifies the risks entailed by dependence upon illicit substances when his work for economic survival within the informal tourism economy also continually exposes him to a behavioral trigger that undermines his health. We contend that it is exactly these kinds of complexities and tensions that characterize the ways that precarity among migrants is produced, managed, and, in some ways and for delimited periods of time, mitigated.

In all of our ethnographic sites, migrants who engaged in different forms of sexual labor demonstrated agency and creativity in the ways they navigated social and legal systems that endangered many of them in their daily lives. For many migrants who find themselves far from their home communities, sexual labor can have the paradoxical effect of both exacerbating their structural precariousness and also allowing a certain degree of freedom from community censure in which to explore different forms of sexuality and intimacy. Nigerian sex workers, for example, described how they became much more proactive in sex with their clients in Europe, unlike the more passive role they took with their husbands and boyfriends in Nigeria (Plambech 2016). The increase in sexual initiative is not simply because of the need to attract clients, but also because "Europe is not my country," as one of the women explained during an interview. Geographic and social displacement means a renegotiation of the boundaries of sexuality – breaking gendered sexual norms, in some cases, in order to accommodate the desires of the sexual market, when one is far removed from the normative controls of family and community. Some of those who return to Nigeria are unafraid of flaunting this newly acquired sexual and economic confidence. As Becky, a young Nigerian prospective migrant, described to Plambech, "These women who return from Europe, they are so sexy, they are so beautiful" (Plambech 2014a). Becky's implication is that such women are defying gendered proscriptions for appropriate Nigerian femininity, even as she finds this to be an appealing model.

The performance of sexual and emotional labor in romantic relationships and in marriage by these migrants has implications for their relation to the state. Intimate relationships with local residents may be (but are not necessarily) a source of material, social, and emotional support and may also lead to a regularization of their status. Marriage with a local citizen is a remote, but nevertheless present, fantasy for many of the migrants we interviewed in our respective sites. Even when marriage is blocked as a path toward regularized legal status, sexual capital can provide migrants with access to other important resources. During the protracted waiting period for asylum seekers in Hong Kong, for example, they have no formal means to live autonomous lives or to pursue personal advancement. They can, however, capitalize on their physical and sexual capital as men in relation to migrant domestic workers, who are predominantly women from the Philippines and Indonesia. As one male asylum seeker from West Africa told Cheng: "When I arrived in 2003, the government did not give us anything. Like many others, I had to have relationships with domestic helpers because they would buy us food, and clothes, and give us money." Although some African men regard their relationships with local girlfriends as the performance of emotional and sexual labor for money, clothes, and meals, many see these relationships as a site for pursuing "real love," rather than (or along with) papers and other goods. Yet, the urgency of their need for documented status is always a part of the relational context. As one West African man complained about his girlfriend of seven months for not committing to marriage: "We African men have to take care of our women. But we can't work, so we don't have money. We have to have ID to take care of them!" Being an asylum seeker puts one's masculinity on hold in an extralegal space of illegitimacy, incompetence, and impotence. As Cheng observes, "[A]sylum-seeking men pursuing intimate relationships and marriage with local women constitutes a way to not only reclaim their masculinity, but also to subvert the regulation of the racial-border regime, crafting one but not the only transgressive mode of future-making in their highly circumscribed lives" (Cheng 2021).

The migration regime, therefore, could be said to open up a new, albeit fraught, space for migrants' negotiation of sex, gender, and sexuality. While Dominican deportees' narratives expressed a deep frustration with the need to resort to the informal economies of sex and drugs, which further heightened their drug dependencies, some also made reference to how these exchanges reflected their status as *tígueres* – referring to a particularly Dominican masculine figure that has received considerable ethnographic consideration (Padilla et al. 2018). The *tíguere* is a man who demonstrates his use of cunning and knowledge of informal street economies – skills which Dominican men who have been deported often acquired while in the US – to survive in the competitive context of the informal economy. "*Trabajador social*" (social worker) was how one interviewee, Juan, described his informal tourism work post-deportation – which, for five years, had primarily consisted of finding drugs and sex workers for tourists and organizing tourist excursions – all facilitated by his command of the English language. Juan's use of "social worker" as a professional descriptor is reflective of a general tendency among local tourism workers to linguistically emphasize the interpersonal and professional dimensions of their so-called "soft" skills, that is, their capacity to fulfill the pleasure-related needs and social desires of tourists.

By contrast, Nigerian migrants to Europe generally speak excellent English and would easily be able to communicate with many tourists, yet they find it difficult to find jobs in tourism. Beauty, one of the women in Plambech's study of Nigerian migrants in Italy, explained that African migrants were often not considered for jobs waiting tables, taking orders, or serving inside restaurants. Instead, African migrant workers were usually put to work in restaurant kitchens, for example as dishwashers. At the restaurant where Beauty worked, the migrants earned €3.5 an hour, working 12 hours a day. They had to pay three days' wages to the driver who would drop them off at the kitchen entrance, because they were not allowed to take the free bus and walk from the resort to the bus stop on the main road (both their Italian employer and his Nigerian manager explained that they could not walk between the bus stop and the hotel because the tourists would be scared if "there were BLACKS around" in the resort area). Thus, the migrants ended up paying a quite large sum of their own salaries so that white tourists would not have to interact with them in any way, or ever encounter those who clean their plates.

Hence, the difficulties that migrants face in finding steady jobs in Europe are also clearly shaped by xenophobia and racism. Furthermore, for women like Princess, another participant in Plambech's study, there was more money in selling sex or even just exchanging phone numbers for food than washing dishes in a restaurant. One day, Princess and Plambech were at the local market. A young Nigerian man approached Princess and asked for her phone number. "If you want my phone number, you have to buy something for me," she said flirtatiously. He trudged behind her into what Princess and her friends called the "African shop." She chose a large yam, a frozen chicken, and three tins of tomato sauce. He paid but looked a bit surprised, since it was apparently more expensive than he had planned. In exchange for these comestible gifts, she gave him her phone number.

Based upon such findings throughout our ethnographic material, we consider intimate relations as a domain for human action that is produced in tension with the exclusionary and delegitimizing effects of the border regimes in the neoliberal era. Migrants inevitably develop creative means to survive, to elude institutional mandates, and to forge solutions to seemingly intractable problems of policing and impoverishment. These expressions of agency by those who are targeted by the regulatory regimes of migration and deportation underline the ways that border regimes are not only prohibitive, but also generative of social and cultural phenomena. For some migrants who are excluded from formal employment, the exchange of erotic and intimate labor for money, material resources, social connections, and/or emotional support constitutes a form of productive agency, one which offers the possibility of a desirable future.

State interventions, border regimes, and normative discourse

The cases we have presented here illustrate the diverse ways in which migrants' performance of erotic and intimate labor becomes pertinent, not only for their ability to make ends meet economically, but also creates possibilities for social and legal advancement. In some of our cases, migrants' aspirational projects for financial well-being, documented status, and stable employment are not only tied to how well they perform sexual and emotional labor, but also to a measure of their "luck" – for example, in meeting the right potential partners or dodging an immigration crackdown. However creative individuals are in negotiating for their own survival, they are always doing so in the midst of powerful migratory regimes that repeatedly create double binds for individual actors. These double binds not only make individual action precarious; they also make collective action challenging.

For the institutions of the state and its (increasingly limited) social services, sexual victimhood and sexual threat become two powerful tropes to delegitimize migrants who are seen to be transgressive by fact of their migration, which is discursively portrayed as a refusal to occupy prescribed racialized and gendered locations. Policy and media narratives may trumpet the immorality of "faked marriages," even as they may focus on the dangers of "prostitution" or the inhumanity of "sex trafficking" at the same time (Bernstein 2010; Cheng 2019; Soderlund 2011). Implicit in a range of state, NGO, and media responses to migrants is the bestowal of legitimacy – and thereby state protections – to individuals according to their racial locations and the "appropriateness" of their genders and sexualities (Bernstein 2010). Moralizing talk – whether formally bureaucratic, circulating in popular media, or *via* networks of informal gossip – is one way to make humanitarianism regulatory while also denying that the state or society might have any social responsibility to asylum seekers or other migrants.

In Copenhagen's Red Light District, for example, a group of about fifty Nigerian migrant sex workers are the subject of intense concerns from neighbors, politicians, the police, NGOs, and anti-trafficking activists. This "concern" gives rise to the humanitarianization of a security regime that is premised upon sexual regulation. The Copenhagen police arrest sex workers in the Red Light District and areas with many Nigerian women because they are purportedly "too sexual," "too aggressive," and too inclined to "touch family fathers inappropriately" (Plambech 2014b). A Copenhagen Police press release in 2013 explained, "It's an area we continue to focus on because these women openly offer sexual services to passersby in a very proactive way and that is a behavior that disturbs residents and other individuals.... We expect these night raids will probably be followed by more" (Plambech 2014b).

The women are then charged for working without documents, as well as destitution (lacking the means of subsistence), and taken into detention. Later, the women are assessed by the governmental Center Against Human Trafficking (CMM) to try to identify if any of them may have been trafficked. In one police raid tracked by Plambech, seventeen women were arrested, two were identified as trafficked, and the rest were scheduled to be deported (Plambech 2014b). Thus, humanitarian desires to rescue "sex slaves" co-exist in Copenhagen with public complaints and perceptions of sex workers as hypersexual and constituting a public nuisance. As is also the case in other European cities, Copenhagen's Red Light District is situated at the juxtaposition of migration control and humanitarian desires to rescue women from sex work and human trafficking. It is a site where both the anti-immigrant position and the humanitarian position reproduce exoticized ideas of "Africa" as evil, dangerous, and filled with "traffickers," and of "African women" as being what a Danish policeman described as "very aggressive when offering sex" (translation by Plambech).

At the shelters in Nigeria for women returning from Europe, conflicts arise between the women and the NGO workers, who are often nuns, because the women do not want to perform the domestic chores assigned to them, often directly and vocally opposing them. In the nuns' explanation, it is because "(i)nstead of working, they just want to sleep with men and have money, instead of doing those things that require discipline ... only some girls are principled and ready to do a dignified job" (Plambech 2017). The shelter for "trafficked women" is thereby a site where ideals of respectable femininity set the rules, and where women who have sex for money are configured as undeserving subjects of protection (Plambech 2016). In the context of highly constrained resources due to neoliberal austerity, such discourses can have a significant effect on migrants' life chances, justifying their ever-greater abandonment by the state and social service agencies.

The simultaneous impetus to protect and to punish reveals a great deal about the nature of state benevolence. For instance, migrant workers in India and deportees returned to the Dominican Republic are policed spatially, restricted to geographic zones where their presence is legitimized for brief periods of time. In India, these zones include public day-wage labor markets, where soliciting short-term contracts for paid work is allowed in the morning but dispersed after a few hours. In the Dominican Republic, these are tourist areas where deportees might garner income, but into which they must be escorted by foreign tourists, or they may always be in danger of expulsion. Within tourism zones, Dominicans perceived as deportees or sex workers are heavily policed and are often arrested on arbitrary allegations of illegal activities, or physically removed from the tourism area by the tourism police. In both of these cases, the "border" is not rendered through the physical barrier of a national boundary but, rather, through the discourse of protection and its delineation of who is unworthy of protection.

Borders are also transposed onto the intimate lives of individuals. Asylum seekers came to be framed as security threats, and their elimination as evidence of "good governance" by the Hong Kong government in the late 2010s. The denial of dependent visas to asylum-seeking spouses of local residents was one means to ensure their eventual removal. Before 2016, asylum seekers were already subjected to extra scrutiny and a much longer wait than the Immigration Department's pledge of "six to nine weeks" for dependent visa processing, but they would eventually get the visas if they fulfilled the stated requirements – one of which was "no known record to the detriment of the applicant." Since 2016, restrictions have been tightened and waiting times were lengthened, while dependent visa rejections were made on "suspected offences" rather than criminal records. One couple applying for a dependent visa had the husband's visa application rejected in mid-2016 after two years of document submission, interviews, and home visits by immigration officers. Over the next three years, they exhausted their energies and money to hire a lawyer and reapplied three more times, to no avail. The financial burden, social isolation, and loss of hope for the couple eventually led to an abortion, and the husband returning to his home country. Visa denial is an administrative practice that reinforces the asylum-seeking partner's inadmissibility into the citizenry, but also indirectly punishes the resident spouse for an intimate association with the "wrong" person (Castañeda 2019). It is a state practice pertinent to the racialization of border control that may support certain intimate relations and sex as work, while also

150 Plambech, Padilla, Cheng, and Shah

undermining longer-term prospects for intimate, social, and reproductive lives between migrants and citizens.

One of the findings of our cross-site analysis has been the fact that the regulatory practices of the state or the public are not the only means by which migrant sexuality is regulated and controlled. Amongst marginalized and persecuted groups, such as the migrants we have studied, competition for limited resources and the urgent need to demonstrate legitimate claims to migration often result in mechanisms of social control that are internal to migrant communities. In many ways, the groups of vulnerable migrants we studied here are small, and, for the most part, relatively bounded because of their irregular status and isolation from what might be defined as "the host society," while they are also unstable and fluid. Migrants are often reliant on each other for information about jobs, police, immigration, and other authorities, but they are also competitive with each other for the limited resources available, and under constant threat of being discovered, persecuted, or removed. Fellow migrants are therefore a potential source of support but also possible threats to one another's well-being. We observed that, in several of our cases, this conundrum sometimes gave rise to relations of distrust between migrants rather than relations premised upon solidarity. This distrust could arise even amongst those who had followed the same migratory trajectories,

In the narratives of Nigerian sex workers, detention and deportation often occurred because their madam or other Nigerians had connections with the police. Jealousy and aggression may be pervasive in these social relations. One woman explained that she had been the target of a spell which cast her as a visible "illegal" on her forehead, making her visible as such to the police (Plambech 2016). Others believed that their madams reported them once they had paid off their debts and could potentially start making money independently. In these explanations, deportation emerges not only as a technology of migration control that benefits the state, but also as an informal tool for social control among other migrants. In the informal economy of the street corners of Mumbai, impoverished workers policed one another in a context in which paid work is extremely scarce, and so-called "unskilled" workers far outnumbered available day-wage labor jobs. In this case, non-seasonal workers, who had a more "local" claim to Mumbai than did seasonal workers, used the rumor that a competing set of women workers, who were also of lower caste than themselves, were soliciting sex work from the spaces of the labor market as well as undercutting the day-wage rate for manual labor jobs in construction. Thus, in this Indian context, normative ideologies of gender and sexuality were used not only by the state but were sometimes deployed by one group of migrants against another group, so as to reduce labor market competition.

Similarly, in Hong Kong, many African refugee men openly condemned refugee African women for being "prostitutes," saying that they should not show up at church and sell sex afterwards.[11] Cheng's research has also documented the use of homophobic stereotyping within the African refugee community, which led to a gay male refugee being evicted from his apartment when his fellow refugee housemates discovered his sexual identity. The sexual policing within the refugee community had the effect of exacerbating vulnerability and exclusion for those who were considered by other community members to be "sexual deviants."

Among men employed in the informal tourism economies in the Dominican Republic, barriers to collective action were created by the interaction among the intense policing of tourist spaces by the Dominican tourism police, the racialization of informal workers in tourist zones, the pervasive assumption that local men are inherently dangerous to tourists, and the normative sexual discourses deployed by migrants themselves. Markers of racial differences in these "danger zones" accentuated the visibility of local men who work in informal economies, many of whom were presumed to be surviving through illicit activities such as the sale of sex and drugs and were socially perceived to be dangerous by many locals. Gossip and rumors amongst the migrants could also easily lead to suspicion or arrest by authorities, resulting in their removal from the area, informal "blacklisting" that could complicate access to tourism work in the future, the confiscation of tourism identifications that allow access to certain spaces, or even arrest and incarceration. For these reasons, many of the men interviewed by Padilla described the importance of "keeping to oneself," of avoiding close friendships that might turn sour, and of "not talking too much." Even apparently positive social connections amongst migrants were viewed as treacherous by many of these men, who were afraid of becoming targets of suspicion and control.

The impetus among Dominican migrants to remain isolated from others as a form of self-protection reverberated in the other sites as well. Nigerian sex workers would, for instance, term themselves a "zipped lip girl" to explain how they avoided gossip, by not saying anything to anyone about anything (Plambech 2016). Yet, in accepting the potential loss of social capital and the creation of social distance in their networks, migrants also rendered themselves more isolated and vulnerable to abuse, since they were hindered in their ability to exchange information with other migrants.

Indeed, migrants' illegitimacy in relation to the border regime and their competition with each other in the informal economy rendered collective action of any sort difficult. Few people in any of these spaces saw the possibility or benefit of directly engaging in activism. The anxiety within the communities further produced normative discourses that reinforced criticisms of attempts at public protests in some of these spaces. The only woman in a refugee rights group in Hong Kong had been the target of gossip, mainly from other women refugees, for her high-profile mobilization and participation in various protests and online platforms. The running complaint that "Geneva (pseudonym) is *everywhere!*" was a suggestion that her actions drew undue attention to herself and, relatedly, the entire refugee community. Similarly, when a workers' advocacy organization set up an office near the public day-wage labor market in Mumbai, women avoided the office at first, for fear of being accused of conducting sex work or meeting illicit boyfriends there. Women began accessing the space only when it was moved to a different office space, where all activities in the office were visible from the street.

In all of our cases, transgressive expressions of gender and sexuality became sites through which the securitization of borders – whether political, economic, spatial, or moral – was enacted. Transgressive acts also became sites for justifying institutional mechanisms that further restricted movement and reproduced migrant precarity. In each of our case studies, we observed that in some instances the dynamics of gossip and rumors within migrant communities had the effect of not just preventing social cohesion but also diverting attention from the systemic injustices that made them vulnerable and deportable in the first place.

Conclusion

Our four ethnographic case studies demonstrate the deep imbrications among migration, gender, sexuality, racialization, and global economic forces that simultaneously necessitate and preclude informal workers from migrating for a sustainable livelihood. These case studies may be understood as springing from global forces, like the policies and practices of neoliberalism, enacted across very different geographic and regulatory regimes, even as there are local distinctions in the articulation of the specific actors, institutions, and sites of control. We have brought these case studies into conversation with each other as a means for understanding the ways in which ideas about sexuality and migratory regulations are conjoined, even while their imbrications may remain elided. That is to say, borders are contingent, produced, and constantly in a state of iteration, as are the migratory subjects who constitute them through the acts of crossing or transgressing borders.

Our examples further show that both foreign and domestic migrants who are often vying for extremely limited resources are subject to the regulatory impulses of official border regimes, as well as cultural discourses from mainstream media, NGOs, and local migrant communities. At times, these regulatory impulses manifest through migrants being identified by the state or by one another as a sexual danger, buttressing the idea that both internal and external boundaries serve to produce a community of value. These communities of value provide moral legitimation for the institution of various borders and boundaries, including the state enclosure of national and regional borders, communal enforcement of local or regional boundaries and of divisions within labor markets, and the enclosure of capital itself. Specifically, the creation of portions of the world in which it is impossible to earn a sustainable livelihood, or, in the case of war, to sustain life itself, sets people in motion, whether within or across national borders. Governmental and normative regulation of these many boundaries limits people's access to anything other than informal economic activity. Thus, the limited opportunities available to these migrants helps to sustain the expansion of informal economies as the site of more and more people's economic lives even as capital becomes concentrated in fewer and fewer people's hands.

Whereas most of the migrants we have studied found themselves regulated in ways that kept them working in informal economics, we also document the limited reach of such regulatory regimes into the erotic and intimate imagination and agency of migrants. We use the idea of the "potency of sex" to refer, in part, to migrants' resiliency in the face of the apparatus of these regulatory regimes, as well as the ways in which migrants deploy bodily and social resources, what we have referenced as "sexual capital," counteracting the regulations that serve to ultimately delimit their options for survival. In other words, the couplet of sexual victimhood and sexual danger has to be constantly reinvented to identify new threats to the community of value, while new forms of sexual agency and expression emerge to poke, prod, and sometimes unhinge the border regimes and attendant instances of regulation.[12]

The productive incoherence between regulation and resilience that has marked migratory experiences over the past several decades creates a series of double binds for migrants. Migrants are positioned as both a threat to the community of value and in need of protection from bad actors. They are positioned as the subjects of humanitarian aid and also treated by "host" countries as suspicious and in need of regulation, a situation that is morally legitimated by racialized discourses about normative gender and sexuality. They are able to survive in precarious situations by working in informal economies, but this work can also intensify policing by the state, by dominant society, and by other migrants, making these situations even more precarious. And even as precarious work in informal economies is deemed worthy of policing, it is also effectively treated as economically valuable. Sometimes, as in the case of the Dominican Republic, the value of migrants' work is created through direct government policies that induce labor in informal economies by blocking labor in other sectors; sometimes, as in the case of African migrants to Europe, value is created through the indirect but nonetheless powerful force of racialized discourses that refuse normative gender and sexuality to migrants while also hypersexualizing them.[13]

Migrants must then do their best to negotiate the ambivalences created by these double binds. In the Dominican Republic, it may be possible to inhabit a socially recognizable form of masculinity that enables both sex work and normative ideals of men providing for their families. And African immigrants to Europe may embrace their sexual agency while also keeping to themselves, so as to avoid both normative regulation and state policing.

Migrants, thus, may both embrace their sexual agency and also internalize regulatory logics. Migrants' various forms of engagement with gender and sexuality can reflect attempts to open spaces of legitimation through which to assert their rights to recognition by the state and other institutional arbiters of rights and protections. At the same time, these understandable efforts to achieve legitimacy can sometimes implicate the migrants themselves, reproducing normative discourses of gender and sexuality that relegate those engaged in the sex

154 Plambech, Padilla, Cheng, and Shah

work or illicit informal labor sectors to the margins, leading to greater policing, incarceration, and deportation. Importantly, we understand the mechanisms that result in collective forms of social control among migrants as reflections of the precarity generated by border regimes.

The apparent hardening of state institutions and the increasing fluidity of migrant subjects as shown in the four different sites demonstrate the ways in which borders themselves, both domestic and national, adapt to neoliberal processes of economic informalization and subject making. In the next chapter, another research group will consider some additional strategies people have developed for negotiating the double binds of neoliberal paradoxes and thereby sustaining lives and livelihoods. And, perhaps most importantly, the "Political Power and Practices of Resistance" group will think through some possibilities for building collective power – as well as economic and gender justice more generally.

Notes

1 See, e.g., Adrian Favell and Ettore Recchi (2020).
2 The descriptor "African" reflects the language used by asylum seekers and migrants from the African continent in Hong Kong to describe themselves. Asylum seekers from various parts of Africa often identify themselves as "African" for different purposes, even as they form a very loosely tied community. More discussion is provided below and in Cheng (2021).
3 See Zhang (2002). "The ratio of women to men among Nigerian migrants is striking in comparison to the ratio among migrants from other parts of Africa" (Kastner 2010; IOM 2017). A few women travel *via* airplane and counterfeit documents, the majority *via* high-risk migration through the Sahara Desert, typically through the central Mediterranean migration route *via* Agadez in Niger and then relying on ramshackle boats to sail them from Libya across the Mediterranean Sea to Italy.
4 See Anderson (2013); Bernstein (2012); De Genova (2013).
5 For theorizations of the relationship between sexual capital and Bourdieusian field theory, see, e.g., Hakim (2010); Green (2014).
6 See Bernstein (2018); De Genova (2013); De Genova et. al. (2018); Ticktin (2011).
7 See Kotz (2002); Chwieroth (2007); Shariati (2012).
8 On ongoing primary accumulation, see also Jakobsen (2015).
9 See Pennington and Balaram (2013); IOM (2017).
10 On informal economies, see for example, Agarwala (2009); Li Zhang (2002); Patricia Fernández-Kelly and Jon Shefner eds. (2006); Martha Chen and Françoise Carré, ed. (2020).
11 Other studies have shown that when women become targets of gossip, they are often suspected of engaging in sex work or other forms of sexual deviance (Malkin 2004).
12 See also Carole Vance's (1984) foundational anthology, *Pleasure and Danger*.
13 This interaction reflects the neoliberal afterlife of the combination of "ungendering" and "pornotroping" that Hortense Spillers (1987) has described as a central dynamic of slavery and which we discuss in Chapter 2.

References

Agamben, Giorgio. 1998. *Homo Sacer: Sovereign Power and Bare Life* (D. Heller-Roazen, Trans.). Stanford, CA: Stanford University Press.

Agarwala, Rina. 2009. "An Economic Sociology of Informal Work: The Case of India," *Economic Sociology of Work (Research in the Sociology of Work, Vol. 18)*, 315–342. Bingley: Emerald Group Publishing Limited, edited by Bandelj, N. https://doi.org/10.1108/S0277-2833(2009)0000018015.

Anderson, Bridget. 2013. *Us and Them?: The Dangerous Politics of Immigration Control.* Oxford; New York: OUP. https://doi.org/10.1093/acprof:oso/9780199691593.001.0001.

Bernstein, Elizabeth. 2010. "Militarized Humanitarianism Meets Carceral Feminism: The Politics of Sex, Rights, and Freedom in Contemporary Antitrafficking Campaigns," *Signs: Journal of Women in Culture and Society* 36 no. 1: 45–71. https://doi.org/10.1086/652918.

Bernstein, Elizabeth. 2012. "Carceral Politics as Gender Justice? The 'Traffic in Women' and Neoliberal Circuits of Crime, Sex, and Rights," *Theory & Society* 41, no. 3: 233–259. https://www.jstor.org/stable/41475719.

Bernstein, Elizabeth. 2018. *Brokered Subjects: Sex, Trafficking, and the Politics of Freedom.* Chicago, IL: University of Chicago Press.

Brotherton, David & Luis Barrios. 2011. *Banished to the Homeland: Dominican Deportees and their Stories of Exile.* New York: Columbia University Press. https://www.jstor.org/stable/10.7312/brot14934.

Byrd, Jodi A., et al. 2018. "Predatory Value: Economies of Dispossession and Distributed Relationalities," *Social Text* 36, no. 2 (June): 1–18. https://doi.org/10.1215/01642472-4362325.

Castañeda, Heide. 2019. *Borders of Belonging: Struggle and Solidarity in Mixed-Status Immigrant Families.* Stanford, CA: Stanford University Press.

Chávez, Karma R. and Eithne Lubhéid, eds. 2020. *Queer and Trans Migrations: Dynamics of Illegalization, Detention, and Deportation.* Urbana, Illinois: University of Illinois Press.

Chen, Martha and Françoise Carré, eds. 2020. *The Informal Economy Revisited.* London and New York: Routledge.

Cheng, Sealing. 2012/2013. "Embodying the Sexual Limits of Neoliberalism" *The Scholar and Feminist Online* 11, no. 1–2; (Fall/Spring). https://sfonline.barnard.edu/gender-justice-and-neoliberal-transformations/embodying-the-sexual-limits-of-neoliberalism/.

Cheng, Sealing. 2019. "Echoes of Victimhood: On Passionate Activism and 'Sex Trafficking,'" *Feminist Theory.* https://doi.org/10.1177/1464700119881303.

Cheng, Sealing. 2021. "Choreography of Masculinity: The Pursuit of Marriage by African Men in Forced Displacement in Hong Kong," *Feminist Review.* Forthcoming.

Cheng, Sealing, and Eunjung Kim. 2014. "The Paradoxes of Neoliberalism: Migrant Korean Sex Workers in the United States and 'Sex Trafficking,'" *Social Politics: International Studies in Gender, State and Society* 21 no. 3: 355.

Chwieroth, Jeffrey. 2007. "Neoliberal Economist and Capital Account Liberalization in Emerging Markets," *International Organization*, 61, no. 2 (Spring): 443–63. https://doi.org/10.1017/S0020818307070154.

Constable, Nicole. 2014. *Born Out of Place: Migrant Mothers and the Politics of International Labor.* First edition. Berkeley, CA: University of California Press.

De Genova, Nicholas. 2003. "Migrant 'Illegality' and Deportability in Everyday Life," *Annual Review of Anthropology* 31: 419–447. https://doi.org/10.1146/annurev.anthro.31.040402.085432.

De Genova, Nicholas. 2013. "Spectacles of Migrant 'Illegality': The Scene of Exclusion, the Obscene of Inclusion," *Ethnic and Racial Studies* 36 no. 7: 1180–1198. https://doi.org/10.1080/01419870.2013.783710.

De Genova Nicholas., et al. 2018. Introduction to Special Thematic Issue on "The Autonomy of Migration within the Crises," *SAQ: South Atlantic Quarterly* 117, no. 2 (April): 239–65.

Duggan, Lisa. 2003. *The Twilight of Equality?: Neoliberalism, Cultural Politics, and the Attack on Democracy*. Boston, MA: Beacon Press.

Favell, Adrian and Ettore Recchi. 2020. "Mobilities, Neo-Nationalism and the Lockdown: Will the European Union Survive?" *Compass*, 14 April, https://www.compas.ox.ac.uk/2020/mobilities-and-the-lockdown-of-europe-will-the-european-union-survive/.

Fernández-Kelly, Patricia, and Jon Shefner, eds. 2006. *Out of the Shadows: Political Action and the Informal Economy in Latin America*. University Park: Pennsylvania State University Press.

Freeman, Caren. 2017. *Making and Faking Kinship: Marriage and Labor Migration between China and South Korea*. Ithaca, NY: Cornell University Press.

Green, Adam Isaiah ed. 2014. *Sexual Fields: Toward a Sociology of Collective Sexual Life*. Chicago, IL: University of Chicago Press.

Hakim, Catherine. 2010. "Erotic Capital," *European Sociological Review* 26, no. 5: 499–518. https://doi.org/10.1093/esr/jcq014.

Hart, Keith. 2009. "On the Informal Economy: The Political History of an Ethnographic Concept," CEB Working Paper No. 09/042 2009. Available from: https://dipot.ulb.ac.be/dspace/bitstream/2013/54329/1/RePEc_sol_wpaper_09-042.pdf.

Harvey, David. 2004. "The 'New' Imperialism: Accumulation by Dispossession," *Socialist Register* 40: 63–87. https://socialistregister.com/index.php/srv/issue/view/441.

HK Golden Forum. 2009. "Hong Kong Women will not jump off the roof after marrying African men," 3 September. (港女跟非洲男人結婚後，不會跳樓).

International Organization for Migration (IOM). 2017. *Human Trafficking through the Mediterranean Route: Data, Stories and Information Collected by the International Organization for Migration*. Rome, Italy: IOM.

Jakobsen, Janet R. 2015. "Economic Justice after Legal Equality: The Case for Caring Queerly," *After Legal Equality: Family, Sex, Kinship*, edited by Robert Leckey, 77–96. New York: Routledge Press.

Kastner, Kristin. 2010. "Moving Relationships: Family Ties of Nigerian Migrants on Their Way to Europe," *African and Black Diaspora: An International Journal* 3, no. 1: 17–34. https://doi.org/10.1080/17528630903319813.

Kotz, David. 2002. "Globalization and Neoliberalism," *Rethinking Marxism* 12, no. 2: 64–79. https://people.umass.edu/dmkotz/Glob_and_NL_02.pdf.

Malkin, Victoria. 2004. "'We Go to Get Ahead': Gender and Status in Two Mexican Migrant Communities," *Latin American Perspectives* 31, no. 5: 75–99. https://doi.org/10.1177/0094582X04268402.

Mishra, Khushbu and Jeevant Rampal. 2020. "The COVID-19 Pandemic and Food Insecurity: A Viewpoint on India," *World Development* 135: 1–3. https://doi.org/10.1016/j.worlddev.2020.105068.

Nigam, Shalu. 2017. "An Ordinary Life Enslaved by a Card: Coercively Linking Aadhaar with Hunger is no Solution," 28 October. Available at SSRN: https://ssrn.com/abstract=3060959.

Nyers, Peter. 2019. *Irregular Citizenship, Immigration, and Deportation*. London: Routledge.

Padilla, Mark, Colón-Burgos, José Félix, Varas-Díaz, Nelso, Matiz-Reyes, Armando, & Parker, Caroline Mary. 2018. "Tourism Labor, Embodied Suffering, and the Deportation Regime in the Dominican Republic," *Medical Anthropology Quarterly*, 32(4): 498–519. https://doi.org/10.1111/maq.1244

Pennington, Jenny & Brhmie Balaram. 2013. "Homecoming: Return and Reintegration of Irregular Migrants from Nigeria," London: The Institute for Public Policy Research. https://www.ippr.org/publications/homecoming-return-and-reintegration-of-irregular-migrants-from-nigeria.

Plambech, Sine. 2014a. *Becky's Journey.* Documentary. 24. min. Production. Final Cut for Real. https://vimeo.com/konggulerod/review/106332153/e7b6e40049.

Plambech, Sine. 2014b. "Between 'Victims' and 'Criminals': Rescue, Deportation, and Everyday Violence among Nigerian Migrants," *Social Politics: International Studies in Gender, State and Society* 21, no. 3: 382–402.

Plambech, Sine. 2016. "Sex, Deportation and Rescue: Economies of Migration among Nigerian Sex Workers," *Feminist Economics* Published online: 17 May. https://doi.org/10.1080/13545701.2016.1181272.

Plambech, Sine. 2017. "God Brought You Home: Deportation as Moral Governance in the Lives of Nigerian Sex Worker Migrants," *Journal of Ethnic and Migration Studies* 43, no. 13: 2211–2227. https://doi.org/10.1080/1369183X.2017.1280386.

Sassen, Saskia. 2014. *Expulsions: Brutality and Complexity in the Global Economy.* Cambridge, MA.: Harvard University Press.

Scheper-Hughes, Nancy. 2003. "Rotten Trade: Millennial Capitalism, Human Values and Global Justice in Organs Trafficking," *Journal of Human Rights* 2, no. 2: 197–226. https://doi.org/10.1080/1475483032000078189.

Shah, Svati. 2014. *Street Corner Secrets: Sex, Work and Migration in the City of Mumbai.* Durham, NC: Duke University Press. https://doi.org/10.1215/9780822376514.

Shariati, Mehdi. 2012. "Neoliberalism, Capital Accumulation, and Austerity," *KCKCC E-Journal* 6, no. 1 (March): https://www.kckcc.edu/files/docs/ejournal/volume-six/number-one-march-2012/neoliberalism-capital-accumulation-and-austerity.pdf.

Soderlund, Gretchen. 2011. "The Rhetoric of Revelation: Sex Trafficking and the Journalistic Exposé," *Humanity: An International Journal of Human Rights, Humanitarianism, and Development* 2, no. 2 (Summer): 193–211. http://humanityjournal.org/wp-content/uploads/2014/06/2.2-The-Rhetoric-of-Revelation.pdf.

Spillers, Hortense. 1987. "Mama's Baby, Papa's Maybe: An American Grammar Book," *Diacritics* 16, no. 2 (Summer): 64–81. https://doi.org/10.2307/464747.

Sriraman, Tarangini. (2018). *In Pursuit of Proof: A History of Identification Documents in India.* New Delhi: Oxford University Press.

Ticktin, Miriam. 2011. *Casualties of Care: Immigration and the Politics of Humanitarianism in France.* Berkeley, CA: University of California Press.

United Nations Development Programme. 2020. "Red Actúa: Segunda encuesta sobre el impacto socioeconómico de la COVID-19" (Red Actua: Second survey on the socioeconomic impact of COVID-19) (September). https://www.unicef.org/dominicanrepublic/informes/red-actua-infografia-segunda-encuesta-sobre-el-impacto-socioeconomico-de-la-covid-19.

Vance, Carole. 1984. *Pleasure and Danger: Towards a Politics of Sexuality.* Boston, MA: Routledge & Kegan Paul.

Vecchio, Francesco. 2014. *Asylum Seeking and the Global City.* London: Routledge.

Yang, Hairong. 2012. "What If Your Client/Employer Treats Her Dog Better Than She Treats You?": Market Militarism and Market Humanism in Postsocialist Beijing," In *Global Futures in East Asia: Youth, National and the New Economy,* edited by Ann Anagnost, Andrea Arai, and Hai Ren, 50–173. Stanford, CA: Stanford University Press.

Zelizer, Viviana A. 2002. "Intimate Transactions." In *The New Economic Sociology: Developments in an Emerging Field*, edited by Mauro F. Guillén, Randall Collins, Paula England, and Marshall Meyer, 274–300. New York: Russell Sage Foundation.

Zhang, Li. 2002. *Strangers in the City: Reconfigurations of Space, Power, and Social Networks Within China's Floating Population*. Palo Alto, CA: Stanford University Press.

6
POLITICAL POWER AND PRACTICES OF RESISTANCE

Mario Pecheny, Janet Jakobsen,
Ana Amuchástegui, and Maja Horn

The goal of this volume has been to develop a conversation amongst scholars living and working in different areas of the world (Argentina, Denmark, the Dominican Republic, Hong Kong, India, Mexico, Nigeria, South Korea, the United States, and the US Virgin Islands) about their understandings of neoliberalism, the imbrication of gender and sex in neoliberal political economies, and current possibilities for achieving justice.

Through our conversations across sites, we have come to understand neoliberalism as a *concatenation* of differential, often productively incoherent, projects – some political, some economic. Some places are the direct subject of structural adjustment policies imposed by transnational institutions, some have moved beyond these direct policies toward new social and political formations, and some were never subject to structural adjustment directly but have nonetheless experienced a range of neoliberal effects, such as a proliferation of non-governmental and semi-governmental organizations. Interactions among gender, sexuality, economics, and politics also vary across this range of neoliberal policies, practices, and effects. Sometimes, gender and sexuality are the legitimating site for policies that bundle together economics and changes to the structure of the state, like those pertaining to "sex trafficking" (Chapter 4). In other instances, sexual politics are an implicit dimension of broader policies on issues ranging from migration (Chapter 5) to the growth of financial services accompanied by a concomitant expansion of inequality (Chapter 3).

Not only does neoliberalism include a bundle of distinct policies and practices, but contemporary governmentality is also produced by practices that have been layered over time. One of the major arguments of our project is that neoliberal transformations both maintain many of the old contradictions of capitalism and democracy, and also introduce new tensions and taxing levels of incoherence.

DOI: 10.4324/9781003252702-6

Part of what we have explored throughout this book is the persistence of modern policies, practices, and their attendant contradictions, which do not simply disappear. In this sense, neoliberalism is not a brand-new formation. Rather, it is a particularly lethal form of capitalism. So, for example, neoliberal governmentality organizes *life* into a zero-sum logic: the idea that everything you get is always at the expense of others, and/or at the expense of yourself. You cannot have cooperative gains or any kind of positive surplus in which possibilities become more abundant for everyone. We cannot all win, and so everyone tries to save themselves, creating a situation in which, if one is willing to harm those who are variously precarious, one might be able to survive. Neoliberal governmentality also increasingly organizes *lives* into a zero-sum game: some categories of the human population (in terms of class or race or nation or generation, for example) have become or are perceived to be superfluous and disposable. There is no place for everybody in this world. And some categories of living beings (animals, plants) have entered in this zero-sum game and have also become superfluous: there is no place for everyone/thing anymore.

Neoliberalism also creates new forms of organization that build on old contradictions and transform them into new paradoxes. The promises of liberalism as the political complement to capitalism were never true, but these promises remained credible for some people. Now belief in equal democracy or that individual choices matter to life chances seem more visible as a simulacrum. The promises of liberal democracy have sometimes provided a glimpse of some other alternative, but seemingly more and more frequently the obviousness of their falsity means there is no glimpse of something else. So, the effects of neoliberalism are paradoxical: many people actively work for more democracy even though they may well also know that it is a lie – the very means for reproducing inequality. Sometimes, these actions are cynical. For example, those in political power often make purported investments in democratic processes and accountability in the hopes of helping their electoral chances, even as they also embrace illegal or semi-legal activities to get "elected." And, in response, voters and activists also fight for more democracy, all the while knowing that these efforts are not going to work to produce a politics separate from money and monied interests. People want some kind of justice within capitalism, but many also doubt justice will ever be realized.

The double bind created by these paradoxical effects is present in liberalism, as well as neoliberalism. But neoliberal policies have narrowed the space of legitimate action in a number of areas – in Latin America, the weaknesses of electoral democracy, the constant violation of the rule of law, and the dubious promises of the age of development have given way to the harsh certainties of an age of austerity. In the United States (US), active voter suppression remains persistent and, since 2020, has intensified, including repeated attacks on the 1965 Voting Rights Act, attempts to control the Census so as to control voting access, and the gerrymandering of Congressional Districts.[1] Even as democratic possibilities

Political power and practices of resistance **161**

have narrowed, the influence of wealthy donors has increased, particularly after the 2010 Supreme Court's Citizens United ruling, in which money was made the equivalent of political speech that must flow "freely" (Bai 2012). Transnationally, increased use of surveillance technologies and moralistic campaigns against sex trafficking have reduced space for the survival economies that are, for many people, the most rational approach to life in a world that paradoxically promises equality and justice and delivers intensified inequality and legal systems that protect the beneficiaries of that inequality.

In this chapter, we consider some of the specifics of how systems of power relations interact with sexual politics so as to constitute neoliberal governance, and we explore how people enact resistance to the strictures of this social formation. We analyze the effects of neoliberalism as a paradoxical governmentality (Foucault 1991) that draws upon state and corporate power, along with practices across a range of sectors (medicine and healthcare, education, popular media, and cultural production). Thus, the concept of governmentality allows us to analyze both state power and large-scale institutions intertwined with local relations in which interpellations to autonomy, freedom, performance, immediacy (e.g., immediate satisfaction: love, money, professional success), and efficacy are incorporated and embodied by individual subjects.

With the concept of governmentality, the idea of sovereign power, of a monolithic state, and of well-established and well-known cleavages (us *v.* them: workers *v.* capitalists, women *v.* men, periphery *v.* center, etc.) shifts toward an analysis of diffused relationships and subjectivities. This understanding of neoliberal governmentality reflects what Lascoumes and LeGales (2007) call "to govern through instruments:" these instruments structure practices of neoliberalism well beyond those of direct state policy, including local, national, and global norms, virtual media, and NGO-ization (i.e., the transformation of radical social movements into financially accountable, formally institutionalized non-governmental organizations and networks).

Yet this shift does not necessarily imply that the state is no longer an important object of analysis. Micro-relations of power are variously related to, limited by, and in tension with the state, which has, and is experienced as having many faces and voices. It is not a plural state as liberal discourse might once have claimed – a democratic arena (even if an unfair and unequal one) – but rather a set of interacting logics and relationships that are experienced simultaneously as oppressive, indifferent, disenfranchising, empowering, and supportive.

Together, these practices create processes of subjectivation (Foucault 1980; Flynn 1985; Butler 1997). Through a series of case studies drawn from Mexico, the US, and the Dominican Republic, we will consider in this chapter both the effects of neoliberal subjectivation and creative responses through art and activism by which people survive in the face of increasing precarity. These responses can create possibilities for different political outcomes, and the inspiration to imagine vastly different worlds.

Neoliberalism, governmentality, and the fractured state

In articulating the complexities of contemporary political possibility, Mario Pecheny (2012/2013) has argued that Latin America has oscillated between neoliberalism and "post-neoliberalism." Neoliberal policies have been instituted in many Latin American countries, shifting people's lives in ways that having continuing effects, and these effects now interact with newer policies and practices. Thus, many Latin Americans live in post-neoliberal conditions in the sense both of the era after the imposition of neoliberalism, and the era in which a formation after neoliberalism (at least in political terms) is taking effect.

Pecheny argues that a multi-layered set of policies – drawn from time periods and policy formations marked by liberal modernity, neoliberalism, and post-neoliberalism – also produces a fracturing within the state itself, as the state simultaneously undertakes practices of direct state violence, normative discipline, and control and securitization.[2] Further fracturing people's political experiences, the state both seeks legitimation for these actions and pursues them as if there were no need for legitimation. For example, in the Dominican Republic, the state has both instituted new legalized forms of migration control and has continuously carried out illegitimate arrests and deportations of Haitian immigrants that fundamentally side-step basic human rights guarantees and any form of governmental accountability. Similarly, the legislature in Mexico has recently (2017) approved the Interior Security Law, which allows the President to instruct the military to carry out police functions without any scrutiny or accountability for human rights violations. And the US has also tended to follow this approach of state action and violence that is both legitimated and not. The US-led wars in Iraq and Afghanistan, for instance, were "pursued for freedom, against terrorism and weapons of mass destruction, to save brown women from brown men and just because" (Cherniavsky 2017, 143).[3]

Importantly, the fractured actions of the state are both differentially distributed across populations and experienced differentially by any individual person. In the first instance of differential distribution, in Argentina and other countries, the denial of indigenous people as right holders and the endemic institutional violence against them in favor of transnational megaprojects, like mining, show a pattern of illegal/illegitimate violent action against one group as a way of gaining legitimacy among a right-wing constituency. In the US, freedom is instituted through security measures that enable the freedom of movement for some populations – those that are white and economically privileged – by controlling the movements of other populations, including African Americans policed at the neighborhood level, the national security surveillance of Muslims, and the ongoing surveillance of immigrant communities that forms a key component of border control.

In the second instance, any individual will have different experiences of state power. The same people whose lives are literally saved by having health care provided by the state in the US may also regard that very health care as

Political power and practices of resistance **163**

government overreach. Thus, early demonstrations against the Affordable Care Act, also known as "Obamacare," decried the law as government interference with health care and included people carrying signs that said, "Get your hands off my Medicare," despite the fact that Medicare is also sponsored by the US government. In response to the COVID-19 pandemic, many of the same politicians who denounced the wearing of face masks as a national security measure were among the first to receive coronavirus vaccines (Richardson 2020).

The differential distribution of effects is enabled by the fact that subjects experience the State as displaying multiple faces of power: decision makers, bureaucrats, health practitioners, teachers, researchers, security forces, social workers, police, and representatives of the legal system. Some people may have mainly a "one-face" experience of the state as oppressor and agent of exclusion, but most people also sometimes experience the state in the form of an actor with whom they might productively engage, or as an arena for their own actions, or a place for contest and claims-making. Even people who have been categorized in ways that have historically excluded them, such as transgender individuals or drug users, have experienced the state in its many faces: the entity responsible for their systematic exclusion and repression, as well as the more or less efficient providers of health care.

Citizens are thus caught up in a "double bind" (Bateson 1972) in which the state presents itself as both a site of oppression and a source of aid.[4] "In order to protect you, the state may threaten you; for you to be free, the state pursues more and more invasive measures for controlling individuals and groups and nations; the state recognizes you as a subject of rights, but the police and bureaucratic officials will harass you when you claim them; or, in some countries, the state will create a sense of security for your health by providing anti-retroviral drugs, but the health protection is so unstable that this certainty might switch into uncertainty at any moment" (Pecheny 2017). In this double bind, certainty is always uncertain, freedom is unfree, and security measures intensify danger for most people.

One effect of these paradoxes is a subjective experience of the state as irrational in its actions. Fractured experiences of the state/experiences of the state as fractured destabilize people as political subjects because one has to make an effort all the time to decipher what the state is doing today and what it is going to do tomorrow; then one has to figure out what one wants to say and do, or not do, in response. This experience of the fractured, paradoxical, and irrational state, the double bind it creates for political subjects is, in fact, a form of political subjectivation. Because neoliberal governmentality is itself paradoxical, neoliberal subjectivation produces ambivalent affective responses. Political subjects may both love and hate the state as they negotiate life in relation to shifting economic possibilities and a state that is experienced as highly regulatory and overly involved in the lives of individuals and, at the same time, also frustratingly inaccessible and likely to undermine life possibilities at any moment. This experience creates the sense of facing contradictory demands which are impossible to fulfill, even as

164 Pecheny, Jakobsen, Amuchástegui, and Horn

it is impossible to ignore them or to live as if they do not exist. And this experience of the state as both necessary for and destructive toward the sustainability of one's life can be reiterated across institutions as discourses of governmentality both create and constrain life possibilities.

Take the state's demand to wait that is the foundational experience of many people, including refugees as described in Chapter 5.[5] In Mexico, for example, victims of feminicide or forced disappearance are promised expedited investigation and justice, which are seldom delivered in spite of years of waiting. The waiting is so prolonged and pervasive, that there is a growing movement of relatives looking independently for their disappeared ones. Whereas this example involves direct expectation of the state, waiting can also be mediated: the use of the time of others or when others use your time by making you wait. Thus, these forms of waiting involve not just the government but a broader sense of governmentality in which discourses across institutions reiterate this type of experience.[6] So, for example, when thinking about the experience of time in relation to neoliberalism, we can see how the effects of governmentality include the state, and also extend beyond its specific actions. And whether direct or mediated, the experience of waiting can become a mode of subjectivation, a process in which one's life is formed by waiting and waiting and waiting for answers from the state or from other institutions, or even from one's more intimate relations.[7] Will you get housing from the government or medicine from an insurance company, or will you get the document that allows you to be a resident and gain access to legitimate employment? Will your daughter's killer ever be found and tried? Will your son, disappeared by police forces, ever come back?

We also see how neoliberal governmentality can induce double binds for people and then demand that individuals resolve them. For example, neoliberal instantiations of time can involve both the demand to wait and an intensive "speed-up" – faster and faster communications, intensive demands for faster and more "efficient" production from labor, more rapidly destructive wars, less time between major disasters (hurricanes, fires, floods). People living in Puerto Rico in 2017, for example, experienced both the speed-up of two major hurricanes in the space of a few weeks, and the slow-down of disaster relief that did not manage to restore electricity to many parts of the island for months.[8] In the world of work, scholars, intellectuals and artistic professionals are not unfamiliar with longer processes of evaluation and reporting, superimposed with growing demands for efficiency and hyper-productivity. The crucial shift that the analysis of paradoxes allows is to connect neoliberal speed-up to neoliberal waiting. As with regulation and freedom, the two poles are distributed differentially across populations and experienced differentially by individuals.

Even for those who are dedicated to activism, or resistance, or movements for social change, daily life is likely to be organized through instruments of governmentality that make any course of action ambivalent and its potential effects paradoxical. What relation to the state should one claim or advocate when the state acts as both a source of individual and global problems and one of the few

Political power and practices of resistance **165**

avenues to solutions? Neoliberal discourses suggest a turn away from the state toward "individual agency" and "personal responsibility," but neoliberal policies also reduce or eliminate the available means and favorable conditions to achieve personal or social goals. How is one to successfully enact "agency" in a more and more globalized, expulsive, and extractive economy? How to be an engaged political subject when meaningful change on virtually any issue is caught up in ambiguities? How, for example, can one make claims for the importance of addressing climate change when almost any consumable good is polluting, is based on exploitation, and produces garbage? These paradoxes, ambivalences, and incoherencies imply that historical forms of resistance – e.g., those who choose either to work within the state, to create a drag on capitalism, or direct resistance against the state – will not be particularly effective. Instead, approaches that recognize the paradoxical workings of power may have more chances for success, even if success becomes harder to define.

Case studies in gender and neoliberal governmentality

As the examples that we deal with in this chapter will show, the fractured, multi-faceted, and paradoxical nature of neoliberal governmentality extends across not just the state and economy, but many fields of life, including public health and medicine, and the experience of illness and disease. Ana Amuchástegui documents the lives of women living with HIV in Mexico City. Their lives are in part livable because they are medicalized, but at the same time such medicalization requires those living with HIV to manage both their chronicity and their relationship with health services as agents of governmentality. This incoherence is not unique to those living with HIV, but in Amuchástegui's field work, we see that it is intensified: those things, like medical care, that allow you to continue more or less living, that even give you happiness, are those that irritate you deeply, define you by the strictures of necessity and by lack. Moreover, at the same time that many of the governmental practices extend various medicalized discourses that position women as passive victims of disease, state-sponsored medical peer groups also help women to understand themselves as actively living and creating life chances. In other words, the state is both the producer of suffering and the site to which people – and political movements – turn in the hopes of alleviating that suffering. It is a paradoxical experience – the peer group practices can extend the expert knowledge and governmental control of state and institutional medicine even as they create a sense of possibility for women living with HIV. The very practices that allow you to live also keep you in a heteronomous subjectivation.

Amuchástegui is interested in how the desire for life can be realized differently in peer group settings than in the doctor's office, as peer group participants articulate a different assemblage of living with HIV than that allowed by medical care alone, even as the women's lives and possibilities are not entirely autonomous from the sphere of medical practice. One of the questions for resistance,

166 Pecheny, Jakobsen, Amuchástegui, and Horn

then, is how to pull ambivalent desires toward different social formations, ones that may not be utterly autonomous from neoliberalism but that nonetheless slip through or past some of its double binds. In order to understand what makes for effective practices of resistance, it is helpful to explore in more detail the workings of governmentality in relation to neoliberal paradoxes.

Case study 1. Women, HIV and antiretroviral treatment in Mexico: a pastoral relationship

Access to HIV treatment and care has been a universal right in Mexico since 2003. As the result of a long political struggle on the part of social movements (not free from conflict themselves), HIV care in public health services was achieved through a contradictory process in which the success of rights claims depended on the same state that was the movements' political adversary.[9] At the same time, the state's power and its practices with regard to HIV have been contradictory, enacted through neoliberal policies that both enable and refuse support for life with HIV. Practices of resistance to the denial of life possibility for those with HIV have carried their own ambivalences and paradoxes, as we briefly detail through this case study of a peer advisory intervention carried out by women living with HIV in two government clinics in Mexico City.[10]

This fieldwork showed the emergence of a *subject of adherence* (to HIV treatment), a subject who is produced through a pastoral relationship that requires its addressees to collaborate actively. Women's subjection to this *pastoral of the soma* (Rose 2001) is, paradoxically, a fundamental condition for their autonomy and agency, as well as for sustaining life itself. Thus, their active participation in the biopolitical project for the control of the AIDS epidemic not only effects subjectivation, but also sets the stage for their own *projects of happiness* (Ayres 2001).

The relationship between biomedical practices and women's appropriations of prescriptions of care involves diverse mechanisms of mediation that are also variously paradoxical. For instance, while one of these mediations elicits women's *obedience* to technical prescriptions, patients are also normatively positioned as *subjects of rights* in accordance with the body of law that protects people living with HIV in Mexico. Health care practices are thus ruled by bioethical and normative principles of "gender equality, sexual diversity, and non-discrimination," as well as by human rights legislation. In this sense, the *self-evident rationality* claimed by medical discourses often clashes with women's *right to self-determination* in relation to treatment and health care.

Furthermore, medical authorities expect this *subject of obedience* to follow instructions without question, although that expectation is constantly frustrated. The material and vital condition of the subject, their life force, creates the potential for fracture between medical practice and obedience to its injunctions. Hiding their symptoms, not being constant with their treatment and concealing information from their providers, as well as skipping their appointments, are seen as *faults* that come out of women's poor education, lack of common sense, and

Political power and practices of resistance **167**

even ingratitude towards the institutions providing care, when women's actions can also respond to other conditions of life beyond the circumscribed designation of "medical patient."

Responsibilization is another mediating mechanism between health institutions and patients' experiences and identities, as it holds women responsible for their own health outcomes, concealing the ways in which structural processes shape these outcomes. In this context, adherence to treatment, insofar as it is the product of a pastoral relationship, is a way to conduct individuals' behavior in order to cultivate subjects who are free to self-manage and who enact that freedom along a relatively narrow prescribed path (Rose 2000; see also Adam 2005). The *responsible* subject is, first of all, a *free* subject who can make her own decisions and is willing to face the consequences of these decisions. In Rose's (2000, 324) words, "freedom technologies ... have been invented to rule *through* and not *despite* the autonomous choices of relatively independent entities."

> The doctor said: "If I tell you you're not dying; will you stop crying?" "Yes." "How long do you want to live?" And I said ..." My daughter's eight, so I would like to live at least ten years more, so I can see her become an adult and take care of herself." And the doctor told me: "It's easy! Nowadays, you can live up to twenty, thirty, or as many years as you wish, as long as you take care of yourself." From that moment on, I said, "That's true, it's entirely up to me." (Mariel, diagnosed 11 years ago, widow, one daughter, Mexico City)

Responsibilization enhances the *subject of obedience* even as it disguises the incompetence of the reductionist biomedical approach. Negative outcomes are not understood as flaws of the medical system, but instead are attributed to the moral failings of the individual. Although responsibilization places the responsibility for health in the patient's hands, this particular mediation also matches neoliberal policies that tend to dismantle people's ability to make claims as the subjects of rights through moralization and individualization.

Expertization, as defined by Pecheny, Manzelli, and Jones (2002), also mediates between biopolitical interventions and women's experiences of living with the virus, as their responsibility as patients induces them to take on the role of experts.[11] While medical staff are positioned as the competent authority regarding scientific knowledge and biomedical technologies, women are expected to become "experts" in order to monitor their symptoms and manage their HIV as a chronic condition. A medicalized body is, thus, relationally constructed in order to be understood as a set of systems and organs that need to be decoded, in the case of HIV, at a *cellular* level. This way, both ends of the pastoral relationship work to facilitate the process of *expertization*; patients and staff alike strive to build a common language that may allow them, for instance, to interpret lab results (viral load and CD4 (T cell) count) and turn them into trustworthy indicators of patients' health. Irene tells her story: "The doctor explained to me that

168 Pecheny, Jakobsen, Amuchástegui, and Horn

I didn't need to worry about my viral load. The viruses that I had in my blood are so low, they can't even be counted because I'm giving the fight for my life. She said she could tell I was following my prescription very precisely" (57 years old, diagnosed ten years ago, domestic worker, Morelos).

Expertization, responsibilization, and other governmental technologies can be thought of not merely as operations of power, but also as lines of desire; in other words, as *agencements*. As Deleuze (1988) explains: "To desire is to construct *agencement*, to construct an assemblage." In this sense, assemblage works as a description of how desire leads one to assemble life possibilities out of different elements that may not fit together but that nonetheless can effectively form a basis for acting in the world. Yet, *agencement* itself is multifaceted in that gaining the power to act on the basis of assemblages also makes one the agent of those assemblages — whether those that constitute medical practice or those of political life.

In the life-sustaining assemblages women living with HIV construct, peer counseling can become an essential anchoring element. Peer counseling works as an allied strategy for therapeutic adherence, not from an appeal to obedience, but from appeal to desire and from a space of solidarity rather than hierarchy. In this space, women have developed subtle ways of negotiating the effects of biopower, including a refusal to establish an identity saturated by seropositivity. "I am a woman living with HIV" is a useful identity for an initial relationship with health services, but participants resist it, in this case, thanks partially to the interventions of peer advisors. In fact, when participants in group sessions complained repeatedly about their "illness," peer advisors would exclaim: "Stop saying you are sick; you just have a diagnosis!"

Based on the construction of a collectivity of mutual support, peer counselors carry out a task of *demedicalizing* diagnosis in order to give it a different dimension: *a commitment to health and to life*. Their own bodies are the material sign of the antiretroviral treatment's effect. Thus, they construct a message that is different from the one sent by medical knowledge — which understands medical prescription as the goal to *control the disease* — and turn it into a message that understands treatment as a *living condition*, a condition they will have to live with if they want to stay in this world: biopower inevitably dialogues with this potency inasmuch as it is understood as something other than the sum of preventive actions taken to keep the body in check, and more like the expression of the intensity and joy of living (Campos 2009).

Case study 2. Ambivalent responses to paradoxical governmentality: Trump and the ascendance of nationalist neoliberalism

Some of the same technologies of government described in Amuchástegui's case study, such as responsibilization, can also help in an analysis of the political forces that led in 2016 to the election of Donald Trump to the presidency of the US and to the crystallization of what we have termed "nationalist neoliberalism." Janet Jakobsen's case study explores how Trump addressed many people's love-hate relationship with the neoliberal state. Trump's campaign drew upon a populist rhetoric to address people's desire for different policies than those offered by the neoliberal state, even as his administration enacted both some of policies desired by nationalist populism (such as the tariffs and "trade wars") and policies that intensify neoliberalism (including massive tax cuts for the wealthy). As with the paradox of actions tracked by Amuchástegui, the same action – a vote for Trump – can represent both a resistance to (or even a rejection of) neoliberalism and an embrace of intensified neoliberal governance. Trump's combination of white nationalism, populism, and neoliberal economics presented an assemblage that combined both a belief in the neoliberal emphasis on responsibility and resentment at neoliberalism's economic effects. And for individuals responding to the fractured state, Trump also embodied a particular form of aggressive masculinity that allowed his supporters to simultaneously submit to the authoritarian tendencies of his government and to feel that their support for him freed them from governmental authority. As with Amuchástegui's case, commitments to governance can be intertwined with the desire for something different, and this intertwining effectively creates a political double bind, in which even resentment of neoliberalism can be bound to an extension of neoliberal policies.

Because neoliberalism is so often conflated with globalization, the idea of nationalist neoliberalism may seem paradoxical (Dreiling 2016). But we have argued that the years since 2016 have seen a continuation or even intensification of some aspects of neoliberalism, such as austerity, privatization, and precarity, along with a turn toward nationalism with increased securitization of national borders and some movement away from global trade. Trends toward nationalist neoliberalism can be seen in various parts of the world, including Brazil (Faiola and Lopes 2018), Poland (Santora 2019), and the UK (Landler and Castel 2020), and, in the US, these trends were crystalized by the 2016 election of Trump to the presidency.

Trump's defeat and the election of Joseph Biden in 2020 has shifted some policies, such as the governmental response to the COVID-19 pandemic, but the overall movement toward connecting nationalism with neoliberalism has not been reversed. For example, although Biden's administration has pursued global diplomatic alliances, Biden has repeatedly emphasized his focus on government support for American manufacturing before global economic connections, a position not so far from Trump's "America First" slogan (Sorkin et al. 2020).[12] Similarly, when it comes to border control, Biden's administration has signaled an openness to allowing asylum claims to resume while also "sending a strong signal that the change in administration does not mean it is suddenly easy to get asylum here. This is intended to discourage migrations, a form of deterrence" (Sargent 2020). The path chosen by the Biden Administration might best be termed "nationalist neoliberalism-light" sustaining much of the approach while removing the worst economic and political cruelties of nationalist neoliberalism.

The analytic frame provided by the concept-metaphor of the "paradoxes of neoliberalism" puts Trump's election and nationalist neoliberalism in the context of the ambivalent affective responses people have to the neoliberal state. Trump's campaign promised both to fight for the "deconstruction of the administrative state" (as stated directly by then-senior advisor Steve Bannon shortly after Trump's inauguration) and to maintain or even build up specific parts of the state through, for example, spending on infrastructure projects (Rucker and Costa 2017).[13] While there is much debate over the reasons for Trump's electoral victory, one way to interpret the debate is that voters themselves are variously ambivalent, that they desire different (and perhaps even opposing) things with regard to neoliberal policies. In other words, voters in the 2016 US elections might have been driven simultaneously by their affective investment in neoliberalism and by concerns about – even a protest against – neoliberalism.[14]

Some political commentators thought that the effects of the COVID-19 pandemic would break through the productive incoherence of Trump's promises.[15] But, as Ana Amuchástegui points out, neoliberal responsibility is inculcated through processes of subjectivation that activate the "personal" sense of the individual as responsible for his or her own life regardless of social supports. And personal responsibility became a central theme of Trumpian responses to the coronavirus pandemic. State Governors who followed Trump in refusing to impose mandates for wearing masks in public often invoked personal responsibility, and public polling both before and after the 2020 election showed that, for a significant part of the electorate, this message sustained Trump's voting base despite the rising death toll (Noem 2020; Bycoffe et al. 2021).[16] This subjectivation can turn the negative effects of public policy into a sense of personal failing – to be ameliorated by trying harder rather than by demanding policy change. And it can occlude the social benefits to those at the top of social hierarchies that are produced by race, class, and gender, so that being on either the top or the bottom of such hierarchies is not experienced as the effect of social systems but of one's own merits or failings.

"Responsibilization," as identified by Amuchástegui, organizes the desires of individuals – for health care, for jobs, for a sense of self and of self-worth – into an openness to hierarchical authority, such as that of medical professionals. The politics of the Trump presidency present a similar kind of paradox in which some voters hope to claim personal responsibility through an openness to an authoritarian figure who promises to correct the political problems attendant with the loss of access to some of the traditional privileges associated with whiteness and maleness.[17] If anything, the four years of the Trump presidency saw an increasing openness to authoritarian gestures. The paradox of those voters who understand themselves to be most committed to individual freedom being open to such authoritarian rhetoric can, thus, be understood through the assemblage crystallized as "personal responsibility."

Political power and practices of resistance   **171**

This assemblage connects desires for freedom and self-determination to moral values about self-discipline and to the political issues of race, gender, sex, and class. It further connects these issues to the neoliberal economic and political policies of limited government support for the social safety net, and increased control of the security state apparatus. It is an incoherent and even paradoxical assemblage: it promotes "de-regulation" and "freedom," while also depending on intensified regulation of gender and sexuality and of immigration. The assemblage may be driven by desires for self-determination, and yet it supports authoritarian rhetoric and what political philosopher Sheldon Wolin (2017) has called "inverted totalitarianism." But the political formation organized through this assemblage can gain strength from its incoherence, not only appearing to do one thing – promote freedom – while actually doing another – intensifying the regulation of gender, sex, race, and nation – but also by responding to the ambivalent commitments of a political populace that both desires and distrusts state action.

It is unclear if this openness to authoritarianism will remain tied to Trump's persona. Scholars have argued that it represents a longstanding strain of American political life, grounded in the white Christian nationalism of the founding of the US.[18] And other scholars have identified the sustenance of this form of authoritarian nationalism in the Republican Party (Giroux 2006). It is also the case that Trump inhabits a form of masculinity that makes the current right-wing assemblage work. Trump's particular version of masculinity – as a heterosexual white male, an apparently successful businessman, an abuser of women, who is also anti-immigrant and willing to flaunt norms of civility – embodies an aspirational sense of masculine individual freedom, one in which Trump can claim to both be personally responsible for his own success (as a businessman) and simultaneously free, including free of all of the constraint and self-discipline usually associated with responsibility. Trump's subjectivity may be utterly unattainable; it may be the product of television, rather than reality (the personal fragility that Trump has displayed through his Twitter stream shows that it is difficult even for Trump to inhabit), but it is a powerful enough realization of some people's desires that they are willing to subject themselves to its political claims, even when those claims run directly counter to some of their interests.

As Amuchástegui suggests, however, the affective force of subjectivation is open to re-articulation, including articulation through solidarity rather than through the hierarchy of obtaining freedom by obedience to authority. In the case of women living with HIV in Mexico, interaction in peer groups can shift the relation between women's desires to live and their subjectivation as being individually responsible for their lives. Through the social action of peers, Amuchástegui sees the possibility for an opening to a different assemblage of power relations. Similarly, by recognizing the dual – and even paradoxical – sets of desires inculcated by neoliberal policies, it might be possible to articulate both

172 Pecheny, Jakobsen, Amuchástegui, and Horn

economic possibilities and race, sex, and gender relations differently. Our next two examples take up this possibility.

Case studies in traversing the double bind

The political strategy that is often suggested in response to a productively incoherent political assemblage is to create an apparently coherent politics – work with the state or oppose the state; either leave race, gender, and sex aside in order to reassert a coherent class politics and oppose neoliberalism or capitulate to neoliberalism for the sake of diversity (Benn Michaels 2011; Frank 2017). Yet, the incoherence of the assemblage makes ineffective either of the choices presented in such binaristic terms.

The choice to simply oppose the state, for example, leaves many people who are directly affected by state policy without recourse. A radical organization, like the Sylvia Rivera Law Project (SRLP) in New York City, recognizes that many poor, trans, and gender non-conforming people need to deal with the state to change their documented gender status even if SRLP also opposes the regulation of binary gender and gender categorization itself (SRLP 2016). If one seeks coherence by appealing only to the limits of gender categories, however, then any engagement with the categories – particularly as enacted by the regulatory state – would be anathema. But, of course, some people are better positioned to ignore the state than others, and those who are already targeted for state surveillance – poor people of color – are often those who can least afford to live with a disjunction between their documents and their lives. Similarly, with efforts to reform marijuana laws: some people can expect never to have to engage with the police over their possession, use, or sale of marijuana, whereas, for others, the possession of even small amounts of marijuana can lead to imprisonment. Legal reform of various kinds – including reform of drug laws and of policing – can be a crucial part of improving life chances for those people regularly targeted by the police (Mueller, Gebeloff, and Chinoy 2018).

Recognizing the complexities of marginalized lives, queer studies scholar José Esteban Muñoz developed a method that doesn't trap us on any single side of a binary opposition, a strategy that Muñoz terms "disidentification." To "disidentify" in relation to subjectivation opens up the type of creative possibilities that women in HIV peer support groups in Mexico City employ to turn medical protocols toward possibilities for intensity and joy in living. Muñoz (1999, 31) defines "disidentification" as follows:

> Disidentification is about recycling and rethinking encoded meaning. The process of disidentification … is a step further than cracking open the code of the majority; it proceeds to use this code as raw material for representing a disempowered politics or positionality that has been rendered unthinkable by the dominant culture.

Joy is not the response imagined by the majority of people living with HIV, but disidentification in relation to subjectivation enables forms of paradoxical action in relation to dominant political formations. Trans artist and activist Tourmaline (2016) has termed this type of response, "making a way out of no way." As Dean Spade (2012/2013), founder of the Sylvia Rivera Law Project, has noted, trans lives are thought by the dominant culture to be impossible, and yet trans people have learned to develop lives that enable survival and thriving. Muñoz focuses on practices of disidentification involved in queer performance art. He documents performances across several decades that refuse normative categories, including the category of "queer" itself. He notes how "queer" can devolve to a normatively white and male category, but that performances by queers of color distance queerness from this normative pull. And the art and performance cultures documented by Muñoz are often connected to practices of political activism.[19]

Case study 3. Queer survival economies and organizing practices in the US

The Queer Survival Economies project, developed by longtime activist Amber Hollibaugh, was established to address the double bind of neoliberal subjectivation. Specifically, the project aimed to address the relationship between the "invisible lives and targeted bodies" of queer and gender non-conforming people, particularly people of color, who work in various survival economies, but who are rarely addressed as the subjects of labor organizing. As Hollibaugh and Margot Weiss (2015, 19) argue in the essay "Queer Precarity and the Myth of Gay Affluence": "LGBTQ people make up a disproportionately high number of the people in many low-wage sectors.... But the particular struggles of queer and gender non-conforming people remain sidelined, both in scholarly work and in the LGBT and labor movements themselves."

Even as the lives of economically precarious queer and gender non-conforming people are invisible to scholarship, to labor organizing and social movements, and to the governmental knowledge that can undergird access to services, these lives are also targeted for surveillance by both employers and the state. The jobs available to queer people are often those with the highest levels of employer surveillance, whether the clock-punching, intense management, and workplace cameras of low-wage retail labor or the police surveillance of grey economies like sex work and cash exchanges. Thus, even as the needs and contours of life for many workers are virtually invisible to the state and to movements for social change, they are also hypervisible to and hyperaware of "instruments of governance," particularly those involving surveillance in both the workplace and the streets. Moreover, there is no simple way out of the double bind of invisibility/targeting. Making life in queer survival economies more visible could simply increase surveillance and targeting, and/or such visibility could effectively pull queer lives into conformity with normative categories. Economically

174 Pecheny, Jakobsen, Amuchástegui, and Horn

precarious and non-conforming people might effectively gain visibility at the cost of increased surveillance and/or excising queerness from their lives.

If queer people try to earn visibility as working people, they face the paradoxes induced by the fact that the labor movement in the US has a long history of being organized around an explicitly straight idea of "the worker": a normative, male worker in industrial production, who earns a "family wage."[20] This normative worker was the insistent focus of the Trump campaign in 2016 and of press coverage that often seemed concerned only with the interests of the "white working class."[21] This normative worker became the only worker that mattered in mainstream political discourse, despite the fact that fewer and fewer households are organized around a single (white and male) family wage earner, and fewer and fewer jobs are in traditional industrial production. Nonetheless, manufacturing remains the focus of policy in the Biden Administration as well, including both energy policy and trade policy (Porter 2020). Queer Survival Economies suggests that, instead of this focus on the normative worker, activists can make a claim for the economic legitimacy of sustaining possibility in the face of precarity while refusing the categories of normativity – whether those of work or family or race or sex or gender.

For Queer Survival Economies, new forms of labor organizing allow for political practices similar to those Muñoz describes as disidentification. Organizing that refuses the normative categories of subjectivation, effectively disidentifying with the paradigmatic sense of "the worker," presents the opportunity to cut across traditional political fault lines in new ways. Journalist and activist Sarah Jaffe (2016) has documented the activism of the Workers' Project in Fort Wayne, Indiana as an instance of this type of organizing: "Ten years ago, before Donald Trump made anti-immigrant scapegoating into popular politics, a group of organizers in Fort Wayne, Indiana were trying to figure out how to bridge the divide between white workers and undocumented Latino workers.... They were doing their best to create a model for the rest of labor as the old model crumbled around them. The Workers' Project exists to organize the broader community around issues that matter to working people. It is not a union, but it is supported by union members; it is not a community organization, but it is open to the community." This assemblage of community labor organization does not need to separate the work of meeting the material needs of a community from organizing that community for a different political future.

As Hollibaugh and Weiss (2015, 24) suggest, "This might mean making the links between racial, sexual, and gendered discrimination visible, as when Restaurant Opportunity Center of New York (ROC-NY) sought to connect front-of-the house sexual harassment to back-of-the-house racial discrimination – an education in 'seeing gender,' as one staff member put it." Part of the project of queer economic justice, then, is recognizing the continuing effects of gender-, sex-, and race-segregation on labor markets and organizing to connect workers' needs with social change.[22] Innovative organizing can cross lines between community service and radical organizing, and/or between traditional

Political power and practices of resistance **175**

union workers and workers in the "new" economy. For instance, community-based centers like ROC-NY or the Indiana Workers' Project described by Jaffe address the needs of workers who have been excluded from traditional labor movements, like domestic workers, day laborers, restaurant, and retail workers. The goal of organizing that takes queer survival economies seriously is to expand these boundaries even further to include sex workers and workers in all informal economies. The hope is to connect worker organizing to the breadth of activist practices that challenge the normative effects of gender, sex, and race – and, in so doing, to address the economic exigencies and paradoxes of neoliberalism by creating justice for all workers.

Case study 4. Artistic practices of survival and other possible futures in the Dominican Republic

By the late 1990s, the Dominican Republic decisively embraced neoliberal economic strategies that culminated in 2004 with the country joining the Central American Free Trade Agreement with the US (hereafter CAFTA-DR). The radical opening to international market forces did not result necessarily in a receding of the importance of the state. As have many other countries in the Global South, however, the Dominican Republic did see an increasing disenchantment with conventional political strategies directed at the state and a proliferation of non-governmental organizations (NGOs) (Hawthorne 2009). As Amuchástegui has described with regard to medical practice in Mexico, many of these NGOs developed programs emphasizing *responsibilization* and *expertization*, rather than activism or other forms of collective action. In this context, a new generation of writers and visual artists emerged in the late 1990s, whose works attested to the detrimental effects of the neoliberal state and the new forms of precarity it produced. These artists also questioned whether these new narratives of responsibilization could address people's needs.

A key member of this creative generation shaped by neoliberalism is the nationally and internationally renowned Dominican writer and musician, Rita Indiana Hernández. Hernández's *oeuvre* stretches from the late nineties to the present, and the gender non-conforming writer and performer is, according to Sydney Hutchinson (2016), "maybe the only out lesbian in Dominican public life today" (173). The critical edge of Hernández's work, first in the literary realm and later in popular music, stood out to academics early on, and, with her rise in popularity, has reached broader audiences; as Hutchinson (2016, 174) describes, "her critiques of Dominican attitudes towards race, sexuality, migrants, and other issues are the most explicit, novel, and disconcerting of any in Dominican public life today."

This brief case study is particularly interested in some of these "other issues" with which Hernández has become increasingly concerned, namely Dominican neoliberal state politics and corruption and how these have left the Dominican people behind. In Hernández's early literary work, there is a total divestment

176 Pecheny, Jakobsen, Amuchástegui, and Horn

from the state and of any kind of conventional forms of political mobilization, leading some critics to describe her writing as divested from politics, but in her more recent work Hernández has increasingly been engaging in critical strategies that go beyond simple binaries of working within or against the state (or capitalism).

Hernández (2003) first came to national renown with her novel, *Chochueca's Strategy* [*La estrategia de Chochueca*] published in 2000. The title itself refers to a beggar, "Chochueca," whose survival strategy consisted of approaching the homes of the recently deceased to ask for donations of their clothing. "*La estrategia de Chochueca*" – Chochueca's strategy – emphasizes an overstepping of all social customs and notions of propriety. In so doing, seemingly abject subjects and materials from the margins are turned into a new kind of life through a form of material reappropriation that does not follow standard avenues of capitalist accumulation and circulation. Putting these materials to use in new, subversive ways allows them to act as a drag on capital. This kind of strategy flies in the face of ideas of personal responsibility induced and reproduced by neoliberalism and the processes of subjectivation we have discussed. Instead, Hernández's novel emphasizes loose social alliances and alternative social relations not centered on identity but on a shared rejection of the social "common sense" as supported by the neoliberal state and prevalent national discourses. This shared, but not common, sensibility can function as a counterweight to the state.

Recently, Hernández has turned to a more direct engagement and confrontation with the Dominican state, its neoliberal prerogatives, and its practices of clientelism and corruption, indicating a broadening of her critical strategies. In 2009 Hernández founded a new music group, "*Rita Indiana y los Misterios*" (Rita Indiana and the Mysteries), which rapidly gained widespread fame in the country and made her a well-known figure, beyond literary circles, in the Dominican mainstream. By the end of the year, the band had played many sold-out concerts and was nominated for the most important creative industry prize, the *Casandra*, in the category "Revelation of the Year." By 2010, the group led by Hernández was awarded a recording contract in the US and launched the album "*El Juidero*," the success of which culminated in a performance at New York's Central Park Summer Stage in 2011.

In contrast to her earlier writings, that are largely divested from state politics, Hernández takes direct aim in her songs at Dominican politics and taps into the widespread popular disenchantment and even cynicism that Dominican politics has produced, especially the governments of Leonel Fernández (1996–2000; 2004–2012). Her song "*No ta llevando el Diablo*" [We are going down with the devil], shows how Dominican reality belies the discourse of progress that was especially ubiquitous under Fernández's government (as discussed in Chapter 2). The song starts, "*Del hoyo salimos y en el terminamos // Con hoja de zinc de diente y bajando president /// Masticando vidrio como una empananada // Licenciada en pan vacío la barriada*" (We came out of the hole and there we end up // With zinc plates as teeth and drinking Presidente beer // Chewing glass like an empanada //

Graduate of the barrio without bread). The song decries how Dominicans are still lacking basic necessities and nothing ever seems to change; as the singer declares, she has been "*Dándome este fin de mundo desde chiquitita*" (Living this end of the world since I was little). According to the song, the fault lies clearly with those in power who give the Dominican people only "*bagazo*" (husks of sugar cane) and keep for themselves the valuable "*pulpa*" (pulp). These references to sugar cane evoke a long history of economic exploitation in the region that the song suggests continues up until today and portrays the Dominican state as one that has fundamentally failed.

Although the song dismisses the ever-present "progress" and "modernity" narratives that the Dominican government and outside voices constantly evoke, it does venture briefly into another mode of futurity. At one point the song fore-tells that "*El hoyo explotará mañana // Y saldrán las doñas a tragar granadas*" (The hole will explode tomorrow // And the doñas will come out to swallow grenades). Interestingly, in this revolt, it is those who are often the least likely to be con-sidered political subjects, "*doñas*," older, stay-at-home, respectable women, who take the lead and face the inevitable pushback (the grenades). What this suggests is how political resistance can no longer be imagined in the Dominican Republic as emerging from within the conventional realm of politics; instead, it is those on the gendered margins of political life that might one day foster resistance and rise up to protest effectively. This tone of hopefulness is, however, mixed with great bitterness and the song ends with the repeated chorus "*No ta llevando el Diablo*" (We are going down with the devil); the song's vision of futurity thus appears as a persistently distant but nonetheless promising vision of a different possi-ble trajectory. Given the Dominican state's longstanding narrative monopoly on discourses of progress and change, such alternative imaginings of other possible languages of futurity take on political urgency. The success of "*El Juidero*" (2010) made Hernández a break-out star in the Latin American music scene and one of the most famous and recognizable celebrities in the Dominican Republic. This kind of fame and success, however, came with "too many drawbacks for Rita I. Hernández, who decided to stop touring and pursuing her musical career further" (Hutchinson 2016, 206). Foregoing the fruits of her impressive rise to fame and to the consternation of many, Rita Indiana Hernández retired from the public eye for several years to refocus on her literary work.

However, about six years later, in 2017, Hernández made an unexpected brief comeback with a new song (Hernández 2017) and music video (Quintero 2017) titled "*El Castigador*," The Punisher, that was written in response to the rise in popular protests in the Dominican Republic against government corruption and impunity. Hernández re-emerged into the public eye with an explicit battle cry against Dominican state politics and corruption, that continued to be carried out by Fernández' successor Danilo Medina (2012–2020). In contrast to her earlier literary work, this song explicitly critiques the Dominican state and demands greater accountability and change; "*El Castigador*" denounces how "*se regordean en lujos // que paga el miserable*" (they fatten themselves on luxuries // that the wretched pay). The song decries the hunger of the poor and their inability to pay for the education of their children in the sense that state reform or a better functioning of the state becomes desirable. "*El Castigador*," for example, critiques the (*leyes atrasadas*: backward laws,) and asks the state to correct its path, to punish corrupt politicians, and calls for political reform. This anti-corruption/anti-impunity movement in the Dominican Republic identified itself by the color green, and in one of her first concerts in years in the Dominican Republic, Hernández performed tellingly with a green scarf.

Hernández's recent turn to the state points to how, after Dominican society's NGO-ization in the 1990s and citizens' widespread divestment from conventional political strategies, there has been a return to engagement with the state, albeit in new forms. Even in the age of neoliberalism, the state remains a central force in shaping Dominican lives precisely because of how it remains driven by neoliberal economic prerogatives that affect the majority of Dominicans in fundamentally detrimental ways, as discussed further in Chapter 2. Hernández's work, thus, attests to a need for multiple strategies *vis-à-vis* the state, since no single strategy – neither legal reform within the state, nor the revolutionary destruction of the state – will automatically meet the needs of those who are both aided and oppressed by the state. Even as the state is seen as both corrupt and incompetent, Hernández's creative body of work attests to social possibilities created through shifting forms of engagement with the state, from disidentification to working directly to change state policies.

Conclusion: practices of resistance in a fractured world

These cases suggest the potential effectiveness of practices of resistance that negotiate around and through the fractured and paradoxical realities created by neoliberal governmentality. If the state is fractured and neoliberal governmentality is productively incoherent, then the most effective practices of resistance are likely to be complex. In other words, the productive incoherence of neoliberal governmentality requires differential practices. As discussed in Chapter 4, the political scientist Ilene Grabel (2015, 82–3) argues that, given productive incoherence, "[t]he potential for change . . . is located in the disparate, the unplanned, the experimental, rather than in a new '-ism' to replace the eroding neoliberalism." From the standpoint of political possibility, taking paradoxes seriously offers alternative ways of understanding possibilities for social change, even (or perhaps especially) when efforts at creating change are directed toward global phenomena like neoliberalism.

Differential practices can recognize both the problems of the state and its potential to provide some provisional, partial solutions; such practices need not be either entirely autonomous from the state or directly engaged with the state. Similarly, these practices may mobilize discourses of vulnerability, and they may resist the normative idea of the innocently vulnerable. These practices are often most effective when articulated together, but not necessarily to recreate a liberal

Political power and practices of resistance **179**

whole (which may never have existed). Rather, they can be connected in networks that are perhaps looser than those of liberal politics, but also less rigid, and, thus, less likely to create unlivable double binds.

Traversing the double binds of paradoxical political power means that any single path of resistance is likely to lead back into the bind, a trap that multivarious and layered approaches may avoid. Returning to the work of the National Domestic Workers Alliance (NDWA) in the US (discussed in Chapter 2), their projects combine both action directed at the state and a critique of political economy that demands much more than state action. As one path of action, NDWA pursues the passage of legislation to protect the rights of domestic workers. These efforts are based on analysis of domestic workers' status as part of a group of workers excluded from the legal category of labor. Through histories that deny the personhood of some workers in the US, those employed in domestic work, farm work, and various forms of piece work, that are associated with slavery or immigration, have also been excluded from basic labor protections, including the right to time off and basic compensation for severance of employment. In addressing this problem, the passage of a domestic workers bill of rights represents a major victory for domestic workers, as well as a major shift in labor law in the US.[23] Because of its argument for legislative expansion of the category "protected workers," at one level, NDWA's organizing is basic liberal advocacy to expand democracy's protections.

At another level, however, NDWA's organizing expands well beyond this liberal, legal framework. The group's analysis shows that labor historically associated with slavery is not as "free" as other forms of work; the effects of the US history of slavery continue. Moreover, this historical exclusion has created gendered and racialized labor markets that now attract increasing numbers of immigrants from the Global South.[24] The "free market," thus, is not actually free. It does not allow for the free movement of individuals to sell their labor, but instead uses historical barriers and national boundaries to devalue the labor of people of color and immigrants. In response, the political work of NDWA both focuses on the nation-state and crosses national boundaries. Not only are many of the workers who organize with NDWA themselves migrants, but they critique the "freedoms" of the global labor market, and they work in solidarity with related organizations around the world.

Even more profoundly, however, the work undertaken by domestic workers challenges the liberal humanist concept of the autonomous individual who is the subject of modern law, freedom, and wage labor at its core. The title of a report by the Filipinx migrant workers' organization DAMAYAN (2010), "Doing the Work That Makes All Work Possible," insists that people widely recognized as autonomous individuals are not, in fact, autonomous. Rather, those who historically have been able to sell their labor by virtue of protected freedoms have always been and still are dependent on forms of domestic labor provided by others, including family members and paid domestic laborers.

Taking seriously the claims of those who do "the work that makes all work possible" brings race and gender domination to the center of any analysis of

180 Pecheny, Jakobsen, Amuchástegui, and Horn

global capitalism, and action in response to this analysis requires more than an expansion of the liberal humanist social contract. The domestic and excluded workers' movements refuse to give up either a deep critique of the conditions of contemporary capitalism or much-needed advocacy focused on legislative change to gain basic legal protections. In maintaining both prongs of action, the fight for workers' rights provides a model for seeking social change that moves beyond the liberal state, while also refusing to leave domestic and other excluded workers vulnerable to the ongoing injustices instituted in the liberal state. This multi-layered strategy allows social movements to address both the immediate challenges facing people whose lives are precarious and the need for expansive social change.

Correlatively, resistance does not depend on any simple sense of solidarity. Rather, the differential elements of political resistance can be connected through a "transverse solidarity," as described by political economist K. Ravi Raman (2010). Raman studies politics and activism in Kerala, India, and has done an in-depth study of rural activism to get the Coca-Cola company to stop using the water of the community of Plachimada and to cease operations there. Raman provides a detailed ethnography of this movement as "a plurality of contested issues and struggles at multiple sites of power" that eventually allowed a "water-based subaltern movement" to force the transnational Coca-Cola company to change its plans. He argues that the movement was successful by connecting a set of non-equivalent actors into trans-local networks.

The very unevenness of these networks allows for the creation of a patchwork of actions across sectors, simultaneously engaging the state and realms well beyond the state and creating unexpected possibilities for justice. Participants in the Plachimada movement included "a curious mix of environmentalists and social activists: the Gandhians, the moderates, the radical Maoists, and a large number of NGOs" (Raman 2010, 256). To say that this is a diverse and unevenly situated group of people is an understatement. But the ability of the movement to maintain some irregular and undoubtedly contentious solidarity across these groups created a form of popularity that eventually meant the local government had no choice but to cancel the factory license for Coca-Cola's operations.

In crossing political boundaries, trans-local action could also work through some of the double binds created by the paradoxes of neoliberalism, engaging resistance to the exploitation and domination of both globalization and nationalism. More importantly, this type of approach might allow those who seek justice to traverse the boundaries of not only the national and the global, but also those dividing the cultural from the economic, gender justice from anticolonial struggle, or sexual politics from worker justice.

As we have argued throughout this book, gender and sexuality provide key sites for analyzing the workings of political power in relation to neoliberal policies and practices. The case studies in this chapter illustrate just a few of the ways that gender and sexuality can provide key sites for developing practices of resistance to the damaging social relations instituted by neoliberal imperatives.

Political power and practices of resistance **181**

In particular, the feminist and queer practices we describe offer approaches for doing things differently in relation to the paradoxes of neoliberalism. Creative practices that may come at problems obliquely, whether through political disidentification, artistic practice, or peer support for women living with HIV, allow practices of resistance to move around or slip past the double binds of neoliberal governmentality. Placing peer support on a par with medical expertise in addressing a global pandemic changes the meaning of public health. This shift has been taken up in response to the COVID-19 pandemic, for example, with an abundance of emerging projects focused upon mutual aid, offering new ways of envisioning what is meant by organizing.[25] Locating non-normative workers as potential leaders in labor organizing across sectors similarly changes the shape of labor organizing. Taking seriously survival economies that include sexual labor as sites of activism changes the shape of economic justice. Shifting amongst practices that deny the importance of the state and those that directly engage allows for art and politics that create new openings for life possibilities, even as one continues to live with a fractured state under paradoxical, often oppressive, conditions.

This type of flexible, multivarious, and multi-layered approach to practices of resistance means that, whereas the paradoxes of neoliberalism may lead to any number of double binds, political action need not get stuck there. Recognizing paradox and refusing to identify with its terms allows for the possibility of also refusing the terms of the double bind. No single action or set of actions can provide an effective practice of resistance to the exploitation and domination enabled and intensified by neoliberalism. Rather, differential practices, collaborative action, and complex solidarity can challenge the social conditions that reinforce injustice. Creative, boundary-crossing practices of resistance also open up new and exciting possibilities for justice.

Notes

1 Voter suppression, sometimes through violence, was the immediate response in the US to the passage of the Radical Reconstruction Act of 1867 and the expansion of the franchise through the 15th amendment after the Civil War. Attempts at voter suppression as part of the project of maintaining white supremacy in the US have persisted since. The end of reconstruction led to the institution of voter restrictions, such as poll taxes, in the former states of the Confederacy to prevent African Americans from voting, and challenges to these restrictions were themselves suppressed often through the extra-legal violence of the Ku Klux Klan. The passage of the Civil Rights Act in 1964 and the Voting Rights Act in 1965 reopened the franchise but did not end efforts at voter suppression, which continued through tactics like the gerrymandering of Congressional districts to pack the majority of African American voters into a restricted number of districts (Soffen 2016). The US Supreme Court decision *Shelby County v. Holder* voided a major section of the Voting Rights Act that provided for federal oversight of states with histories of voter suppression. In response, these states passed a range of new restrictions: May (2014); Berman (2015); Hurley (2020). For example, Arizona cut back on polling places in predominantly Latino neighborhoods so as to disenfranchise potential voters now that the federal oversight authorized by

182 Pecheny, Jakobsen, Amuchástegui, and Horn

the Voting Rights Act was gone (Berman 2016). These efforts intensified through the Trump Administration, including through various attempts to manipulate the results of the 2020 Census, which forms the basis for Congressional districting (among other things). Throughout the 2020 election cycle, Trump also cast doubt on the legitimacy of voting and electoral processes, culminating on 6 January 2021 in a crowd storming the US Capitol, where Congress had convened to certify the results of the 2020 election and Joseph R. Biden's election as President of the US. Biden's election was certified, and he was inaugurated on 20 January 2021 (Snyder 2021). One of the responses by Republican lawmakers to their loss in the 2020 presidential election, as well as in a special run-off election for two Senate seats in the state of Georgia, has been to intensify voter suppression, particularly through the passage of new state laws. The new election law in Georgia restricting voting hours and including administrative changes to how votes are counted has garnered intense media attention, including corporate and sports boycotts of the state, but a number of other states, including Florida, have nonetheless passed related legislation (Brennan Center for Justice 2021).

2 Eva Cherniavsky (2017, 10), also describes this fracturing, arguing that neoliberal transformations include: "the divorce of capitalism and democracy; the demise of disciplinary society; the apparent disinterest of the state in the cultivation of a national people, [with] the effect of eroding a common sense of reality, in which a national or even a local (not to mention a planetary) "we" live in simultaneous time and convergent social and material worlds." One could say that neoliberalism engenders a fracturing of modernity and a correlative fracturing of any political "we."

3 Since their initiation, the US has continued to pursue any number of unofficial wars, and the number has now expanded so much that it seems there is no longer any need, nor much concern, on the part of US citizens to know about military action. Even when the deaths of US soldiers reveals that the US military is active in parts of the world, such as Niger, that have not been named as US conflict zones, no public debate ensues (Blinder and Gibbons-Neff 2019).

4 We loosely use Bateson's (1972) concept of double bind in our discussion of the paradoxical nature of the neoliberal state to describe some of the dynamics of people's experiences in relation to state institutions. Within such a bind, two conflicting demands are posed within the same message, each on a different logical level, neither of which can be ignored or escaped. This leaves the subject torn both ways, so that, whichever demand he or she tries to meet, the other cannot be met. Double binds are effective because of their repetition in the context of an inescapable relationship, in which the subject is unable to leave the communicational field either physically or through questioning the authority that issues the message.

5 The Center for Women's and Gender Research at the University of Bergen has similarly developed an analysis of how the state imposes waiting as part of the subjectivation of refugees (https://www.uib.no/en/project/wait).

6 Governmentality, as Foucault (1997a, 87) defines it, is "understood in the broad sense of techniques and procedures for directing human behavior. Government of children, government of souls and consciences, government of a household, of a state, or of oneself."

7 This subjectivation is not intentional in the Weberian sense of imposing one's will or in the most traditional Marxist sense of one class exploiting another, but is nonetheless effective in creating limited possibilities for human beings.

8 Johnson, et. al. (2017); *The New York Times* (2017); Robles (2018). Even the project of counting how many people died as a result of the hurricanes in 2017 was delayed, with a major commissioned report having been barely started on its promised publication date of May 2018 (Fink 2019).

9 In the context of an epidemic concentrated on "men who have sex with men," trans women, male sex workers, intravenous drug users, and cis women with HIV engaged

Political power and practices of resistance **183**

ambivalently with gay men's organizations as the only way to access treatment. For a long time, their needs remained invisible within this male-dominated activist arena.

10 There is no question that the HIV epidemic has been articulated and experienced as a biopolitical issue within the framework of neoliberal governmentality. Even radical HIV activist organizations, such as the Treatment Action Coalition in South Africa or ACT UP in the US, focused much of their effort on obtaining government support for medical research, treatment, and prevention of AIDS. The disease has been constituted through discourses of truth articulated by competent state authorities, who have developed specific intervention strategies on behalf of life and health. These strategies involve subjectivation to neoliberal governmentality. See, e.g., Foucault (1997b); Rabinow and Rose (2006); and Biehl and Eskerod (2005).

11 "[It refers to] the process through which people [living with chronic conditions] acquire a certain amount of knowledge that draws them away from a situation of ignorance, especially regarding medical knowledge, and brings them closer to those who hold legitimate knowledge in that field, in other words, the professionals. Such knowledge can be "discursive" (it can be expressed, through speech) or "practical" (tacit, action-knowledge)" (Pecheny, Manzelli, and Jones 2002, 32).

12 As commentators such as Adler and Wertheim (2020) have pointed out, Biden's move to international alliances is also an effort to reconstitute a form of American pre-eminence as the "leader of the free world" over and against non-democratic nations who are positioned as the "enemies" of democracy, much as migrants are positioned in a Trumpian version of "America First."

13 The infrastructure spending promised by Bannon disappeared quickly from the Trump Administration's agenda, as Bannon himself was also fired from the Administration after a few months (Scher 2017).

14 There was extensive debate after the 2016 elections in the mainstream US media, which ran along two main lines – was it mainly racism or class anxiety that drove Trump voters, and whether Trump's election was an intensification of or a resistance to neoliberalism. Over time, some of those who had argued on behalf of class anxiety and resistance to neoliberalism alone shifted toward a recognition that complex and even contradictory factors could be at play. For recognition that the white working class is dedicated to racism and xenophobia as well as jobs, see The Editors (2017). See also Edsall (2018).

15 See, e.g., Sullivan (2020).

16 The productive incoherence of Trump's policies and pronouncements remained effective for a significant portion of the population such that, in the end, more people voted for Trump in 2020 than in 2016, but Biden improved on the votes for 2016 Democratic Presidential candidate Hillary Clinton by even more (and, importantly, some of that improvement came in key states that swung the Electoral College for Biden rather than Trump) (Wasserman et al. 2020; Cook Political Report 2016).

17 Trump made just such promises in his speech at the Republican Convention accepting the nomination for President. Trump paired the claim that "I alone" can fix the problems of the American nation with a refrain of "I am your voice," sometimes printed in all capital letters: "I AM YOUR VOICE," in the version distributed to the news media (Politico Staff 2016; Applebaum 2016).

18 Robinson (2019); Parker and Towler (2019); Haney Lopez (2015); Lichtman (2008).

19 There were important connections between cultures of art production and AIDS activism in the 1990s and between art and activism for organizations like Queers for Economic Justice (QEJ) in the 2000s. Art, such as the photography of Syd London, helped not only to document and promote new forms of queer organizing, such as the moment when QEJ and labor organizers marched in solidarity for the first time in the New York City Pride Parade, but also to create a sense of community and culture – to make a queer world – by representing social gatherings and the community built by QEJ (Hollibaugh 2011).

20 See Chappell (2010) and Self (2012).

184 Pecheny, Jakobsen, Amuchástegui, and Horn

21 Thomas Edsall's columns in *The New York Times* provide a good example of the insistent press focus on the concerns of the "white working class" from the Trump era (see, for example, Edsall 2018) into the Biden Administration. See Edsall (2021).
22 Hollibaugh served for a time as co-Executive Director of Queers for Economic Justice (QEJ). The papers for QEJ, which was founded in 2002 and closed in 2014, can be found at Cornell University archives: https://rmc.library.cornell.edu/EAD/htmldocs/RMM07802.html.
23 NDWA has supported the passage of a Domestic Workers Bill of Rights in nine states and similar legislation was introduced at the national level in 2019, sponsored by Pramila Jayapal in the US House of Representatives and Kamala Harris in the US Senate. See, e.g., Campbell (2019) and National Domestic Workers Alliance (2020).
24 Nadasen and Williams (2011).
25 On the salience of peer networks during the COVID-19 pandemic, see Spade (2020).

References

Adam, Barry. 2005. "Constructing the Neoliberal Sexual Actor: Responsibility and Care of the Self in the Discourse of Barebackers," *Culture, Health & Sexuality* 7, no. 4: 333–346.

Adler, David and Stephen Wertheim. 2020. "Biden Wants to Convene an International 'Summit for Democracy': He Shouldn't," *The Guardian*, 22 December. https://www.theguardian.com/commentisfree/2020/dec/22/biden-wants-to-convene-an-international-summit-for-democracy-he-shouldnt.

Applebaum, Yoni. 2016. "I Alone Can Fix It," *The Atlantic*, 21 July. https://www.theatlantic.com/politics/archive/2016/07/trump-rnc-speechalone-fix-it/492557/.

Ayres, José Ricardo. 2001. "Sujeito, intersubjetividade e práticas de saúde," *Ciencia & Saúde Coletiva* 6, no. 1: 63–72. https://doi.org/10.1590/S1413-81232001000100005.

Bai, Matt. 2012. "How Much Has Citizens United Changed the Political Game?" *The New York Times Magazine*, 17 July. https://www.nytimes.com/2012/07/22/magazine/how-much-has-citizens-united-changedthepolitical-game.html.

Bateson, Gregory. 1972. *Steps to an Ecology of Mind: Collected Essays in Anthropology, Psychiatry, Evolution, and Epistemology*. First edition. Chicago, IL: University of Chicago Press.

Berman, Ari. 2015. *Give Us the Ballot: The Modern Struggle for Voting Rights in America*. New York: Farrar, Straus, and Giroux.

Berman, Ari. 2016. "There Were 5-hour Lines to Vote in Arizona Because the Supreme Court Gutted the Voting Rights Act," *The Nation*, 23 March. http://www.thenation.com/article/there-were-five-hour-lines-to-vote-in-arizona-because-the-supreme-court-gutted-the-voting-rights-act/.

Biehl, João and Torben Eskerod. 2005. *Vita: Life in a Zone of Social Abandonment*. 47160th edition. Berkeley, CA: University of California Press.

Blinder, Alan and Thomas Gibbons-Neff. 2019. "'I Cry Everyday': Families of Soldiers Killed in Niger in 2017 Are Still Waiting for Answers," *The New York Times*, 26 April, https://www.nytimes.com/2019/04/26/us/us-soldiers-killed-niger.html.

Brennan Center for Justice. 2021. "State Voting Bills Tracker," 24 February, https://www.brennancenter.org/our-work/research-reports/state-voting-bills-tracker-2021.

Butler, Judith. 1997. *The Psychic Life of Power: Theories in Subjection*. Stanford, CA: Stanford University Press.

Political power and practices of resistance **185**

Bycoffe, Aaron, Jasmine Mithani, Christopher Groskopf, and Dhrumil Mehta. 2021. "How American's View Biden's Response to the Coronavirus Crisis," *FiveThirtyEight*, 22 April (last updated). https://projects.fivethirtyeight.com/coronavirus-polls/.

Campbell, Alexia Fernández. 2019. "Kamala Harris Just Introduced a Bill to Give Housekeepers Overtime Pay and Meal Breaks," *Vox*, 15 July, https://www.vox.com/2019/7/15/20694610/kamala-harris-domestic-workers-bill-of-rights-act.

Campos, Gastao Wagner de Sousa. 2009. *Método Paideia: Análisis y Co-Gestión de Colectivos.* Buenos Aires: Lugar Editorial.

Center for Women's and Gender Research. "WAIT," University of Bergen. https://www.uib.no/en/project/wait.

Chappell, Marisa. 2010. *The War on Welfare: Family, Poverty, and Politics in Modern America.* Philadelphia, PA: University of Pennsylvania Press.

Cherniavsky, Eva. 2017. *Neocitizenship: Political Culture after Democracy.* New York: NYU Press.

Cook Political Report. 2016. "Presidential Results by Year," https://cookpolitical.com/presidential-results-year.

DAMAYAN Migrant Workers Association and the Urban Justice Center with the assistance of Ninotchka Rosca. 2010. "Doing the Work That Makes All Work Possible: A Research Narrative of Filipino Domestic Workers in the Tri-state Area," *Community Development Project*, 23 October, www.cdp-ny.org.

Deleuze, Gilles Abecedario.1988. https://vimeo.com/132742319. (transcription available at) http://estafeta-gabrielpulecio.blogspot.mx/2009/08/gillesdeleuze-abecedario-entrevistas.html.

Dreiling, Michael C. 2016. *Agents of Neoliberal Globalization: Corporate Networks, State Structures and Trade Policy.* New York: Cambridge University Press.

Edsall, Thomas B.. 2018. "Opinion | The Democratic Party Is in Worse Shape Than You Thought," *The New York Times*, 20 January. www.nytimes.com/2017/06/08/opinion/the-democratic-party-is-in-worse-shape-thanyou-thought.html.

Edsall, Thomas B. 2021. "Should Biden Emphasize Race or Class or Both or None of the Above?" *The New York Times*, 28 April, https://www.nytimes.com/2021/04/28/opinion/biden-democrats-race-class.html.

Faiola, Anthony and Marina Lopes. 2018. "Bolsonaro Wins Brazilian Presidency," *The New York Times*, 28 October. https://www.washingtonpost.com/world/the_americas/brazilians-go-the-polls-with-far-right-jair-bolsonaro-as-front-runner/2018/10/28/880dd53c-d6dd-11e8-8384-bcc5492fef49_story.html.

Fink, Sheri. 2019. "Puerto Rico's Death Toll Could Exceed 4,000, New Study Estimates," *The New York Times*, 29 May. https://www.nytimes.com/2018/05/29/us/puerto-rico-deaths-hurricane.html.

Flynn, Thomas R. 1985. "Truth and Subjectivation in the Later Foucault," *The Journal of Philosophy*, 82, No. 10 (October): 531–40. https://doi.org/10.2307/2026360.

Foucault, Michel. 1980. "Truth and Subjectivity," *Howison Lecture*. Berkeley, CA. https://gradlectures.berkeley.edu/lecture/truth-and-subjectivity/.

Foucault, Michel. 1991. "Governmentality." In edited Graham Burchell, Colin Gordon, and Peter Miller. *The Foucault Effect: Studies in Governmentality.* Chicago, IL: University of Chicago Press.

Foucault, Michel. 1997a. *Ethics: Subjectivity and Truth.* Edited by Paul Rabinow. First edition. New York: The New Press.

Foucault, Michel. 1997b."Historia de La Medicalización," *Educación Médica y Salud* 11, no. 1: 3–25. http://terceridad.net/Sistemasdesalud/Foucault,%20M.%20Historia%20de%20la%20medicalizaci%F3n.pdf.

Frank, Thomas. 2017. *Listen Liberal: Or, What Ever Happened to the Party of the People.* New York: Picador.

Giroux, Henry. 2006. "The Emerging Authoritarianism in the United States: Political Culture under the Bush/Cheney Administration," *symploke*, 14, No. 1/2: 98–151.

Grabel, Ilene. 2015. "Post-Crisis Experiments in Development Finance Architectures: A Hirschmanian Perspective on 'Productive Incoherence,'" *Review of Social Economy*, 73, no. 4: 388–414.

Haney López, Ian. 2015. *Dog Whistle Politics: How Coded Racial Appeals have Reinvented Racism and Wrecked the Middle Class.* New York: Oxford University Press.

Hawthorne, Sierra. 2009. "Benevolence and Blunder: NGOs and Development in the Dominican Republic," *Georgetown Journal of International Affairs* (Summer/Fall): 133–41/.

Hernández, Rita Indiana. 2003. *La estrategia de Chochueca.* Second edition. San Juan: Editorial Isla Negra.

Hernández, Rita Indiana. 2017. "El Castigador," *Official Video*, 29 March. https://www.youtube.com/watch?v=9-J_n1H2qT4.

Hollibaugh, Amber. 2011. "A New Tradition … Queers for Economic Justice and Labor Walk in Solidarity at NYC Pride March," *Huffpost*, 25 August. https://www.huffpost.com/entry/queers-for-economic-justice-nyc-pride_b_884530.

Hollibaugh, Amber and Margot Weiss. 2015. "Queer Precarity and the Myth of Gay Affluence," *New Labor Forum (Sage Publications Inc.)* 24, no. 3 (Fall): 18–27. https://doi.org/10.1177/1095796015599414.

Hurley, Lawrence. 2020. "Supreme Court Throws Out Challenge to Trump Census Immigrant Plan," Reuters, 18 December, https://www.reuters.com/article/us-usa-court-census/u-s-supreme-court-throws-out-challenge-to-trump-census-immigrant-plan-idUSKBN28S240.

Hutchinson, Sydney. 2016. *Tigers of a Different Stripe: Performing Gender in Dominican Music.* Chicago, IL: University of Chicago Press.

Jaffe, Sarah. 2016. "In GOP Country, a Small Labor Organization Offers a Model for Fighting Trumpism," *The Nation*, 4 November. https://www.thenation.com/article/in-gop-country-a-small-labor-organization-offers-a-model-for-fighting-trumpism/.

Johnson, Alex, et al. 2017. "Hurricane Irma Skirts Puerto Rico, Leave 1 Million without Power," *NBC News*, 7 September. https://www.nbcnews.com/storyline/hurricane-irma/hurricane-irma-skirts-puerto-rico-lashing-it-powerful-winds-flooding-n799086.

Landler, Mark and Stephen Castle. 2020."Britain and E.U. Reach Landmark Trade Deal on Brexit," *The New York Times*, 24 December, https://www.nytimes.com/2020/12/24/world/europe/brexit-trade-deal-uk-eu.html?searchResultPosition=3.

Lascoumes, Pierre and Patrick Le Gales. 2007. "Introduction: Understanding Public Policy through Instruments—From the Nature of Instruments to the Sociology of Public Policy Instrumentation," *Governance: An International Journal of Policy, Administration, and Institutions*, 20, no. 1 (January): 1–21.

Lichtman, Allen J. 2008. *White Protestant Nationalism: The Rise of the American Conservative Movement.* New York: Atlantic Monthly Press.

May, Gary. 2014 *Bending Toward Justice: The Voting Rights Act and the Transformation of American Democracy.* Durham, DC: Duke University Press.

Michaels, Walter Benn. 2011. "Let Them Eat Diversity: An Interview with Walter Benn Michaels," *Jacobin*, https://jacobinmag.com/2011/01/let-them-eat-diversity.

Mueller, Benjamin, Robert Gebeloff, and Sahil Chinoy. 2018. "Surest Way to Face Marijuana Charges in New York is to Be Black or Hispanic," *The New York Times*, 13 May. https://www.nytimes.com/2018/05/13/nyregion/marijuana-arrests-nyc-race.html.

Muñoz, José Esteban. 1999. *Disidentifications: Queer of Color and Performance Politics.* Minneapolis, MN: University of Minnesota Press.

Nadasen, Premilla and Tiffany Williams. 2011. "Valuing Domestic Work," *New Feminist Solutions* 5. bcrw.barnard.edu/wp-content/nfs/reports/NFS5-Valuing-Domestic-Work.pdf.

National Domestic Workers Alliance. 2020. "Bill of Rights," https://www.domesticworkers.org/bill-rights.

Noem, Kristi. 2020. "Thanksgiving and Personal Responsibility," South Dakota State News, 20 November, https://news.sd.gov/newsitem.aspx?id=27492.

Parker, Christopher Sebastian and Christopher C. Towler. 2019. "Race and Authoritarianism in American Politics," *Annual Review of Political Science* 22: 503–19. https://www.annualreviews.org/doi/10.1146/annurev-polisci-050317-064519.

Pecheny, Mario. 2012/2013. "Sexual Politics and Post-Neoliberalism in Latin America," *Scholar & Feminist Online* 11, no. 1–2 (Fall/Spring). http://sfonline.barnard.edu/gen derjusticeandneoliberal-transformations/sexual-politics-and-post-neoliberalism-in-latinamerica/.

Pecheny, Mario. 2017. In discussion with Elizabeth Bernstein (October).

Pecheny, Mario, Hernán Manzelli, and Daniel Jones. 2002. "Vida Cotidiana Con VIH/Sida y/o Hepatitis C. Diagnótisco, Tratamiento y Proceso de Expertización," Buenos Aires: Centro de Estudios de Estado y Sociedad (CEDES). http://www.cedes.org/publicaciones/documentos/SSPP/2002/SSPP200205.PDF

Politico Staff. 2016. "Full Text: Donald Trump 2016 RNC Draft Speech Transcript," *Politico*, 21 July. https://www.politico.com/story/2016/07/full-transcript-donald-trump-nomination acceptance-speech-at-rnc-225974.

Porter, Eduardo. 2020. "Trump, Biden, and 'Made in the U.S.A.': Same Refrain, Different Notes," *The New York Times*. 28 September. https://www.nytimes.com/2020/09/28/business/economy/biden-trump-made-in-usa.html.

Quintero Herencia, Noelia. 2017. *El Castigador [Vídeo Oficial].* Gallo Negro. https://www.youtube.com/watch?v=9-J_n1H2qT4.

Rabinow, Paul and Nikolas Rose. 2006. "Biopower Today; Paul Rabinow and Nikolas Rose; Biopower Today," *BioSocieties; London* 1, no. 2 (June): 195–217. http://search.proquest.com/docview/220871782/abstract/7148C1A0DA8C400EPQ/1.K.

Raman, K. Ravi. 2010. "Transverse Solidarity: Water, Power, and Resistance," *Review of Racial Political Economics* 42, no. 2: 251–68.

Richardson, Ian. 2020. "U.S. Senator Joni Ernst Gets Backlash for Past Comments After Taking COVID-19 Vaccine; Grassley, Axne Also Plan to Take it Soon," *The Des Moines Register*, 22 December. https://www.desmoinesregister.com/story/news/politics/2020/12/22/covid-19-vaccine-u-s-sen-joni-ernst-gets-backlash-past-comments/4010812001/.

Robinson, Russell K. 2019. "Justice Kennedy's White Nationalism," *University of California Law Review*, 53, 1027–72. https://escholarship.org/uc/item/0g116625.

Robles, Frances. 2018. "Puerto Rico Spent 11 Months Turning the Power Back On. They Finally Got to Her," *The New York Times*, 14 August. https://www.nytimes.com/2018/08/14/us/puerto-rico-electricity-power.html.

Rose, Nikolas. 2000. "Government and Control," *The British Journal of Criminology* 40, no. 2: 321–39. http://www.jstor.org/stable/23638480.

Rose, Nikolas. 2001. "The Politics of Life Itself," *Theory, Culture & Society* 18, no. 6 (December): 1–30. https://doi.org/10.1177/02632760122052020.

Rucker, Philip and Robert Costa. 2017. "Bannon Vows a Daily Fight for 'Deconstruction of the Administrative State,'" *Washington Post*, 23 February. https://www.washingtonpost.com/politics/top-wh-strategist-vows-a-daily-fight-fordeconstruction-of-the-administrative-state/2017/02/23/03f6b8da-f9ea-11e6-bf01d47f8cf9b643_story.html?noredirect=on&utm=term=.54e2eff4f903.

Santora, Marc. 2019. "In Poland, Nationalism With a Progessive Touch Wins Voters," *The New York Times*, 10 October. https://www.nytimes.com/2019/10/10/world/europe/poland-election-law-and-justice-party.html.

Sargent, Greg. 2020. "The Biden Team does not seem Spooked by the Ghost of Stephen Miller," *The Washington Post*, 22 December. https://www.washingtonpost.com/opinions/2020/12/22/biden-team-does-not-seem-spooked-by-ghost-stephen-miller/.

Scher, Bill. 2017. "Why Bannon Lost and the Globalists Won," *Politico Magazine*, August 18. https://www.politico.com/magazine/story/2017/08/18/why-bannon-lost-globalists-won-215506.

Self, Robert O. 2012. *All in the Family: The Realignment of American Democracy since the 1960s*. New York: Farrar, Straus, and Giroux.

Snyder, Timothy. 2021. "The American Abyss," *New York Times Magazine*, 9 January. https://www.nytimes.com/2021/01/09/magazine/trump-coup.html.

Soffen, Kim. 2016. "How Racial Gerrymandering Deprives Black People of Political Power," *The Washington Post*, 9 June. https://www.washingtonpost.com/news/wonk/wp/2016/06/09/how-a-widespread-practice-to-politically-empower-african-americans-might-actually-harm-them/.

Sorkin, Aaron Ross, et al. 2020. "The Biden Spin on 'America First,'" *The New York Times*, 2 December. https://www.nytimes.com/2020/12/02/business/dealbook/biden-economy-workers.html?searchResultPosition=2.

Spade, Dean. 2012/2013. "'Impossibility Now' (Video and Slideshow), in 'Gender Justice and Neoliberal Transformations',," edited by Bernstein and Jakobsen, *Scholar & Feminist Online* 11, no. 1–2 (Fall /Spring). http://sfonline.barnard.edu/gender-justice-and-neoliberal-transformations/impossibility-now/.

Spade, Dean. 2020. *Mutual Aid: Building Solidarity During this Crisis (And the Next)*. London: Verso.

Sullivan, Andrew. 2020. "COVID-19 Will Be the Real Swing Voter," *Intelligencer*, 10 July. https://nymag.com/intelligencer/2020/07/andrew-sullivan-covid-19-will-be-the-real-swing-voter.html.

Sylvia Rivera Law Project. 2016. "How to Legally Change Your Name in New York City," https://srlp.org/resources/namechange/.

The Editors. 2017. "The White Working Class," *The American Prospect*, 1 June. http://prospect.org/article/white-working-class.

The New York Times. 2017. "Hurricane Maria Updates: In Puerto Rico, 'The Story Destroyed Us',," *The New York Times*, 21 September. https://www.nytimes.com/2017/09/21/us/hurricane-maria-puerto-rico.html.

Tourmaline. 2016. "Making a Way Out of No Way," Keynote address at Scholar and Feminist Conference 41: Sustainabilities, February 27. http://bcrw.barnard.edu.

Wasserman, David, et al. 2020. "2020 Popular Vote Tracker," *Cook Political Report*. https://cookpolitical.com/2020-national-popular-vote-tracker.

Wolin, Sheldon. 2017. *Democracy Incorporated: Managed Democracy and the Specter of Inverted Totalitarianism*. New Edition. Princeton, NJ: Princeton University Press.

INDEX

Page numbers in *italic* denote figures

agencement 168; *see also* assemblage
agency: individual 165; sexual 27n23, 153
AIDS/HIV 2, 21–3, 25, 61n40, 78–83, 95, 100n14, 165–8, 171–3, 181, 182n9, 183n10, 183n19
Allende, Salvador 37
Alvarez, Sonia 11
ambivalence 6, 9, 12, 20, 24, 27n20, 56, 123, 134, 153, 163–6, 168, 170–1, 182n9
AMMAR 122
Amuchástegui, Ana 2, 13, 21, 23, 25, 80, 165, 168–71, 175
anti-trafficking 18, 21, 93, 95, 110, 112–28, 129n6, 129n8, 130n20, 130n21, 130n22, 148
Argentina 4, 13, 18, 22, 24, 110, 121, 123–4, 126–8, 130n18, 159, 162
Argentine Workers Central Union (CTA) 122
Arruzza, Cinzia 35
assemblage 13, 56, 165, 168–72, 174
austerity 4, 7, 9, 36, 42, 46, 57n9, 91, 115, 118, 135, 149, 160, 169

Bedford, Kate 14
Bernstein, Elizabeth 2, 22, 26n12, 27n23, 62n43, 114, 129n6
Betances, Emelio 47, 60n35, 61n36
Bhattacharya, Tithi 35
Bhattacharyya, Gargi 7, 17, 41–2

Biden, Joseph 43, 60n27, 169, 174, 182n1, 183n12, 183n16, 184n21
Biehl, João 78–80
biopolitics 72, 75–6, 97, 128, 166–7, 183n10
biopower 72, 74, 168
Black Sexual Economies (BSE) 17, 27n27, 40, 47
body multiple 6, 38; social 6, 9, 26n11, 27n25, 38
borders: control 20, 24, 92, 109, 111, 127, 135, 142, 149, 162, 169; cross- 109, 135, 137–8; international 24, 109, 138; national 1, 9, 24, 109, 111, 124, 152, 169; political 138; regimes 20, 25, 139–41, 146–7, 151–4; regional 138, 152; *see also* security
boundaries 18, 23, 41–2, 45, 55, 74–5, 100n7, 123, 128, 138, 140, 142, 145, 147, 149, 152, 175, 179–81
Brady, Mary Pat 53, 63n52, 63n53
Brazil 5, 58n9, 78, 135, 169
Brennan, Denise 47–8
Brigada Callejera 21–2
#BringBackOurGirls (#BBOG) 23, 78, 84, *85*, 86, 88, 97, 99
Brooks, Peter 74
Brooks, Siobhan 11
Business Organized NGOs (BONGOs) 11
Butler, Judith 35, 73, 83, 86, 100n16
Byrd, Jody 37, 140

190 Index

Cabezas, Amalia 47
Campbell, Jocelyn 52
capitalism: global 50, 53, 180; industrial
  35; racial 14, 16–18, 21, 27n26, 36–8,
  40–2, 50–1, 56, 86, 138; redemptive
  112, 115, 118
carceral politics 14, 27n23; *see also*
  feminism
Castro, Roberto 82
Center Against Human Trafficking
  (CMM) 148
Central American Free Trade Agreement
  with the US (CAFTA-DR) 175
Chávez, Karma 144
Cheng, Sealing 10, 22, 24, 127, 140,
  145–6, 150
Chile 5, 37
Christian: evangelical 110, 112–14, 129n9;
  moralism 97, 110; nationalism 43, 171
Clinton, Bill 53, 63n52
Coalition Against Traffic in Women
  (CATW) 116
Cohen, Cathy 18, 40
coloniality 37, 39–41, 45–7, 50–1, 56,
  58n11, 73, 92, 138, 140
Constable, Nicole 144
Copenhagen 15, 148; Red Light
  District 148
COVID-19 1, 3, 9, 22, 26n13, 44–5,
  53, 60n27, 99, 134–5, 163, 169–70,
  181, 184n25
Cypher, James M. 5

Dae-Jung, Kim 115
DAMAYAN 179
Davis, Adrienne D. 17, 27n27, 40, 47
Deleuze, Gilles 100n12, 168
deportation 10, 25, 48–9, 51, 53, 119,
  134, 136, 139–43, 146–50, 152,
  154, 162
Derby, Lauren 46
deregulation 171; *see also* regulation
differential consciousness 25
disidentification 172–4, 178, 181
disposability 8, 44
domestic violence 11, 84
domestic work 1, 14, 17, 23, 35, 36,
  39–42, 45, 50–6, 57n6, 61n43, 115,
  179; *see also* labor; migration
domestic workers 12, 15–16, 21, 40,
  51–3, 62n44, 62n45, 62n46, 62n50, 82,
  144–5, 168, 175, 179
Domestic Workers United 52, 62n50
Dominican Republic (DR) 3, 10, 13, 17,
  21–3, 25, 41–51, 55–6, 59n25, 60n36,

  61n38, 61n39, 61n40, 62n46, 90,
  134–6, 138, 141–3, 149, 151, 153, 159,
  161–2, 175, 177–8
double binds 20, 24–5, 134, 137, 142, 147,
  153–4, 160, 163–4, 166, 169, 172–3,
  179–81, 182n4
Duggan, Lisa 14, 37, 141
Dworkin, Shari L. 82

Economic Development Commission
  (EDC) 89–92, 101n19
European Union (EU) 9, 26n16, 109,
  119, 121
expertization 167–8, 175

familialism 52, 62n47
Fassin, Didier 75–6, 99n1
feminism: carceral 112, 114, 128; and
  neoliberalism 100n15; social justice 15,
  34; transnational 2
Ferguson, James 87
Ferguson, Roderick 39
Fernández, Leonel 61, 176–7
financialization 7, 9, 141
formal economy 39–40, 49, 51, 56–7
Foucault, Michel 6, 26n12, 72, 74, 83,
  99n4, 100n12, 182n6
free trade zones 42–3, 46–9, 59n25,
  60n34, 60n35, 60n36
freedom: economic 43; individual 170–1;
  reproductive 113; sexual 55, 113
Freeman, Carla 43
Friedman, Milton 5

gender: analysis 16; hierarchies 16, 43–4,
  47; identity 49, 83, 136; injustice 34,
  114, 123; relations 1, 15–16, 38,
  48, 59n17, 123, 172; *see also* justice;
  transgender
George, Abosede 10, 13, 23, 36
global: economies 9, 12, 23, 48–9, 53,
  152, 169; financial crisis 129n3; North
  1, 5, 13, 16, 18, 36–7, 43, 50, 52, 59n23,
  136, 142; pandemic 3, 5, 181; relations
  2, 9; South 1, 5–6, 13, 16, 18, 36–7, 50,
  52, 59n23, 142, 175, 179; system 19–20,
  59n25, 87; trade 8, 169; woman 2, 13;
  see also capitalism; governance
globalization 9–10, 43, 50, 87, 113–14,
  117, 122, 126, 169, 180
governance: global 118; neoliberal 3, 10–11,
  14, 18, 24, 76, 78, 98, 110, 161, 169
governmentality: neoliberal 4, 13, 19, 43,
  78, 160–1, 163–5, 178, 181, 183n10;
  paradoxical 161, 168

Index **191**

Grabel, Ilene 110, 129n3, 178
Green, Linda 53
Gregory, Steven 46–7, 61n38
Grosfoguel, Ramón 37–8, 45, 58n12
Gross Domestic Product (GDP) 9, 61n39, 62n46
Guerrero, Zelem 52

Harris, Kamala 40, 184n23
Harvey, David 5, 26n12, 46, 57n3, 141
Hernández, Rita Indiana 175–8
heterosexuality 18, 40, 95, 113
Higgins, Jennifer 82
Ho, Josephine 11
Ho, Karen 90
Hoffman, Susie 82
Hollibaugh, Amber 27n28, 40, 173–4, 184n22
Hong Kong 10, 25, 134, 136–8, 140, 143–5, 149–51, 154n2, 159
Horn, Maja 23, 25, 57n6
Huber, Anthony 98, 102n37
human rights: activist 112–13; campaign 86; issue 110, 130n18; women's 113, 115–17, 126
humanitarianism 75, 85, 88, 98, 128, 148; militarized 112, 114
Hutchinson, Sydney 175

India 2, 4, 98, 134–5, 137, 143, 149–50, 159, 180; see also Mumbai
individualism 5, 8
informal economy 3, 39, 41–2, 47, 49, 51, 57, 122, 134, 136, 138–41, 143, 146, 150–3, 154n10, 175
insecurity 1, 98, 111, 135
International Monetary Fund (IMF) 5, 7, 36–7, 46, 58n11, 60n30, 91, 115, 118, 121
International Organization for Migration (IOM) 124

Jaffe, Sarah 174–5
Jakobsen, Janet 4, 23, 25, 26n12, 38, 169
James, C. L. R. 12
justice: economic 16, 23, 174, 181; gender 2–3, 12, 15–16, 20–1, 23, 34, 36–7, 41, 57n1, 110–11, 118, 122–3, 126, 128, 154, 180; social 1, 12, 15–16, 24, 34, 75, 92, 110–11, 122–3

Karim, Lamia 14
Kauanui, J. Kēhaulani 11–12, 26n19, 27n19
Kaye, Kerwin 13, 22–3
Kempadoo, Kamala 17, 36, 47
Keynsianism 9

Kirchner, Néstor 123
Klein, Naomi 4, 26n13, 37
Kristof, Nicholas 114

labor: domestic 16, 41, 50, 63n54, 123, 179; formal 42, 47, 51, 143; informal 23, 42, 47, 51, 115, 139, 141, 154; productive 16–17, 38, 54; reproductive 16–17, 35, 38, 42, 54, 97; sexual 24, 48–9, 55–6, 109, 125, 145, 181; see also domestic work; sex work
Lancaster, Roger N. 14
Lascoumes, Pierre 161
Latin America 5, 44, 46, 60n31, 96, 125, 160, 162, 177; see also Brazil; Chile; Mexico
LeGales, Patrick 161
LGBTQI 14, 27n23, 101n28, 144, 173
liberalism 8, 22, 57n1, 73, 87, 160
Lowe, Lisa 38–9, 58n14
Lubhéid, Eithne 144
Lugones, Maria 15–16, 38, 58n13

Manalansan, Martin 50–1
Martin, Trayvon 98, 102n37
Medina, Danilo 177
melodrama 74–5, 77–8, 82, 86, 96, 100n7, 100n8, 100n10, 102n38
Mexico 2, 5, 12–13, 15, 21–3, 25, 27n22, 43, 46, 73, 78–80, 85, 100n12, 109, 159, 161–2, 164–7, 171–2, 175
Meyer, Carrie 42, 91
migration: cross-border 109, 135; domestic 135
mobility: economic 49, 143; global 10; women's 43, 127
Mohanty, Chandra 75, 86
Mol, Annemarie 6, 38
Mulvaney, Mick 52
Mumbai 25, 134–5, 137–8, 142, 144, 150–1
Muñoz, José Esteban 17, 36, 172–4
Musser, Amber 39–40

Nadasen, Premilla 50–1, 62n50
National Agency for the Prohibition of Traffic in Persons and Other Related Matters (NAPTIP) 119, 129n16
National Domestic Workers Alliance (NDWA) 12, 53–6, 62n50, 179, 184n23
Navarro, Tami 13, 23, 44
neoliberalism: nationalist 3, 9, 26n8, 43, 168–70; paradoxes of 4, 9, 12, 15–16,

20–2, 24–5, 45, 47, 56, 134, 154, 166, 170, 175, 180–1; post- 5, 13, 18, 162

Ngai, Mae 53, 62n51

Nigeria 5, 10–11, 23–5, 73, 78, 84, 86–8, 100n17, 109, 118–21, 124, 126–8, 130n18, 134, 137–8, 141, 144–8, 150–1, 154n3, 159

non-governmental organizations (NGOs) 5, 7, 11, 72, 75–7, 79–88, 91–2, 95, 109, 117–21, 124–5, 128, 136, 148, 152, 159, 161, 175, 178, 180

Obama, Barack 40, 43, 129n11

Oliviero, Katie 75

Padilla, Mark 10, 22–4, 47–9, 61n40, 136, 151

paradoxes 1–3, 6, 9, 11–13, 15, 20–2, 27n19, 39, 43, 47, 59n16, 134, 142, 160, 163–6, 174, 178; *see also* neoliberalism

Pecheny, Mario 4, 18, 24–5, 162, 167

peer support 2, 25, 172, 181

Pellegrini, Ann 4

personal responsibility 8, 39, 165, 170, 176; *see also* responsibilization

Philippines 8, 98, 145

Pinochet, Augusto 37

Plambech, Sine 10–11, 22, 24, 120, 137, 145–8

policing 3, 11, 20, 34, 75, 99, 111, 114, 118, 135, 144, 147, 151, 153–4, 172

political economy 2–3, 6, 8, 12, 14, 25, 34–8, 71, 110, 121, 128, 179

Poo, Ai-jen 56

populism 4, 128, 169

poverty 44, 46, 52, 63n52, 90, 118–20, 135, 139; anti- 14–15

precarity 13, 21–5, 44, 48, 50, 54–5, 59n23, 71, 73, 82, 87–9, 91, 96–7, 99, 117, 122–3, 134–5, 139, 141, 145, 152, 154, 161, 169, 174–5

privatization 6, 10–11, 26n13, 61n38, 76, 78, 91, 109, 121, 139, 141, 169

productive economy 41–2

productive incoherence 24, 110, 129n2, 129n3, 153, 170, 178, 183n16

prostitution 80, 92–6, 112–18, 120, 122–7, 129n6, 130n20, 148, 150

Public Distribution System (PDS) 137

Queen Idia 120, 126

queer materialism 16, 18, 36, 38, 40, 42, 56

queer survival economies 25, 40, 173–5

Quijano, Aníbal 16, 38

race 6–7, 15, 17–18, 34–5, 38, 40–1, 44, 50, 53, 55, 58n12, 58n13, 59n16, 60n28, 62n51, 73, 75–7, 92, 135, 138, 144, 160, 170–2, 174–5, 179

racial difference 151

racial politics 61n43, 63n51

racism 16, 58n12, 147, 183n14

Raman, K. Ravi 180

rape 39, 92, 94, 101n30

Reagan, Ronald 37

refugees 76, 137, 150–1, 164, 182n5

regulation 10, 12, 24, 122–3, 125, 128, 138, 142–4, 146, 152–3, 164; gender 2, 35, 171–2; moral 24, 80, 84; normative 152–3; sexual 35, 55, 148, 171; social 71

regulatory logics 153

reproductive economy 41–2

resistance 5, 14, 20, 23, 25, 71, 77, 83, 144, 161, 164–5, 169, 177, 179–80, 183n14; practices of 13, 25, 166, 178, 180–1

responsibilization 167–8, 170, 175; *see also* personal responsibility

Restaurant Opportunity Center of New York (ROC-NY) 174–5

risk 7, 39, 72–3, 76, 78, 80–2, 90, 92, 97, 99n1, 99n4, 101n22, 119, 137, 144, 154n3

Rittenhouse, Kyle 98

Rosenbaum, Joseph 98, 102n37

Samuel (tourism employee) 48–9, 61n42, 136–8, 144

San Francisco 23, 94–6

Sandoval, Chela 25

Sanyal, Kalyan 17, 27n28, 41–2

Sassen, Saskia 140–1

Scott, David 11–12

Scott, Joan 22

Scully, Pamela 86

securitization 24, 77, 97, 100n10, 152, 162, 169

security: apparatus 78, 90, 97, 99n4, 140, 171; border 139–40; national 162–3; private 140; social 8, 53, 62n43, 82, 143

sex: trafficking 2, 12–13, 20, 24, 27n22, 43, 78, 92–6, 101n28, 109–18, 121–8, 128n1, 129n6, 129n9, 130n18, 130n22, 148, 159, 161; work 14, 21–2, 39, 41–2, 50–1, 56, 61n40, 62n43, 92–3, 96, 120–5, 128, 134, 142, 148, 150, 152–3, 154n11, 173

sexual: economy 46–7, 49; politics 6, 12–14, 20, 27n23, 34–5, 41, 50–1,

55–6, 57n2, 57n3, 128, 159, 161, 180; relations 10, 14, 51, 113; rights 122–3; services 49, 61n42, 125, 136, 148; slavery 92, 96; victimhood 112, 116–17, 127, 147, 153; violence 39, 72, 78, 94, 115; *see also* agency; freedom; labor; regulation
sex workers 112, 120, 125, 128n1
Shah, Svati 2, 22, 24, 28n34, 134, 142–3
slavery 16–17, 35, 39–40, 47, 50, 59n22, 62n43, 86, 90, 112–14, 125, 129n11, 130n20, 154n13, 179; *see also* sexual
Smith, David Jordan 118, 120
social reproduction 3, 16–18, 27n26, 35–6, 38, 44, 51, 54
solidarity 150, 168, 171, 179–80, 183n19; complex 181; transverse 180
South Korea 4, 10, 24, 109, 115–18, 121, 124, 126–8, 130n18, 159
Spade, Dean 173
Spillers, Hortense 16, 27n27, 38–9, 58n15, 59n16
Spivak, Gayatri Chakravorty 26n18, 36, 75, 86
state: fractured 25, 162, 169, 181; policy 161, 172; power 11, 161–2; welfare 7, 13–14, 40
structural adjustment 5–7, 19, 36–7, 46, 52–3, 60n30, 90, 122, 159
Structural Adjustment Programme (SAP) 53, 119–20
subject: of adherence 166; of rights 163
subjectivation 161, 163–6, 170–4, 176, 182n5, 182n7, 183n10
suffering 12, 23, 71–5, 77, 80, 84, 88, 97, 99n1, 117–18, 120, 165
survival economies 3, 5, 17–18, 21–3, 27n28, 35, 41, 44–5, 49, 51, 54–6, 123, 137, 139, 161, 173, 181; queer 25, 40, 173–5
sweatshops 114, 126
Sylvia Rivera Law Project (SRLP) 172–3

Tadiar, Neferti 8, 44
Taylor, Marcus 37
Thailand 14
tigueraje/tiguere 48, 61n42, 146
tourism 17, 41–3, 47–9, 51, 59n25, 61n38, 61n39, 61n40, 135–6, 142, 144, 146, 149, 151
Trafficking in Persons Reports (TIP) 94, 111, 114, 116, 124, 126, 129n11
Trafficking Victims' Protection Act (TVPA) 111, 115–16, 126–7, 129n12

transgender 12–13, 15, 24, 35, 50–1, 93, 109, 112, 123, 163
Trimarco, Susana 124–5
Trump, Donald 4, 26n8, 27n22, 43, 60n27, 129n6, 168–71, 174, 182n1, 183n12, 183n14, 183n16, 183n17; Administration 12, 52, 182n1, 183n13, 184n24

United Nations (UN) 100n13, 111, 113; Protocol 115, 116, 125–7
United States (US) 3–5, 7–14, 22–5, 26n8, 26n13, 27n23, 27n24, 37, 39–44, 46, 48, 50–6, 57n9, 58n11, 60n27, 61n40, 61n43, 62n43, 62n44, 62n46, 62n49, 62n50, 62n51, 63n52, 73, 75, 78, 88–9, 91, 93–4, 98, 101n22, 109, 111–16, 118–19, 121, 124–8, 129n6, 130n22, 136, 141–3, 146, 159–63, 168–71, 173–6, 179, 181n1, 182n1, 182n3, 183n10, 183n14, 184n23; US Bill of Rights 12, 179, 184n23; *see also* San Francisco
US Virgin Islands (USVI) 13, 23, 44, 73, 78, 88–90, 101n22, 159
Usuanlele, Uyilawa 120

value: economic 7–8, 134; market 26n13; moral 74, 86, 140, 171
Veron, Marita 124–5
victims 74–8, 80–1, 83–4, 90, 93–7, 99, 101n28, 101n30, 101n32, 116, 123–7, 129n9, 130n20, 130n22, 139, 164–5
villains 74, 76–8, 86, 90, 93–4, 97–8
vulnerability: neoliberal 13, 23–4, 63n53, 71–109, 111, 151, 178

waiting 8, 10, 18, 42, 137, 143, 145–6, 149, 164, 182n5
Weiss, Margot 173–4
Werner, Marion 46
Williams, Tiffany 50–1, 62n50
Willis, Brian 93
Wilson, Ara 14
Wolin, Sheldon 171
work: agricultural 50–1, 56, 62n43; factory 8, 42, 47–8, farm 50, 179; *see also* domestic; sex
worker: care 50; childcare 62n48; factory 8; *see also* domestic workers; sex workers; work
World Bank (WB) 5–7, 14, 36–7, 44, 46, 58n11, 61n38, 91, 100n13, 119–20

Zimmerman, George 98

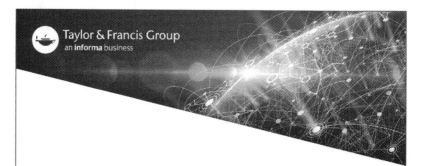

Printed in the United States
by Baker & Taylor Publisher Services